Japanese Politics and Government

D0087352

This book investigates Japanese politics in the postwar era from theoretical and comparative perspectives. After providing historical context, it offers an in-depth exploration of postwar political institutions, political reform in the 1990s, the policymaking process, and the politics of economic growth and stagnation. The author draws attention to key policy issues including women and work, immigration, Japanese aging/low fertility society, and Constitutional revision. By delving into Japan's international relations, the book sheds light on Japan's security and trade policies, Japan's role in the Asian region, and Japan's bilateral relations with the U.S., China, South Korea, and the EU.

Themes and questions addressed throughout the text include:

- How and why did Japan modernize so successfully when so many other countries fell prey to colonialism and authoritarianism?
- What explains the Japanese economic miracle and its subsequent economic stagnation?
- What accounts for Japan's successful democratization?
- In the international realm, why has Japan achieved economic superpower status without achieving political superpower status?
- What has or has not changed since the historic election of the Democratic Party of Japan in 2009, and why?
- What is the future trajectory of Japanese politics?

Connecting Japan to larger themes in comparative politics and linking Japan's history, institutions, policymaking process, and international relations to experiences and structures in other countries, this book is essential reading for any course on Japanese or Asian Politics.

Alisa Gaunder is a Professor of Political Science at Southwestern University, USA. Her previous publications include the *Routledge Handbook of Japanese Politics* (Routledge 2011) and *Political Reform in Japan: Leadership Looming Large* (Routledge, 2007).

Japanese Politics and Government

Alisa Gaunder

Routledge
Taylor & Francis Group

LONDON AND NEW YORK

First published 2017
by Routledge
2 Park Square, Milton Park, Abingdon, Oxon OX14 4RN

and by Routledge
711 Third Avenue, New York, NY 10017

Routledge is an imprint of the Taylor & Francis Group, an informa business

British Library Cataloguing in Publication Data
A catalogue record for this book is available from the British Library

Library of Congress Cataloging in Publication Data
Names: Gaunder, Alisa, 1970- author.
Title: Japanese politics and government / Alisa Gaunder.
Description: Abingdon, Oxon ; New York, NY : Routledge, 2017. | Includes
  bibliographical references and index.
Identifiers: LCCN 2016040540| ISBN 9780415826693 (hardback) |
  ISBN 9780415826709 (pbk.) | ISBN 9781315228594 (ebook)
Subjects: LCSH: Japan–Politics and government–1945-
Classification: LCC JQ1631 .G379 2017 | DDC 320.952–dc23
LC record available at https://lccn.loc.gov/2016040540

ISBN: 978-0-415-82669-3 (hbk)
ISBN: 978-0-415-82670-9 (pbk)
ISBN: 978-1-315-22859-4 (ebk)

Typeset in Times New Roman
by Taylor & Francis Books

For Ian

Contents

List of tables   viii
Acknowledgments   ix

1   Introduction: Why Japan matters   1

2   The making of a modern state   9

3   The postwar settlement   21

4   The postwar political system   31

5   Political parties   49

6   Elections and electioneering   68

7   The economic miracle   83

8   Economic slowdown   96

9   Policymaking   110

10 State–society relations   122

11 Prime ministerial leadership   135

12 National security and foreign policy   149

13 Conclusion   163

Index   171

List of tables

1.1	A comparison of GDP and population size in 2015	1
5.1	Current composition of the lower house (as of July 14, 2016)	65
6.1	Party seat representation in the lower house under the SNTV/MMD system	70
6.2	Party seat representation in the lower house under the post-1994 electoral system	72
9.1	Number of female members of the lower house	116
11.1	Postwar prime ministers	140

Acknowledgments

Writing a book is always a journey with surprises along the way. For me, the biggest surprise was the opportunity to take on a University leadership role with only four chapters of this text complete. Balancing the role of Dean of the Faculty with my passion for writing and Japanese politics involved a lot of experimentation and trial and error as I learned how to set and protect writing boundaries. To this end, two people proved critical to my success. President Edward Burger supported my commitment to the teacher-scholar model and approved defining my summer workdays as half research and half administrative work. I have realized that writing and research energize me and I am so thankful for this support. Barbara Jean, my administrative assistant, however, is the true hero. She protected my weekly research time during the semester and daily research time during the summer. Without her assistance, I would have never finished this book. I cannot thank her enough for this and so much more. I also appreciate the patience and support of my editors at Routledge, Stephanie Rogers, Leanne Hinves, Lucy McClune, and Rebecca Lawrence.

The largest intellectual support for this project came from students in my Japanese politics courses. This text represents years of efforts to explain Japanese politics to students, mostly from Texas, who have not had much exposure to Japan. It is impossible to list them all but several pushed my thinking and improved the way I teach Japanese politics including Kevin Livesay, Lissa Terrell, Tyson Berger, Chris Bailey, Grace Webster, Sarah Morris, Luke Martel, Christina Sohn, Jessica West, Aimee Turner, Jacob Henderson, Elizabeth Hoffman, Cortney Clegg, Amy Hubbard, Shannon Foster, Anthony West, Haley Guida, Jacob Beswick, Mandy Mantzel, Matt Glenn, Adena Young, Marwa Adalla, Dan Kilgore, Rachel Asselin, Alex Blake, Martin Fergus, Kyle Mathis, Alex Caple, Matt DeCesare, Randi Spencer, Taylor Gracia, Lauren Jensen, Blake Stone, Clayton Tucker, Gillian Ring, Michael Korman, Zach Coates, Omeed Azmoudeh, Eryn Quinn, Mary Grace Steigerwald, Arun Jacob, Belle Jo, Chyenne Wooldridge, Grace Garrigan, Brandon Thomas, Sarah Coe, Bonnie Daniel, Meg Greenfield, Nicki Jacks, Ashley Johnson, Claire Jamison, Will Cozzens, and Kylie LeBlanc. Mara Weidmann never took Japanese politics; however, I will never forget when she raised her hand in the middle of my Comparative politics class and asked, "what exactly do you mean the rules of the game matter?" – what an important moment in my teaching career as I realized I needed to unpack this catch phrase. Ben Bracher and Danny Jozwiak directly influenced this book with their research assistance – both were amazing honors students. Hunter Jurgens is a current honors student and generously read some chapters to make sure they were accessible to undergraduates. The enthusiasm and energy I have received from all these students and many more is why I love my job. A special thanks goes to Patricia Maclachlan, T. J. Pempel, and Steve Vogel for providing feedback on the book proposal. I also appreciate Jon Marshall's feedback on the introduction and conclusion. Sarah Wiliarty and Shannon Mariotti provided moral support and advice all along the way.

Finally, I would like to thank my family. My parents instilled in me the confidence and work ethic to pursue my goals. My mother, Eleanor Gaunder, was not alive to see this project, but she contributed to it nonetheless. My dad, Robert Gaunder (aka Papa G.), provides regular after school care for my son and extra support whenever needed. He is one of the main reasons I can balance the various work-life demands. My sister, Laura Gaunder, is an awesome cheerleader who always knows the right thing to say. My husband, Robert McAlister, has been an excellent sounding board and taught me how to be more assertive over the years – something I am forever grateful for. I value his work advice and support, and I love his spontaneity and humor. Finally, I would like to thank my son, Ian McAlister. Ian knows more about this book than anyone else in my family. He can tell you how many chapters are in it and which ones were written when. He loves people and never has complained about camps or daycare. His good attitude and easy going nature have allowed me to continue dedicating time to my work and writing with minimal amounts of guilt. Spending time with him energizes me and drives home what really matters. He is pure joy and it is with the deepest love that I dedicate this text to him.

1 Introduction

Why Japan matters

This book explores Japanese politics in the postwar era. Unless you have been to Japan, are taking Japanese or have been captivated by some aspect of Japanese popular culture (anime, karate, sushi, etc.), it may not be apparent why you should spend a semester studying Japan in general and Japanese politics in particular. In essence the implicit question is, why does Japan matter.

Most cases for why Japan matters start by focusing on its economy. Japan's economy grew at phenomenal rates in the 1970s and 1980s, leading many to classify the growth as constituting an economic miracle. What was even more miraculous about this growth, perhaps, is that it was accompanied by relative income equality (Kabashima 1984). When growth slowed in the 1990s and the focus shifted to China, Japan's presence in U.S. media coverage slowed and interest waned. Still today, Japan is the third largest economy in the world (see Table 1.1). Gross domestic product illustrates the absolute size of the economy. Japan's GDP in 2015 was 4,601,461 million dollars. China surpassed Japan as the second largest economy in 2010, a position Japan had held for over 40 years. Japan's economic performance, however, remains notable especially given the population size difference between Japan and China, and between Japan and the United States. China's population is ten times that of Japan's; the U.S. population is triple that of Japan's (Rosenbluth and Thies 2010: 3). Thus, the per capita output in Japan is impressive.

Table 1.1 A comparison of GDP and population size in 2015

Country	GDP ($ millions)	Population
USA	17,946,996	321,368,864
China	10,866,444	1,367,485,388
Japan	4,123,258	126,919,659
Germany	3,355,772	80,854,408
United Kingdom	2,848,755	64,088,222
France	2,421,682	66,553,766
India	2,073,543	1,251,695,584
Italy	1,814,763	61,855,120
Brazil	1,774,725	204,259,812
Canada	1,550,537	35,099,836

Source: Column 2: CIA. 2015. "The World Factbook." Available online at www.cia.gov/library/publications/the-world-factbook/rankorder/2119rank.html (accessed 25 July 2016).

But, a focus on the economy begs the question why study Japanese politics. The answer rests in the fundamental notions of political economy and comparative politics. Scholars of political economy note the dynamic relationship between politics and economics and the interplay between the market and the state. Domestic politics can influence the economy. Similarly, the way a country organizes its economy can impact politics.

From the perspective of comparative politics, the reasons for studying Japanese are clear – Japan is interesting as a point of comparison. It sheds light on key questions of political science. This introduction discusses the importance of studying Japanese politics from comparative and theoretical perspectives. The objective is to cast Japan as comparable to some countries in certain aspects and other countries in different respects. This text does not paint Japan's politics and economics as unique, but instead it seeks to explore Japan's history, institutions, policymaking process, and international relations in relation to experiences and structures in other countries.

The main themes and objectives of this text connect Japan to larger themes in comparative politics, including but not limited to, (1) How do states successfully modernize? (2) What leads to the establishment of a successful democracy? (3) What is the relationship between development and democracy? (4) How do institutions and institutional legacies influence political outcomes? (5) What is the relationship between culture and structure in Japanese politics and what can this tell us about the relationship between these factors in other countries? (6) What challenges face mature democracies economically and politically, and how do states address these challenges?

Japan is a particularly interesting case for modernization because it is one of the few late developers to avoid colonization. An exploration of the pre-modern period suggests that certain practices established under Japanese feudalism put Japan in a strong position to create a modern state. The role of crisis and international assistance in establishing democracy in the Japanese case is also interesting to consider, especially when coupled with the German experience. At first glance, Japan seems to confirm the notion that development leads to democracy. This assertion becomes complicated, though, when exploring the sequence of events in the Japanese context. Many point to culture as explaining Japan's rapid economic growth. This text, however, unpacks this assertion to explore how the Japanese case sheds light on the relationship between culture and structure. Culture certainly explains why certain practices look different in Japan. It is unclear, though, that culture is the decisive variable in explaining economic development. Finally, the Japanese case illustrates how politics influences outcomes. As we shall see, the connections between politicians, bureaucrats, and interest groups represent strong structural constraints on reform.

The remainder of this introduction provides an overview of these themes while the chapters that follow explore these issues in greater depth.

Themes

Modernization

One of the central questions of comparative politics explores the factors that lead countries to move from traditional to modern societies. Modernization occurs in the cultural, political and economic realms. Traditional societies are characterized by group identities and personal relationships. In contrast, in modern societies the basic unit of identity is the individual. Moreover, impersonal rules govern behavior (Jowitt

1992). Economic modernization is associated with changes in economic organization that promote economic growth.

Comparativists have wrestled with whether all countries follow the same path to modernization. Scholars sympathetic to Marx's historical determinism posit that the internal tensions in society move countries from feudalism to capitalism to socialism/communism (Marx and Engels 1848). In Marxist theory, these tensions that emerge in each country are the same, and thus countries follow the same path to development. According to this logic, all countries would follow a similar path to modernity as Great Britain, the first country to modernize. Empirical evidence calls this theoretical approach into question. Every country did not follow the same path as Great Britain. Several factors influenced variations including when a country started on the path to development, how developed the country was when it started to modernize, institutions and technologies that could be borrowed or improved upon, and guiding ideologies (Gerschenkron 1962).

Japan usually gets placed into the category of late-developer. In many senses, this is true. When the West forced Japan to open its country, it did not have a representative political system nor did it have a private banking system. Japan, however, did have a highly bureaucratized feudal system with a relatively marketized economy for a pre-modern country. These factors help explain why Japan did not fall prey to colonialism or authoritarianism like most of its contemporaries. Indeed, Chapter 2 posits that the historical and institutional legacies of Japan's pre-modern period provide answers to why Japan avoided colonization by the West as it embarked on the path to development. In particular, Japan's strong feudal system, its experiment with Taishō democracy in the interwar years, and the legacies of the Occupation shaped its modern political and economic institutions.

While Japan became a modern state in 1868 with the Meiji Restoration, Japan did not become an economically developed country until the postwar period. When Japan did start on the path to economic development, it flourished with most outside observers classifying Japan's growth as a miracle. Many scholars have sought to explain Japan's rapid economic growth. The reasons behind this growth are contested. Chapter 7 sheds light on the causes of Japan's economic miracle, exploring the role of the bureaucracy, politicians, interest groups, and culture.

Democratization

A country can move from a traditional to a modern society without adopting democratic institutions. That is, the path to modernization can lead to a variety of different forms of governments and economic arrangements (Gerschenkron 1962). What then accounts for Japan's successful democratization? Japan provides an excellent case to explore the relationship between development and democracy. Did the democracy that emerged after the Occupation promote growth or did Japan's rapid economic growth following World War II foster Japan's democratic success? Several chapters focus on the incentives and constraints posed by institutional rules to illustrate how the rules of the game matter in creating viable advanced capitalist democracies. Historical and institutional legacies are also relevant in addressing this question in Japan, particularly the importance of Taishō democracy.

Democracy has been defined in a multitude of ways – both broadly and narrowly. Samuel Huntington suggests that a political system is democratic "to the extent that its most powerful collective decision makers are selected through fair, honest, and periodic elections in which the candidates freely compete for votes and in which virtually all the adult population is eligible to vote" (1991: 7). In short, this definition points to two key features of democracy: contestation and participation. It also suggests some provision for civil liberties and civil rights. That is, freedom of speech and assembly are implied in free, fair elections (Huntington 1991).

Democracy is best conceived as a continuum. Political systems are more or less close to meeting the various criteria of the ideal type of democracy. The exploration of political institutions in Chapter 4 and of political parties and elections in Chapters 5 and 6 evaluates institutions and practices against an ideal type of democracy. Japan then can be placed in comparative perspective with other advanced industrial democracies.

Many look at Japan's democratization as a confirmation of modernization theory. Modernization theory maintains that economic growth provides the structural requisites of democracy. Modernization theory notes a strong correlation between economically developed countries and democratic countries. According to this theory, the process of development fosters growth. Along with growth comes a rising middle class, increasing literacy rates due to greater access to education, greater social mobility and the creation of civil society. Education fosters democratic values. A middle class of well-educated people is also more likely to participate in intermediary organizations that make up civil society (Lipset 1959).

Certainly several empirical examples of economically developed, democratic countries exist. The problem is that it is unclear whether development caused democracy. One could argue that in fact democracy led to development. Political scientists note that causation cannot be confused with correlation. Moreover, this theory while parsimonious becomes particularly difficult to verify from a comparative perspective. What about the poor democracies or rich authoritarian regimes? Even the case of Japan calls it into question. Critics of modernization theory note that it points to factors that sustain democracy, not the factors that create democracy (Rostow 1960).

Japan also poses problems to theories of democratization that focus on culture. Theories of development and democracy often extend the causal chain to include values and beliefs as the spark for economic development and democracy. Modernization theory is implied in these arguments, which make them problematic for all the reasons noted above. A cultural argument maintains that values and beliefs influence the kind of institutions that emerge as a country industrializes. Max Weber, for example, maintained that the Protestant Ethic based on working hard to glorify God while denying the self provided incentives for savings and investment. This capital supported industrialization in Great Britain (Weber 1930). Extending this line of argument, the Protestant Ethic taught the masses to depend on themselves and to work hard in order to become good citizens. The state found these citizens less threatening, and thus democratic reform was more possible. In contrast, in countries such as Russia, where traditional kinship relations remained strong, democracy and development were slowed in the absence of impersonal legal norms (Bendix 1964). Similarly, Confucianism with its focus on the family as the unit of analysis could be seen as impeding the emergence of the individual, a key feature of political and economic liberalism. Explanations that focus on the values and beliefs of certain religions fall prey to the same critiques as Modernization Theory – correlation does not equal causation. The fact that fewer Confucian or Islamic countries are democracies does not mean that religion is the primary reason. In fact, the fact that democracy has emerged in various religious contexts suggests something else is going on.

This discussion illustrates the difficulty in addressing the questions of how, when, and why countries have become democracies. If we look at cases of late modernizers such as Japan, what becomes clear is that establishing and maintaining a stable democracy is difficult and requires substantial crises such as war and Occupation or substantial international assistance such as the Marshall plan in Germany, the U.S. Occupation of Japan and more recently the EU's efforts in Southern Europe. The international environment as well as domestic politics influence whether democracy will take hold. Several chapters will discuss these themes. Chapter 3 explores the postwar settlement. Chapter 4 provides an overview of the political institutions that have framed Japanese democracy. Chapter 7 delves into the question of the relationship between development and democracy.

Institutions

This exploration of Japanese politics also illustrates the role of institutions in influencing outcomes. A political institution is "a set of rules, norms or standard operating procedures that is widely recognized and accepted and that structures and constrains individuals' political actions" (Drogus and Orvis 2012: 25). Institutions are important because they define the "rules of the game." Institutions provide the incentives and constraints political actors face in the policymaking process. The main political actors explored in this text are prime ministers, political parties, politicians, bureaucratic ministries, interest groups, and voters.

The electoral system is an institution that has garnered a great deal of attention in Japan. Chapter 6 investigates how this institution has influenced the behavior of political parties, politicians and voters. Japan has experimented with two different electoral systems for the lower house in the postwar period. The different sets of rules allow political scientists to explore the effect of different electoral rules on behavior. The change of electoral systems also illustrates the importance of exploring the political legacies of past rules. That is, some institutions and practices that emerged under the old electoral rules persist under the new rules due in part to inertia. The practices might change under the new rules, but the larger historical context is always important to keep in mind.

Culture

Culture is another factor that is often cited as influencing political outcomes and behavior. Political culture is defined as a set of attitudes, values, and beliefs. Cultural explanations can be enticing; however, these explanations must be carefully employed. One particular problem with a cultural explanation is that it can treat culture as monolithic – that is, the assumption is that everyone in the country has the same values, attitudes, and beliefs. Such generalizations can then be used to explain everything (Reed 1993). For example, a common generalization that has been used to explain Japan is that the Japanese people avoid conflict and prefer consensus. This generalization has been extended to contend that Japanese are non-litigious. As we shall see, however, several institutions in Japan provide incentives to settle disagreements through third-party mediation. Disagreements are not absent; they are settled in different ways (Haley 1978).

Cultural arguments also need to be carefully examined to guard against tautology. That is, behavior such as non-litigiousness can be used to identify a value such as passiveness or conflict avoidance, and then this value can in turn be used to explain non-litigiousness. In addition, cultural explanations can be used to stereotype or promote nationalism (Reed 1993).

When comparing Japan to East Asian countries, cultural explanations have been used to explain both similarities and differences. That is, there is a tendency to point to similarities in culture when looking at similar outcomes, and differences in culture when noting differences (Reed 1993).

Political culture has often been used to explain differences when comparing Japan to Western countries. For example, as mentioned earlier, initially Confucianism was seen as preventing industrialization. In particular, Confucianism's emphasis on personal relationships, the family, morality, loyalty, cooperation, and hierarchy were seen as impeding development. When Japan developed, however, this explanation was called into question. Some sought to figure out how Confucianism might differ across Asian countries (Fukuyama 1995). That is, does the Japanese variety of Confucianism somehow allow for development whereas the Chinese version does not? One argument suggests that Japan places an emphasis on the emperor as opposed to the family. This deference to authority explains the dominance of the Liberal Democratic Party (LDP) (Fukuyama 1995). The problem with such cultural arguments is that these arguments are often non-falsifiable. One is left to prove how Confucianism is somehow different or stronger in China to produce such varying outcomes. Such explanations also make sweeping generalizations. While certain cultural norms are broadly shared, often features of the polity, such as deference to authority, are not.

Political culture is important and should not be dismissed. In many cases, different values and beliefs can help us understand why processes look different in one country than in another. That is, culture can be an intervening variable that explains why things look the way they do. Moreover, culture is important because it imbues events with meaning. This is different than asserting that culture in and of itself determines the outcome. As we shall see, values and beliefs can influences what certain institutions and practices look like; cultural explanations have less power in explaining the outcomes given that culture only changes very slowly. The cultural explanation will be discussed in greater detail in Chapter 7, which explores the Japanese economic miracle.

Economic challenges of advanced industrialized democracies

Japan has experienced several challenges to growth since reaching economic maturity. Its rapid economic growth extended from the 1960s to the 1980s. Since the late-1980s, it has become apparent that many of the institutional structures that effectively promoted growth have been less well suited to sustain growth. Despite an understanding of this situation, reforms to the political economy have been difficult to implement as politicians, bureaucrats, and certain interest groups have vested reasons to support the status quo. The inability to reform has been even more striking since Japan has experienced economic stagnation since the early 1990s. Chapter 8 addresses many aspects of the political economy that have impeded reform.

The challenges to the Japanese economy are not unique. Japan's response, however, has not always followed that of other countries. One of the largest challenges facing Japan is the fact that it has a rapidly aging population coupled with a declining fertility rate. Japan has been aware of these trends for decades, but it has done very little to address the situation in terms of policies and institutions. Chapter 9 looks at several potential policy areas that could address Japan's aging, low fertility society. Some policies address women, work, and family issues such as the provision of daycare. Other policies focus on ways to increase the labor force through immigration. Some of the inflexibility in the policymaking process explains why little progress has been made on these issues.

Outline of the book

The chapters that follow develop the themes discussed here. Chapter 2 provides the historical context for the development of the postwar political system by exploring the Tokugawa, Meiji and Taishō periods. An investigation of the postwar settlement in Chapter 3 then sets the stage for a more in-depth look at postwar political institutions in Chapter 4. Here, the focus is on domestic politics and institutions, including the Diet, the electoral system, the prime minister, political parties, the bureaucracy, local government, and the legal system. The textbook also highlights the importance of political reform in the 1990s by exploring both the nature of the reform as well as the effects of the electoral, campaign finance, and administrative reforms passed. The chapters on political parties (Chapter 5), the electoral system and electioneering (Chapter 6), and the prime minister (Chapter 11) pay particular attention to the effects of reform by discussing how rule changes have affected the incentives and constraints politicians, voters and parties face. After providing an overview of the political system, the textbook explores the politics of economic growth and stagnation in Chapters 7 and 8. In Chapter 9, it then considers the policymaking process and the changes it has undergone in the postwar period, outlining the role of politicians, the bureaucracy, and interest groups. Chapter 9 also highlights key policy areas, including policies related to daycare, women and work, and immigration. State–society relations enter the discussion in Chapter 10 as the text delves into different types of civil society organizations as well as investigates how different social movements have influenced the political environment. Exploring Japan's national security and foreign relations in Chapter 12 sheds light on Japan's security and trade policies, Japan's role in the Asian region, and Japan's bilateral relations with the U.S., South Korea, China and the EU. The textbook concludes by addressing what has changed since the historic election of the Democratic Party of Japan (DPJ) in the 2009 lower house election, and what political and economic challenges remain in the years to come.

References

Bendix, R. (1964) *Nation-Building and Citizenship: Studies of Our Changing Social Order*, Hoboken, NJ: John Wiley & Sons, Inc.

Drogus, C. A. and Orvis, S. (2012) *Introducing Comparative Politics: Concepts and Cases in Context*, Washington, DC: CQ Press.

Fukuyama, F. (1995) "Confucianism and Democracy," *Journal of Democracy*, 6: 20–33.

Gerschenkron, A. (1962) *Economic Backwardness in Historical Perspective*, Cambridge, MA: Harvard University Press.

Haley, J. O. (1978) "The Myth of the Reluctant Litigant," *Journal of Japanese Studies*, 4: 359–390.

Huntington, S. P. (1991) *The Third Wave: Democratization in the Late Twentieth Century*, Norman, OK: University of Oklahoma Press.

Jowitt, K. (1992) *New World Disorder: The Leninist Extinction*, Berkeley: University of California Press.

Kabashima, I. (1984) "Supportive Participation with Economic Growth: The Case of Japan," *World Politics*, 36: 309–338.

Lipset, S. M. (1959) "Some Social Requisites of Democracy," *American Political Science Review*, 53: 69–105.

Marx, K. and Engels, F. (1848/2011) "The Communist Manifesto," in N. Capaldi and G. Lloyd (eds) *The Two Narratives of Political Economy*, Hoboken, NJ: John Wiley & Sons, Inc.

Reed, S. R. (1993) *Making Common Sense of Japan*, Pittsburgh, PA: University of Pittsburgh Press.

Rosenbluth, F. M. and Thies, M. F. (2010) *Japan Transformed: Political Change and Economic Restructuring*, Princeton, NJ: Princeton University Press.

Rostow, W. W. (1960) *The Stages of Economic Growth: A Non-Communist Manifesto*, New York: Cambridge University Press.

Weber, M. (1930) *The Protestant Ethic and the Spirit of Capitalism*, London: Allen and Unwin.

2   The making of a modern state

This chapter explores Japan's transition from a traditional to modern society. The characteristics of traditional and modern societies are inherently opposed to one another. Traditional societies focus on corporate groups, personal ties, and fixed hierarchies (Jowitt 1992). In feudal Japan the corporate group was one's feudal class. A person was born into one of four groups – samurai (the military class), peasant, artisan, or merchant. This class made a complete claim on a person's identity, and people could not move from one class to another. These classes were hierarchical, and the hierarchy was characterized by a statement of more power as well as greater self-worth. Samurai stood at the top of this hierarchy followed by peasants, artisans, and merchants. One trend that becomes apparent in this brief exploration of Japanese history is how modern elements begin to enter Japanese society and challenge the traditional paradigm. Over time, we see the emergence of impersonal rules and a breakdown in the hierarchical structure, at least informally, as the capital of merchants becomes more and more important despite their low status. These tensions are brought to a head when the West forces Japan to reopen its country.

An exploration of Japan's journey from a feudal society to a modern state also illuminates some of the developmental and transformational patterns of Japanese history. Japan has a tendency to learn from both its neighbors and the West. It has not relied on other countries for capital, just technology and knowledge. It has explored various forms of government and these experiments have led to important legacies and reverse legacies. As we shall see, direct legacies of the establishment of a modern state in 1868 include a parliamentary form of government and a medium-sized electoral system. Reverse legacies are reflected in Japan's attempt to correct some of the problems with the Meiji period including the ambiguity in the Meiji Constitution.

Finally, this chapter will illustrate some of the necessary conditions for the creation of a unified, modern state. It will explore why Japan was able to resist Western colonization and instead build its own imperial state. It also will detail some of the important decisions Japan made as it worked toward becoming an economically developed, unified democracy. The effects of these decisions will be explored both in this chapter as well as the following chapter on the postwar settlement. Ultimately, Japan's first experiment with democracy failed due to the competing interests and growing strength of the military in the 1920s and 1930s. Japan's experience with democracy would prove quite valuable to the Allied powers after the war, however, as it attempted to consolidate democracy in the defeated nation.

Tokugawa Japan

Pre-modern Japan is divided into periods. The final period of the pre-modern era is the Tokugawa period. Tokugawa began in 1600 and extended until the Meiji Restoration in 1868. It is noteworthy for its political stability, isolation, and relatively high levels of education and economic development for a traditional society. Economic development and a move to more impersonal rules have led many to classify Tokugawa as early modern. The transition from tradition to modernity definitely began during this period. The advances made under Tokugawa ultimately aided Japan as it was forced to open to the West.

Prior to 1600, Japan was divided into numerous independent regions. The domains were not unified. Instead, the leaders of more powerful domains sought to extend their influence over large areas of the country and achieve unity. Oda Nobunaga, a feudal lord from a region east of Kyoto, was the first leader to move Japan towards unification. He seized the capital in 1568 and began to gain control of the central region of Japan. Oda's efforts were cut short when a vassal killed him in 1582 (Reischauer 1990: 65–66).

Hideyoshi Toyotomi took over Oda's work to unify Japan. He eventually gained control over western, eastern, and northern Japan. After this, he established feudal domains, standardized the currency, attempted to monopolize trade, and confiscated all the weapons from peasants in an attempt to end warfare. At this point, he essentially froze the feudal classes with samurai conceived as scholarly warriors, followed by peasants, artisans, and merchants.

After his death in 1598, succession was in doubt since the heir was only an infant. The heir was put under the control of five chief vassals. The strongest of the vassals, Tokugawa Ieyasu, eventually took control under his own name. He won power over the entire country at the battle at Sekigahara in 1600. He took the title of shogun in 1603. He put down opponents in 1614–1615 and finally stabilized political control over the country (Reischauer 1990: 66–67).

Both Hideyoshi and Tokugawa saw Christianity as a threat to unification and political stability. These leaders were aware that Christianity often came hand in hand with political domination. Christianity was even more complicated because of its exclusive nature. At first, it was welcomed as a variant of Buddhism. When missionaries rejected this Japanese reception, they lost the support of Buddhist clergy. Hideyoshi eventually banned Christianity in 1587. He enforced this ban a decade later, crucifying nine missionaries and seventeen of their converts (Reischauer 1990: 76).

At first, Tokugawa was more tolerant of Christianity, but in 1606 he began issuing anti-Christian edicts. He started persecuting Christians in 1612. The ban on Christianity was escalated to an even more isolationist policy in 1636 when Tokugawa implemented the policy of "closed country" (sakoku). In order to ensure that Christian influence did not reach Japan, Japanese were no longer allowed to leave the country, and Japanese living abroad were not allowed to return (Reischauer 1990: 76).

The ban on Christianity followed by persecutions of Christian missionaries eventually caused the West to lose interest in Japan. Japan's contact with the outside world became minimal and was limited to controlled interactions with the Dutch outside Nagasaki, Koreans in Tsushima, and Chinese through the Ryukyus (Reischauer 1990: 77).

The timing of the implementation of the closed country policy is significant. Japan's political decision to close itself off was just prior to the Industrial Revolution. During the middle ages, prior to the seventeenth century, the difference between the East and West was not that large. Literacy rates were quite high in the East with about 40 percent of the male population and 15 percent of the female population literate. The East also was developing technology mainly of the moveable kind like compasses, gun powder, and clocks. The West did not go ahead of the East until after the policy of closed country was enforced. The result of this advance was not inherent in Western culture but instead can be seen as a result of Japan's political decision to close itself off from the rest of the world. While Japan did experience economic growth under Tokugawa, it was not able to benefit from some of the advances made in the West during the Industrial Revolution. Moreover, after closing the country the incentives to live in cities diminished. Instead, more rewards came from agriculture in rural areas. These incentives led to the development of agriculture as well as handicrafts. The depopulation of cities took away a favorable environment for developing manufacturing or mass production.

Several positive developments during Tokugawa moved it slowly from a traditional to a pre-modern society, capable of eventually responding to the forced opening by the West in the nineteenth century. While Tokugawa was not highly centralized in a modern sense, it was more unified than most traditional societies. Several policies implemented by the shogun facilitated this unification. One of the most important policies was the system of alternate attendance (sankin kōtai). The policy called for feudal lords (daimyō) to spend alternate years in their feudal domains and at the capital with the shogunate. In order to fund the trips and pay their respect to the shogun, the feudal lords had to produce excess crops and handicrafts. This promoted economic development. In addition, the frequent contact with the shogunate allowed the shogun to maintain tighter control over the domains. In theory, the feudal domain had independent control over local matters. In practice, the system of alternate attendance allowed for greater influence by the shogun (Reischauer 1990: 72–73).

The other significant innovation was the creation of a bureaucracy to coordinate activities between the classes and the shogunate and feudal domains. Succession issues did not plague the Tokugawa shogunate in part because the bureaucracy compensated for the varying levels of competence of the leaders that followed Tokugawa (Totman 1981). Significantly, a bureaucracy is a distinctly modern innovation based on impersonal rules as opposed to personal ties. Personal ties were still dominant during the Tokugawa period, but the development of a bureaucratic structure in the pre-modern period made Japan's eventual shift to a nation-state more smooth and quick.

Education

The long period of peace and isolation under Tokugawa also fostered education. After 1638, samurai were no longer involved in warfare. Thus, while education continued to focus on martial training, the environment made this type of education less relevant. As a result, education expanded beyond martial training. Peasants were often educated in temples. This education provided them the necessary tools to develop into "peasant entrepreneurs" who developed specialized crops and became more capable of effectively using the land. In a sense, these peasants represented an emerging middle class (Reischauer 1990: 85).

Economics

Even though Tokugawa was still feudal, economic growth occurred during this period. Two features of Tokugawa fostered economic growth. First, the shogun controlled about one fourth of the most fertile and prosperous areas of the country, regions that include Tokyo, Osaka, and Kyoto today. The shogun's control of the region provided security and resulted in what some have classified a trade free zone (Reischauer 1990: 80). Moreover, as noted earlier, the system of alternate attendance meant that no domain stood in isolation. Instead, each domain had incentives to produce extra crops or manufactured goods to share with the shogunal court.

Demographics and feudal class

The population eventually stabilized under Tokugawa. Tokugawa Japan was remarkable due to its ability to "self-regulate" and control its population size (Totman 1981: 222). This self-regulation resulted in population control. Marriage regulation and infanticide kept family size small. Families had a smaller number of children and focused more resources on them. They also did not have more children than they could afford to support. The Tokugawa bureaucracy monitored population growth and land use, overseeing a very sophisticated form of economic growth.

The shift of the population from the cities to the countryside not only dampened the incentives to innovate in manufacturing, but it also influenced the relative power of the various feudal classes. Over time peasants gained more power and influence. This class was responsible for the country's prosperity. Meanwhile, the samurai became more reliant on merchants for funds. Samurai did not think to tax trade and instead relied on loans from merchants, weakening the effective power of samurai.

An interesting counterfactual to consider is whether the tensions emerging between the feudal classes had already put Tokugawa on the brink of falling and moving toward modernity prior to the opening by the West. While there is no definitive answer to this counterfactual, there is plenty of evidence that the reality of late Tokugawa differed greatly from its original conception. In particular, the strict hierarchy of the feudal classes was breaking down.

The Meiji Restoration

Ultimately, the arrival of Commodore Matthew Perry hastened Japan's transition from a traditional to a modern society. Commodore Perry was an officer in the U.S. navy who arrived in Japan in 1853 with orders to open Japan to the West. Even today the image of Perry's so-called "black ships" looms large in Japan and is a shorthand reference for Western dominance. Perry's ships were so shocking because Japan had been closed off from the West for over 250 years. When Japan closed its ports, ships were made of wood; after the Industrial Revolution, however, ships were made of steel and fueled with coal. The ships symbolized the advance in technology of the West as well as the power and danger of these innovations in the context of Western imperialism which prevailed at this point. At the time, the United States had its eye on trade with China and whaling. It saw Japan as a critical coaling and watering stop. Japanese rulers held open the possibility that Western colonization was a potential threat. Perry left the Japanese rulers to consider how to respond to this demand indicating he would return in a year for Japan's response.

In 1854 Japan agreed to open two of its ports – Shimoda and Hakodate – to the West. This agreement was followed by a series of unequal treaties initiated by the West. Consul Townsend Harris enacted the first unequal commercial treaty in 1858

(Reischauer 1990: 97). The most pernicious features of this treaty included the provisions regarding extraterritoriality and tariffs. Extraterritoriality held that Western laws held for Westerners in Japan. This provision was a slap in the face but also reflected Japan's status as pre-modern. Japan was not a unified nation-state and as such the West refused to submit to its customs and rules. The commercial agreement held that tariffs on Japanese goods were to remain low and fixed. This provision increased the barriers to growth, prosperity or even economic survival for Japan as it entered upon the path to development.

Japan like all developing countries faced the pressure of having to catch up quickly to developed countries. One way to meet this challenge is to place a tax on imports. The unequal treaty took this option away. In this instance, for example, Japan produced beautiful silk goods, but it did not have the advantages of machinery, factories, or the division of labor. Thus, while the quality of its silk products was high, these products could not compete against the price of the Western goods. The inability to place a tariff on the cheaper silk products made Japanese silk producers uncompetitive. Japan was also forced to open its cities to free trade. The unequal commercial treaties initially resulted in a disruption in domestic handicrafts and manufactured goods, a drain on gold, and low public support.

Perry's arrival sparked a debate on how to best respond to the threat posed by the West. In general, the Japanese response was tinged with xenophobia and anger, but a divide emerged between conservatives who favored resistance and others who favored cooperation, at least initially. The military might and technological prowess of the West suggested that cooperation was the most pragmatic response. The emperor was opposed to signing the unequal treaties, but the shogun eventually did (Reischauer 1990: 95–97).

This divide eventually resulted in the Meiji Restoration. The Meiji Restoration was led by a group of low-ranking samurai from domains in Southwest Japan with the aid of some court nobles. These actors felt that the most effective response to the threat of the West was a change in government. The initial battle cry of the samurai leading the revolt was "sonnō jōi," which means "honor the emperor, expel the barbarians." This cry reflected their strategy and goal. The movement was called a restoration as opposed to a revolution because the goal was to "restore" the emperor to power. In this sense, the emperor was an important symbol of legitimacy (Reischauer 1990: 101). The way of expelling the barbarians became clear once the leaders of the restoration (the so-called oligarchs) took power. With the assumption of power the slogan changed to "fukoku kyōhei" which translates to "rich country, strong military." The implication was that the only way to expel the barbarians was to promote economic development and strengthen Japan's military might (Reischauer 1990: 102).

In comparative perspective, the Meiji Restoration is quite distinct from other revolutions prompted by a desire to modernize. First, the Restoration was characterized by collective leadership, not individual leadership. It also defies many of the typical categories of revolution. It was not a revolution from below nor was it a revolution from above. It also was not a bourgeois revolution; the merchants were not active participants (Reischauer 1990: 112). As we have seen, low-ranking samurai and court nobles led the revolution in response to an external threat, not an internal one.

Some legacies of the Tokugawa period aided the success of the Restoration. Over two centuries of isolation resulted in a unified, homogeneous society that did not suffer from significant religious or ethnic cleavages. The seeds of nationalism were also present in the traditional society, something that allowed the domains to join together in the face of a common threat from the West (Reischauer 1990: 112–113). The relative importance of each of these factors is hard to determine; however, each is important for understanding Japan's transition from tradition to modernity.

Meiji Japan

The modern era is divided into periods based on imperial reign. The first period from 1868 to 1912 is referred to as the Meiji period. Meiji was followed by Taishō (1912–1926), Shōwa (1926–1989), and Heisei (1989–present). The Meiji period focused on the developmental task of consolidation. Once the oligarchs gained power, they forged new institutions to foster legitimacy, unity, and growth.

The oligarchs were able to maintain power in part due to the support of the emperor and the military. The oligarchs increased Japan's financial resources by raising funds through land taxes and loans from rich merchants.

To further extend power and control as well as set Japan on the track of economic development, the oligarchs also began to centralize and rationalize power. Most significantly, perhaps, the oligarchs abolished the feudal class structure. With this, peasants and samurai could engage in trade, not just merchants. In addition, mass conscription was implemented. Under Tokugawa only samurai could carry weapons. Mass conscription ensured the end of the privileged military class. Mass education was also implemented in 1871. This reform facilitated the goal of eliminating class distinctions (Reischauer 1990: 107).

The oligarchs replaced feudal domains with a smaller number of prefectures. They also created several "modern" institutions based on impersonal rules instead of personal ties. For example, they created a judicial system, a modern bureaucracy, a civil service, and centralized banking. Property rights were established and taxes were collected using currency as opposed to rice. This tax revenue was critical as Japan attempted to promote economic growth (Reischauer 1990: 105).

Japan's economic growth focused on building infrastructure and munitions. The government built railroads and adopted the telegraph (Reischauer 1990: 105). It also supplied the capital necessary for industrial development. Inflation, however, caused an amendment to these state-led development policies. As part of a deflation policy implemented by Finance Minister Matsukata, the Japanese government sold many of its mines and private factories to private entrepreneurs (Reischauer 1990: 109). This policy had both economic and social implications. Economically, privatization resulted in greater economic efficiency and a downward pressure on prices. Socially, the policy indicated that people with close connections to the government were more likely to receive favors. Many of the beneficiaries of this policy would go on to create industrial conglomerates (zaibatsu). The zaibatsu families were later seen as a driving force in Japan's military expansion due to the desire for access to more raw materials.

The Meiji Constitution

In 1890 the Diet passed the Meiji Constitution. The oligarchs felt a constitution was a necessary step in their quest to consolidate power. They also reasoned that a Western-style constitution would make Japan more intelligible to the West and serve as a tool to free itself from its "unequal" status. Finally, a constitution would promote unity and inclusiveness.

The Constitution was presented as a gift from the emperor and used to justify continued rule by the oligarchs who led the Restoration. Executive power remained with the oligarchs. A parliamentary system was established with an elected lower house and an appointed house of peers. The election of representatives to the lower house allowed for some participation, but the franchise was extremely limited by sex, age, and tax status. Due to these limitations only about 1.26 percent of the population could vote (Reischauer 1990: 122). The parliament did have some control over funding. The budget rule established by the Constitution held that if the parliament and cabinet could not agree on a new budget, the budget from the previous year would be renewed. Politicians would use this rule during the Taishō period to increase their power in relation to the cabinet. Finally, citizens were only given limited rights. In contrast to the notion of inalienable rights, the rights of citizens under the Meiji Constitution were circumscribed by the "rule of law." That is, citizens only had rights as outlined in the Constitution.

A fatal weakness of the Meiji Constitution was that sovereignty was not clearly established. It was not clear where ultimate sovereignty rested. Instead, as time passed several actors competed for ultimate sovereignty, including the emperor, the oligarchs, the military, politicians, political parties, and the parliament (Reischauer 1990: 140). As we shall see, the military exploited this ambiguity and seized control in the 1920s.

The new Constitution did have one significant effect internationally – it contributed to the eventual elimination of unequal treaties. Extraterritoriality ended in 1899, and Japan gained control over its tariffs in 1911. Japan continued to feel like a second-class citizen in the eyes of the West, though. These feelings would contribute to rising militarism in the early twentieth century.

Taishō Democracy

The Taishō period (1912–1926) is characterized by the dual developments of democracy and militarism. The ambiguity of the Meiji Constitution allowed for these conflicting tendencies to arise. In the short term, militarism would destroy democracy in Japan, but the legacy of the Taishō period is important in understanding the success of postwar Japanese democracy.

As time passed the oligarchs recognized the need to expand political participation, a project that the Meiji Constitution initiated. This recognition emerged as more voices of opposition became apparent. A functional democracy needs to allow for contestation, participation, and representation with some provision of civil liberties and civil rights. The Taishō period from 1912 to 1926 was the period when these principles were pursued and to some extent flourished. The irony, however, is that the ambiguity of sovereignty in the Meiji Constitution allowed for advances in contestation and participation to occur alongside rising militarism.

Demands for greater participation came from opposition forces both inside and outside the government prior to the Taishō period. The responses to these calls for inclusion set the stage for the creation of political parties and their increased status and involvement during the Taishō period. During the Meiji period, there were several types of opposition. Military opposition was most apparent early in the Meiji period with Saigo Takamori's attempt to overthrow the Meiji oligarchs by force. Political opposition from the outside was led by Itagaki Taisuke, who co-founded the first political party in Japan, the Liberal Party (Jiyūtō). Itagaki led the Freedom and People's Right's movement from 1873 to 1890, a movement that was instrumental in bringing

about the Meiji Constitution and the establishment of a lower house with elected officials. This movement was led by intellectuals and did not include the wealthier members of society. Dissenting voices also existed within the oligarchy. Ōkuma Shigenobu
led the elite opposition and founded the Progressive Party. Because this group of
opposition was inside government, its agenda focused on issues of policy and power
within the current system. For example, the progressives fought and lost the battle to
adopt a British-style constitution (Reischauer 1990: 119). As political parties began to
emerge, these parties were constrained both by the ambiguity of sovereignty and the limited franchise. Both weakened their position. Limited franchise in particular prevented
them from establishing a mass base of political support.

Popular demands for participation increased during the Taishō period. These
demands came from various quarters. As Japan began to develop, a small Socialist
movement emerged. The movement was not that radical or big. Still, many in government saw this organization as a potential threat and felt that it was better to increase
opportunities to participate in government rather than shut this voice out. A larger
demand for increased involvement in government came from peasants involved in
tenant unions. At this time, a large percentage of land was still under tenancy (about 40
percent). Tenant unions formed to pressure landlords for better conditions. The number
of peasants involved in the movement was not that large, but the potential for mobilization was great and thus made this movement even more of a threat. These developments pressured conservatives to consider opportunities for expanding contestation and
participation.

The response of the conservative oligarchs to these developments was mixed. The
conservatives led by Yamagata Aritomo supported some policies to constrain participation and others to encourage involvement, at least a particular kind of involvement.
To keep political activity under control the conservatives strengthened the police laws.
The conservatives also ensured that only elites could participate in the bureaucracy by
relying almost exclusively on professional bureaucrats who passed the civil service
exam. The military was also insulated from the public. Both the departments of the
army and the navy were run by active military personnel. Conservatives also limited
the power of political parties by creating large electoral districts. Large multiple-
member districts forced members of the same party to compete against one another.
The large districts also allowed smaller parties to win seats since the percentage of the
vote a party had to win was lower (Reischauer 1990: 125).

Despite these institutional rules and norms, the conservatives also made some compromises to expand political participation. First, the franchise was extended by lowering
the tax requirement. The secret ballot also was introduced (Reischauer 1990: 125).

The Taishō political change in 1912 significantly influenced the power of political
parties in relation to the oligarchs by ensuring that cabinets could not stand without
majority political party support. Prior to the Taishō political change cabinets were dominated
by oligarchs. The constitutional provision that required parliamentary approval for the
passage of the annual budget allowed political parties to gradually gain more influence
over the cabinet which had initially been conceived as "above politics." The shift in
political party influence came after a political crisis in 1912 related to budget negotiations. At this time the army was not satisfied with its budget allocation, and its minister
resigned from the cabinet to indicate its displeasure. This resignation forced the entire
cabinet to resign. The emperor ordered political parties to cooperate with the new
government led by General Katsura but the seiyūkai, one of the political parties at the

time, refused to cooperate. The public weighed in with a "movement to preserve constitutional government," which demanded a cabinet responsible to the parliament. The crisis was settled when the actors found a compromise prime minister and granted the seiyūkai six seats on the cabinet, ensuring a majority voice and its support (Reischauer 1990: 140). Political parties dominated all cabinets following the Taishō political change.

The Taishō political change was significant for several reasons. First, it illustrated some of the endemic problems with the Meiji Constitution, specifically the fact that sovereignty was ambiguous. The Taishō political change revealed the relative power of political actors in Japan. In particular, it showed the weakness of the emperor in relation to other actors – the seiyūkai was able to ignore his order to support the new government. It also showed the ability of the military to disregard or at least challenge other actors. According to the Constitution, the military was only responsible to the emperor (Reischauer 1990: 141). Finally, the Taishō political change revealed that it was no longer possible for the oligarchs to rule without political party support. In this regard, the move from control by the oligarchs to responsible parliamentary government was a remarkable shift that boded well for the transition to democracy.

The period of 1912–1926 is often referred to as Taishō democracy. Once political parties increased their presence and influence, participation was further expanded. Parties experimented with electoral rules. First, the electoral system was changed from large multiple-member districts to single-member districts. A single-member district system favors larger parties with greater organization and resources. After a negative reaction to this system, the parliament adopted a medium-sized district system. A similar medium-sized district system would be adopted after World War II. The tax requirement for voting was completely abolished in 1925, further expanding participation (Reischauer 1990: 143).

Ultimately, however, the competing power of the military overwhelmed the attempt of political parties to consolidate parliamentary government in Japan. The weak Constitution opened this door. The growing economic tensions in the 1920s facilitated the military's quest for increased power.

Economic conditions

Economic growth slowed during the 1920s. The Great Depression in the late 1920s exacerbated this slowdown. In particular, rice and silk prices dropped dramatically. As Japan continued to develop, a dual economy emerged. The dual economy was characterized by a productive industrial sector that received significant government support and a less productive rural sector.

Japan never had an abundance of raw materials, but its limited resources became even more apparent as it continued on the path to development. In order to meet the growing needs for raw materials, Japan became more dependent on foreign sources and markets. Instead of relying on international free trade to meet its needs for raw materials, Japan chose to create and expand its imperial empire.

As the economic problems increased, the support for parliamentary democracy decreased. Divisions within the public also emerged, many related to the dual economy. In particular, the interests of the educated, urban population and the less educated, mostly rural populations diverged.

In 1925, the government abolished the voting tax requirement for men, and it also strengthened the Peace Preservation Law. The Peace Preservation Law of 1925 made it a crime to support political reform or to abolish private property. This law significantly curtailed free speech and weakened the trend toward democracy in Japan (Reischauer 1990: 151).

Militarism

The military enjoyed a privileged position in Modern Japan from its inception. The Meiji oligarchs put the military front and center in their slogan "rich country, strong military." This slogan indicated the direct relationship between economic growth and military expansion that the oligarchs were pursuing.

When Commodore Perry forced Japan to open to the West, all developed countries had colonies. To Japan, imperialism was a path to enter the Western club of industrialized democracies and gain the security, economic, and status benefits that accompanied entrance to that "club." Indeed, over time Japan's primary motivation for acquiring colonies shifted from security concerns to economic and status goals.

The empire Japan built was unique in at least two features – it was small and close to home. At its height, the Japanese empire included Korea, Taiwan, and part of China. The close proximity to Japan allowed for the relocation of Japanese to the colonies to oversee business and political interests.

Initially, Japan set its sights on Korea primarily for security reasons. Korea was quite close to Japan, and many feared that it would come under control of a foreign power such as China. If a stronger power controlled Korea, many Japanese felt the power could use Korea as a foothold to gain control of Japan.

The Sino-Japanese war broke out in Korea in 1894. Japanese and Chinese armies in Korea got involved in a local rebellion by a conservative religious group. This incident escalated into war and a newly industrialized Japan dominated. It destroyed the Chinese fleet and occupied a port in North China. The Chinese and Japanese settled the fighting with the Treaty of Shimonoseki. In this treaty, China gave Japan control of Taiwan, the Pescadores Islands, and the tip of the Liaotung Peninsula and paid a large indemnity. China also acknowledged the full independence of Korea. Finally, the Japanese extorted economic and diplomatic privileges from China that mimicked the unequal treaties established by the West after forcing Japan's opening (Reischauer 1990: 129).

Japan secured its first Western ally in 1902 when it signed the Anglo-Japanese Alliance. Once again, security concerns motivated the alliance. This time, Japan was concerned about Russia. It reasoned that if it allied with Great Britain, this would prevent other Western powers from assisting Russia in an act of aggression against Japan. This treaty also elevated Japan's international status as it was the first military agreement that accorded equal status to a Western and non-Western country (Reischauer 1990: 129).

Japan initiated the Russo-Japanese War in 1904, and once again, Japan emerged victorious. This time its dominance was facilitated by the fact that Russia struggled to supply provisions and troops to the Eastern battle front due in part to the fact that its railway system only had one track. Still, both sides won battles. In the end, President Theodore Roosevelt helped negotiate a treaty ending the Russo-Japanese War on September 5, 1905. Japan greatly benefitted from the terms of this treaty. Specifically, Russia acknowledged Japan's interests in Korea. It also transferred its lease of the Liaotung Peninsula and the railways it had built in Manchuria, a part of China. Finally, Russia ceded the southern half of the Sakhalin islands. After its victories over China and Russia, Japan officially annexed Korea in 1910 (Reischauer 1990: 129–130).

Japan used its alliance with Britain to further expand. It joined World War I against Germany but did not participate in Europe. It received German colonies in the East as a reward for its support of the Allies in the Treaty of Versailles (Reischauer 1990: 130).

In 1915, Japan issued the Twenty One Demands on China. Many of these were economic in nature. China resisted the most far-reaching demands but accepted several demands as well. These demands further consolidated Japan's interests in the region. By the 1920s, Japan was Great Britain's chief revival in China (Reischauer 1990: 131).

Despite its gains in the region, Japan was determined to continue to expand its empire. It began to float the idea of creating a Greater East Asian Co-Prosperity Sphere in the early 1940s (Reischauer 1990: 172). Its motivations for expansions were primarily economic. Interestingly enough, for Japan participation in International Free Trade was not an option for solving its problem of limited resources. In the 1920s and 1930s, Japan continued to feel as if it were being treated as a second-class citizen by the West. The unequal treaties were removed in the early 1900s and Japan did ally with Great Britain. Still, certain domestic policies in the West continued to frustrate Japan. For example, Japanese were not allowed to emigrate to North America and Australia. Japanese exports also met increasing restrictions in the West. In addition, the West was explicitly pressuring Japan to decrease its presence in the China.

The military's response to the increasing international pressures and tensions of the 1920s and 1930s was to take control of the decision making on the ground in China. In 1928, young military officers assassinated a local warlord in Manchuria. The emperor demanded that the officers be disciplined, but the army refused. This assassination was followed by the more serious Manchurian Incident. In this incident, middle-grade army officers blew up a portion of the Japanese-owned Manchurian railway and placed the blame on China. The army used this pretext of sabotage to overrun all of Manchuria. In 1932, Japan created the puppet state of Manchukuo (Reischauer 1990: 159).

These military successes fueled nationalism. Many Japanese became convinced that force was a viable way to secure Japan's interests. These incidents revealed other important trends. First, the fact these actions were carried out by younger military personnel illustrated a division between old officers and younger personnel. While the officers did not support the acts by the younger personnel, the officers did use the accomplishments as a way to pressure the civil government for political changes. The fact that the army ignored the emperor's order to discipline the officers also showed the increasing power of the military versus other domestic actors.

The military brought an end to democracy in Japan with the February 26 Incident in 1936. In this incident several young extremist officers led members of the first division in Tokyo in an attempt to assassinate several top government leaders. The February 26 Incident was the biggest challenge to the government since the Satsuma rebellion in 1877 (Reischauer 1990: 162–163). By 1936, political parties had lost most of their power.

World War II

In 1937, Japan began its war of aggression on China, marking the beginning of World War II on the Eastern front. The incident that sparked the war was relatively minor – Japanese and Chinese troops got into a skirmish near the capital, but China refused a local settlement to the fighting. Japan escalated in response. While Japan tried to secure a victory over China quickly, it was stymied by China's United Front, when the Communists and the Nationalists who had been fighting joined forces to defeat Japan.

The West initially registered its disapproval of Japan's hegemony and quest for the Greater East Asian Co-Prosperity Sphere by implementing economic sanctions. In 1939, the U.S. denounced its commercial treaty with Japan. Then in 1941, the U.S., Great Britain, and the Netherlands implemented an oil embargo on Japan to illustrate their disapproval of continued Japanese aggression in East Asia. These countries would only lift the embargo if Japan withdrew from Asia completely. These conditions forced Japan to choose between a humiliating withdrawal or more aggression. The military refused to support a policy of withdrawal. It had told the Japanese people that it was securing its economic interests through aggression. A withdrawal would disgrace the military in the eyes of the public. The military chose to sail south and break the embargo by seizing resources in Southeast Asia, particularly oil in the Dutch East Indies. It also made a pre-emptive strike on Pearl Harbor forcing the United States to enter the war (Reischauer 1990: 172–174). While Japan experienced early victories against the U.S., it became more desperate as the fighting continued. The U.S. brought the war to an end with the bombings of Hiroshima and Nagasaki.

Conclusion

From its journey from Meiji Japan through the end of World War II, Japan experimented with political and economic arrangements to promote democracy and growth. By the 1930s, it appeared that Japan had reached its goal of rich country, strong military. In the end, Japan's imperial quest was stymied by Asian nationalism, especially in China. Japan also challenged Western interests in China. This challenge led to economic sanctions and a pre-emptive strike on the U.S. by Japan.

The way World War II ended had a significant legacy on postwar Japan. Japan was the first country to experience a nuclear attack. This final attack allowed the Japanese people to see themselves as victims instead of aggressors. In addition, many also saw themselves as victims of a totalitarian regime. As discussed in Chapter 12, this "victim" mentality would color Japan's domestic and foreign policy for decades to come.

References

Jowitt, K. (1992) *New World Disorder: The Leninist Extinction*, Berkeley: University of California Press.
Reischauer, E. O. (1990) *Japan: The Story of a Nation*, 4th edn, New York: McGraw Hill Publishing Company.
Totman, C. (1981) *Japan Before Perry: A Short History*, Berkeley: University of California Press.

3 The postwar settlement

Following the atomic bombings of Hiroshima on August 6, 1945 and of Nagasaki on August 9, 1945, Emperor Hirohito announced Japan's surrender to the Allied Powers in a radio address on August 15, 1945. At the war's end Japan lay in ruins with 40 percent of the area of its cities destroyed from air bombings. The human loss also was significant with most estimates placing the dead and missing around three million, a third of whom were nonmilitary casualities. In addition, Japan's industrial capacity had been devastated. Most industrial production had come to a halt (Reischauer 1990: 184). Food and consumer goods were in short supply and hyperinflation ensued.

It is within this context that the Allied Occupation commenced on August 28, 1945 with General Douglas MacArthur as the Supreme Commander of the Allied Powers (SCAP), and Japan officially signed the surrender papers on September 2, 1945. The Occupation lasted seven years ending in 1952 after the signing of the Peace Treaty. Unlike in Germany where the Occupation was a multilateral affair with Britain, Russia, France, and the United States overseeing various zones of the defeated territory, in Japan the United States was the dominant actor. The absence of other allied powers smoothed the completion of a political settlement with the Japanese approving a new Constitution in 1947, five years before the Germans ratified their Basic Law. As we shall see this Constitution addressed the weaknesses in the Meiji Constitution and paved the way for a vibrant democracy to emerge.

While the path to the political settlement was relatively smooth, partially due to the force of will of the United States, the economic settlement was delayed until the outbreak of the Cold War. Only with the fear of the spread of Communism in Asia did the United States begin to prioritize recovery and rehabilitation in the economic realm. Indeed, this fear would also result in the United States pressuring Japan to rearm and enter into a bilateral security arrangement that would define the postwar period. While a set of conservatives strongly favored rearmament and even revision of the peace clause in the Constitution, centrists, the left, and the public at large were much more wary of these events.

This chapter explores Japan's road to political, economic, and security settlements following the end of World War II. It draws comparisons to settlements made in Germany and Italy, two other defeated powers. It also explores the reverse legacies of the Meiji Constitution and sets the stage for direct legacies to emerge from the Occupation.

The Occupation

The political settlement

Occupation officials in Japan and Germany prioritized the so-called four Ds: denazification, demilitarization, democratization, and decartelization. In Japan, denazification related more to dismantling the authoritarian military rule, which most agree was fascist in character, albeit with an emphasis more on the nation than on race. Both denazification and demilitarization were seen as necessary precursors to the creation of democratic regimes.

The Occupation sought to achieve denazification through war trials and purges. Unlike in Germany where key members of the Nazi party could be identified as the main instigators of the atrocities, a clear leadership group did not exist in Japan. No consensus existed on culpability. Many blamed the emperor. The Occupation, however, decided not to prosecute him, due in part to a fear that such an action would make the public less willing or enthusiastic about SCAP's desire to establish strong democratic institutions. Occupation officials did force the emperor to publicly apologize to the Japanese people via radio address. This action alone shocked many Japanese as the emperor had always served as a near God-like figure with the status of awe, never having addressed the people directly. The Japanese people had never even heard his voice prior to the radio address.

The Tokyo War Trials focused on the military elite as the main perpetrators. General Tōjō and nine other military officials were hanged. Many others were imprisoned. Outside the formal prosecution of war crimes, many other former military personnel, business people, and politicians were purged in an effort to rid government and business institutions of the former military mentality.

The purge had a large impact on the Japanese party system. Unlike Germany, Japan maintained some semblance of elected government throughout World War II. Political parties were banned in 1940, but Japan conducted parliamentary elections in 1942. Politicians that supported the military government were approved by the Imperial Rule Assistance Association (IRAA), but even a few independents won elections. After the end of the war, the SCAP purged any politician who had been approved by the IRAA. The Progressive Party, which was a major party on the right at the war's end, was devastated by the purge since most of its politicians had been approved by the IRAA. The Liberal Party (another party on the right) lost about a fifth of its membership due to the purge. Most notably, the Liberal Party's nominee for prime minister in 1946, Hatoyama Ichirō, was purged before he was able to take office. The Socialist parties also lost about half their Diet members due to the purge. While the purge initially targeted politicians with connections to the wartime government, it expanded during the Occupation to target Communist party members. These politicians had not supported wartime activities. Instead, these purged officials were targeted by the SCAP and conservative parties in Japan's postwar governments.

The bureaucracy was the only institution left virtually untouched by the Occupation purges. It was not that sitting civil servants were completely free from complicity in the former regime. Instead, this choice was out of practical necessity. The Occupation decided it needed some assistance from domestic actors, and the members of the elite bureaucracy were deemed the most appropriate and potentially useful in facilitating SCAP's goals. This decision would eventually have a legacy in the political realm as many of these bureaucrats would become politicians and serve as leaders in Japan's state-led growth.

Just like denazification, demilitarization was a negative goal focused on destroying past institutions. To begin with, the Japanese army and navy were abolished. Investigations of war crimes and purges were carried out. Japan's weapons were destroyed, and its military industrial capacity was dismantled.

In contrast to demilitarization which was a goal that could be achieved in the short term, democratization was a goal with a much longer time frame. The first step on the road to democracy was the formulation of a new Constitution, one that specifically addressed the weaknesses in the Meiji Constitution.

Japan held elections more quickly than Germany following the war's end. Japan's first parliamentary elections occurred under the old Meiji Constitution in 1946. The Liberal Party won a majority and selected Hatoyama Ichirō as prime minister. After he was purged, Yoshida Shigeru became prime minister. The main task of this Diet was to approve the new Constitution. According to Richard Samuels, Yoshida was able to convince others to accept the new Constitution by explaining, "democracy had always formed part of the traditions of our country" (Samuels 2003: 203). Yoshida blamed the failure of the Meiji Constitution on the militarists. He felt that the solution was to promote democracy and pacifism. Finally, Yoshida also recast the role of the emperor in Japanese history by asserting that the emperor had always merely been a symbolic figure (Samuels 2003).

While addressing the past weaknesses of the prewar Constitution, the SCAP also tried to put forth a Constitution that reinstated democratic institutions that flourished under Taishō democracy. Indeed, one of the main reasons Japan is not a blueprint of U.S. institutions of democracy is that Occupation officials recognized the need and value of drawing on structures from Japan's previous experience with democratic institutions. Thus, just like in the prewar period, Japan adopted a parliamentary system of government with a lower house and an upper house. Unlike the Meiji Constitution, Japan's postwar Constitution clearly addresses the issue of sovereignty: sovereignty rests with the people and is secured through the election of representatives to parliament. Instead of defining cabinets as "above politics," the postwar Constitution ensured that the party or parties that had a majority in the lower house of the parliament known as the Diet controlled the selection of the cabinet and the prime minister.

The Constitution expanded suffrage to women and guaranteed equal rights to men and women, something a few activist female Occupation officials pushed with the aid of domestic allies. As a result, Japan's Constitution goes beyond the United States' Constitution by including an equal rights clause. The Constitution also introduced Western-type labor practices in the text of the Constitution with a clause declaring the right to collective bargaining.

The most controversial clause in the Constitution is Article 9, the so-called peace clause. This article states that Japan will not pursue or develop the capabilities to pursue acts of aggression. Article 9 is often referred to as the renunciation of war clause. This article states that Japan rejects war. To this end, according to Article 9 Japan will not maintain land, sea, or air forces for the purposes of war or aggression. The clause nicely supported the United States' goal of demilitarizing Japan. It was also received well by a public that was exhausted from a war effort and disillusioned with militarism (Reischauer 1990: 192).

The Constitution went into effect on May 3, 1947. Many argue that the Americans forced the Japanese to accept this foreign-influenced document, pointing to the fact that Occupation officials threatened to put the emperor on trial for war crimes if parliament rejected the document. Despite these strong-arm tactics, the Constitution stands today as the unrevised guiding document of democracy for Japan.

Once the Constitution was approved, Japan held new elections. In 1947, the Socialist Party won a majority and selected Katayama Tetsu as prime minister. This coalition was weak, though, because Socialists were in coalition with Conservatives. It only lasted ten months. In the following election another coalition of left and right parties came to power. It was only able to stay in power for eight months. In the 1948 election, the Socialists lost two-thirds of their seats and split over the peace treaty being negotiated with the allies. Yoshida Shigeru was appointed prime minister in 1948 and would serve in this capacity until 1952. He worked well with the Occupation and effectively protected Japan's interests in economic development.

The left and right were divided in the first decade following the end of the war. Responding to the incentives of the new political institutions and the dictates of party competition, parties merged in 1955. On the left, the right Socialists and the left Socialists merged to form the Japanese Socialist Party (JSP). This merger prompted the Liberal and Democratic parties to form the Liberal Democratic Party shortly thereafter. These mergers ushered in the 1955 system of LDP dominance and the main lines of competition from 1955 to 1993.

The economic settlement

The path to an economic settlement was much more harried. In the beginning, Occupation officials were not interested in rehabilitating the economy of the former aggressor. In the mind of most U.S. policymakers, Japan had received the just desserts of its actions.

Early Occupation policies focused on deconcentrating the industrial conglomerates (zaibatsu) seen as promoting Japanese imperialism in an effort to get greater access to natural resources and markets. Occupation officials oversaw the passage of anti-monopoly legislation. These laws included the Fair Trade Law and the Economic Power Excessive Concentration Elimination Law (1947). These laws called for the dissolution of zaibatsu. Holding companies were destroyed and the zaibatsu families (which included names still familiar to us today such as Mitsui, Mitsubishi Sumitomo, and Yasuda) were broken up. SCAP, however, struggled to implement these deconcentration policies in a timely fashion. By the time that the comprehensive antimonopoly provisions were reconsidered as part of the reverse course only eleven groups had felt the full weight of these regulations.

In addition to deconcentration policies, the Occupation introduced fair market rules. Legislation to promote fair market rules included the Anti-Trust Law and the Securities Exchange Law. These provisions were meant to promote transparency and ensure fair market competition.

The uncertainty of the deconcentration policies hampered industrial innovation in big businesses. In the interim, small- and medium-sized enterprises flourished. With more flexibility and less regulation, these enterprises provided the initial economic energy that began to fuel Japan's road to recovery. The small- and medium-sized enterprises focused on consumer goods such as cooking appliances, electronics, etc. Many of these companies successfully converted the production of wartime products to consumer goods (Dower 1999: 533).

Some sectors of the economy were targeted for recovery. Domestically, the focus was on coal, steel, electricity, and chemical industries including fertilizer. Shipbuilding and textiles also received attention as key export sectors in need of development. A government policy labeled "priority production" then focused resources in these sectors of the economy (Dower 1999). The targeted sectors received direct government subsidies and loans through the Reconstruction Finance Bank (RFB). The country's scarce resources and labor were thereby directed to these sectors. While this system did promote growth, it also facilitated corruption. Soon businesses learned that connections to the state along with "gifts" could help secure loans from the RFB. This type of corruption was exposed in the Shōwa Denko scandal that broke in October 1948. This scandal implicated the sitting Prime Minister Ashida Hitoshi and Deputy Prime Minister Nishio Suehiro as having accepted bribes from Shōwa Denko, a chemical fertilizer company, in return for favorable loans from the RFB. Prime Minister Ashida was forced to resign and Nishio was imprisoned. The legacy of close government–business relations characteristic of priority production would endure after the end of the Occupation, as would the corruption that often accompanied such relations.

Other postwar economic reforms targeted agriculture, labor, and education. The Occupation sought to eliminate land tenancy. To this end, the government oversaw the redistribution of land by buying the holdings of landlords and selling the holdings to tenants at very reasonable rates. This reform increased the number of independent farmers. The Occupation also promoted the formation of labor unions as institutions that could hold industry accountable and thus promote democracy in the economic realm. Labor movements were also made legal through this series of legislation that included the Labor Union Law (1945), the Labor Relations Adjustment Law (1946), and the Labor Standards Law (1947). Finally, to promote an educated workforce the Occupation oversaw the extension of compulsory education from six to nine years (Dower 1999: 245–7).

Inflation proved to be a larger threat to Japan's economic recovery after World War II. As tensions between the United States and the Soviet Union increased in the late 1940s and the fault lines of the Cold War became more apparent, especially with the outbreak of the Korean War in 1950, the United States began a so-called reverse course in the economic realm. In February 1949, the United States sent an expert economic team led by Joseph Dodge to make policy recommendations to get inflation under control in Japan. The so-called Dodge Mission forced the Japanese Diet to overbalance the budget. This policy necessitated a reduction in government subsidies. Loans from the RFB were also halted. In addition, Dodge moved to stabilize the yen by establishing a fixed exchange rate that undervalued the yen at 360 yen to the dollar. These policies got inflation under control but also resulted in pervasive unemployment and less domestic consumption. Balancing the budget also meant that fewer funds could be allocated to public works, welfare, and education (Dower 1999: 541).

The reverse course also forced a reconsideration of the antimonopoly legislation. Zaibatsu had originally been targeted due to their complicity in Japanese imperialism. Once the Occupation decided it was important to revive Japan's industrial sector in the wake of the Cold War, it relaxed the restrictions on shared stockholdings and mergers. These revisions allowed for the emergence of postwar industrial conglomerates labeled keiretsu. The keiretsu system was not a carbon copy of the zaibatsu system. According to John Dower, "Whereas the old zaibatsu were rigidly pyramidal groupings, keiretsu relationships tended to be more horizontal, open and internally competitive" (Dower 1999: 545). The major keiretsu groups included Mitsui, Mitsubishi, Sumitomo, Fuji,

Daiichi, and Sanwa. Most of the new keiretsu groups had ties to the old zaibatsu system, although the new system was no longer family based. Instead, stockholdings were broader. The keiretsu system was also less exclusive – keiretsu banks dealt with companies outside the keiretsu and companies from the keiretsu dealt with banks outside the keiretsu. State funding, however, was a more integral part of the postwar industrial conglomerates (Dower 1999: 545). The reduced regulation of industry combined with the increased demand for industrial materials and military products sparked by the Korean War helped catapult Japan's economic growth. By the mid-1950s, Japan's economy had returned to prewar levels.

Many of the features of postwar Japanese capitalism emerged during the Occupation. High levels of capital concentration and bureaucratic guidance of industrial policy characterized the postwar economy. The connections between government and business were bolstered by the fact that the banking system was not reformed under the Occupation. Instead, private city banks which had had ties to zaibatsu during World War II were allowed to over-loan targeted industries following the restrictions placed on the RFB by Dodge. These city banks in turn received funds from the Bank of Japan which was administered by the Ministry of Finance, one of the two bureaucratic agencies involved in promoting and some would say directing Japanese growth in the postwar period. The city banks essentially took over the functions of the RFB following the Dodge reforms (Dower 1999: 544–545). Each city bank in turn was connected to a keiretsu grouping. These city banks took over the central role that holding companies had played for zaibatsu (Dower 1999: 545).

Security policy

Following the end of World War II, the primary goal of the Occupation was to demilitarize Japan. Demilitarization was a negative goal – it meant the destruction of the old regime. It was a short-term goal that was carried out with relative ease.

Achieving this goal meant shutting down or repurposing all industries built to support the military industrial complex. This disarmament allowed the Occupation to focus its political goals of democratization without the influence of the military.

The Occupation pursued demilitarization in several steps. The first step was to dismantle Japan's empire. This step involved repatriating nearly six million Japanese nationals who had moved to areas under the control of Imperial Japan. Russia was given control over the Northern Territories, and the United States was put in charge of Okinawa. Disarmament meant converting the ministries of the army and navy to the first and second demobilization ministries. All munitions plants were shut down. War criminals were also brought to trial. This piece proved a bit problematic as it was less clear who should be held responsible for the atrocities of war. In the end, seven military officials were hung, including General Tōjō Hideki, the head of the Japanese Imperial Army and prime minister during most of World War II. The Occupation also conducted far-reaching purges of military, business, and government personnel connected to Japan's Imperial aggression. All purged officials were banned from government service, a ban that was rescinded after the end of the Occupation. These purges opened up space for new leaders to emerge, especially from the bureaucracy, the one area protected from the purge efforts (Reischauer 1990: 189–190).

The final step of demilitarization was to delink the State and the Shintō religion. The practice of the Shintō religion was permitted, but the State could no longer provide support. This step was deemed necessary given that Shintō had become a tool used by Imperial Japan to foster nationalism (Reischauer 1990: 190).

Rearmament

The outbreak of the Korean War on June 25, 1950 opened the door for a conversation about rearmament. The Korean War brought the Cold War into the Asian region. The tensions between the Soviet Union and the Allies had been much more pressing in Germany's postwar settlement. The division of Germany was the most vivid expression of the rising tensions of the Cold War in Europe. Japan seemed further removed from this conflict until the outbreak of the Korean War. In particular, the Korean War allowed those in favor of rearmament to argue that it was necessary for Japan's self-defense.

The initial steps to self-defense involved the creation of the National Police Reserve in 1950. The National Police Reserve was created just weeks after the outbreak of the Korean War. Its creation came following a directive sent by General MacArthur to Prime Minister Yoshida. General MacArthur had been opposed to remilitarization up to this point. The outbreak of the Korean War, however, required that U.S. troops stationed in Japan be sent to Korea. It also left a demilitarized Japan vulnerable. As a result, the directive called for the creation of a 75,000-person police reserve and an expansion of the coast guard by 8,000 people. Prime Minister Yoshida denied that the National Police Reserve was a new military. He supported this claim by pointing out that these forces were not capable of supporting a war effort (Samuels 2003).

The outbreak of the Korean War also hastened the United States' efforts to end the Occupation and restore Japan as a country in good standing internationally. In particular, the United States wanted Japan firmly in the camp of liberal Western democracies. To this end, John Foster Dulles worked throughout 1950–1951 to negotiate the San Francisco Peace Treaty between Japan and the 48 allies. With the signing of this treaty, Japan received full independence. Japan also was not charged war reparations. In fact, the Allies did not enact any negative economic punishments as part of the agreement (Reischauer 1990: 200–1).

At the same time, the United States negotiated a security agreement with Japan. Unlike Germany, which entered a multilateral security agreement with NATO, Japan relied solely on this bilateral agreement with the United States. As part of this agreement, the United States stated it would defend Japan against external threats. This agreement also expanded the Police Reserve Forces and changed its name to the National Security Forces. The National Security Forces were to respond to internal threats and natural disasters. Finally, in 1954 the Diet passed the National Self-Defense Act, which created Ground, Maritime, and Air National Self-Defense Forces (SDF).

In the U.S.–Japan Security Agreement, Japan agreed not to produce or use weapons of mass destruction. In return, it received a security guarantee from the U.S. against outside aggression. To this end, Japan agreed to have U.S. troops stationed on its territory and to remilitarize for internal threats to security. Under this treaty, the U.S. remained in charge of the Ryukyu Islands. The most controversial provision allowed the United States to control its troops on Japanese soil without communicating with the Japanese government. U.S. troops could also be deployed to deal with internal threats in Japan. In addition, the treaty forced Japan to cut its diplomatic ties with China. Later, it would sign a separate peace treaty with Taiwan (Dower 1999: 552–3).

Prime Minister Yoshida supported having U.S. troops in Japan. He allied with General MacArthur to secure this outcome. Yoshida defended the need for a continued U.S. presence in Japan by pointing to the outbreak of the Cold War and Japan's unwillingness to amend Article 9 that renounces war and prevents Japan from raising troops.

A reverse course also occurred in security. The reverse course in security focused on the role of police forces and rearmament. In 1952, the Subversive Activity Prevention Law went into effect. This law increased the State's control over strikes as well as public assemblies and demonstrations. In addition, the conservatives in power at the time centralized the police forces.

The re-evaluation of rearmament was more complicated. The divisions over rearmament cut across the left and the right. The creation of the SDF, however, predated the formation of the JSP and the LDP. The controversy over rearmament and fear over the potential revision of Article 9 of the Constitution actually provided incentives for the left and right Socialists to merge in 1955. The creation of the JSP was followed by the merger of the Liberal and Democratic Parties into the Liberal Democratic Party in 1955 later that same year.

In general, the left opposed rearmament. Its vision was of Japan as a peace nation. It supported unarmed or minimally armed neutrality. In particular, Socialists opposed capitalism and alignment with the West. The U.S.–Japan Security Agreement involved both implicitly supporting capitalism and an alliance with the West. The Left's position had strong support from labor unions and the media.

The right was divided on the issue of rearmament. The conservative side, which included Asida Hitoshi and Hatoyama Ichirō, was willing to consider the possibility of rearmament. Certain conservative supporters such as farmers and ex-military personnel were even more enthusiastic in their support of rebuilding Japan's military strength. Many conservatives supported revising the Constitution; they also wanted to regain control over Japan's national foreign policy agenda. Yoshida Shigeru, the prime minister during most of the Occupation period (from 1946–1947 and 1948–1954), did not favor rearmament. He was more interested in promoting Japan's economic development. Yoshida felt that rearmament would hamper economic growth and antagonize Japan's neighbors. He favored relying on the United States' security guarantee (Samuels 2003). The public and the East Asian region had the same position – neither constituency favored rearmament. The public also was afraid that Japan might be forced to participate in conflicts initiated by the United States. The region saw Japan's potential of returning to an aggressor as too high to risk rearmament.

The U.S.–Japan Security Treaty

The first U.S.–Japan Security Treaty was signed in 1951 and went into effect in 1952. This arrangement was less favorable for Japan. Many referred to it as an unequal treaty harkening back to the first commercial treaties negotiated between the U.S. and Japan in the late 1800s. As stated earlier, the most controversial provision stated that the United States could influence domestic disputes in Japan. When Prime Minister Kishi took office in 1957, he tried to strengthen Japan's defense capabilities. Kishi was a polarizing figure to begin with given that he was a formerly purged official. He was a class-A war criminal due to his service as Munitions Minister under Tōjō. He also was heavily involved in the development of Japan's interests in China. His focus on defense as prime minister was seen as an attempt to undermine Japan's postwar democracy.

As part of his efforts to increase Japan's control over its own defense, the Kishi administration oversaw the renegotiation of the U.S.–Japan Security Treaty in 1960. This treaty sought to strengthen the "mutual" nature of the security arrangement. Japan and the United States were to consult each other when threatened on Japanese soil. Despite the revisions to make the arrangements more mutual, some provisions still provoked controversy. In particular, the left objected to the article that outlined the status of forces in Japan. Critics saw the article that allows the United States to use its troops and bases in Japan for combat purposes beyond the defense of Japan as threatening Japan's sovereignty. Kishi and the LDP pushed the initial treaty through the lower house of the Diet, securing a vote without the presence of the opposition. The opposition boycotted Diet sessions and attempted to delay the ratification of the treaty. Demonstrations and protests intensified after Kishi's visit to the United States. Kishi largely ignored the domestic uproar. President Eisenhower had to cancel his plans to visit Japan following the signing of the treaty after his initial envoy to Japan was attacked by demonstrators. Kishi was forced to resign in response to public outrage. The treaty ended up being ratified by default. The lower house ratified the treaty without the presence of the opposition. The upper house failed to act within the required 30 days. As a result, the treaty went into effect (Reischauer 1990: 241–3).

The U.S.–Japan Security Treaty has left several important legacies on Japanese politics. To begin with, it defined the division between the left and the right under the 1955 system of LDP dominance. The JSP and LDP formed as each side attempted to strengthen its ability to define Japan's position in the postwar world order. The JSP never backed down from its opposition to the U.S.–Japan Security Agreement even decades later when the issue was no longer as salient with the public. Its inability to redefine its position eventually led to its virtual demise in the 1990s.

The controversy over the U.S. bases in Japan has continued to hamper U.S.–Japan relations throughout the postwar period. The U.S. bases in Okinawa have been particularly contentious. These bases cover large portions of the island and have been cited for noise and environmental pollution. High-profile crimes by U.S. military personnel have only intensified tensions.

Finally, the security arrangement has long been credited for supporting Japan's economic miracle. Many have argued that the fact that Japan did not have to provide for its own defense in the postwar era allowed it to focus its resources and personnel on growth.

Conclusion

The goals of the postwar settlement changed over time. Initially, the United States and its allies did not want to rehabilitate the Japanese economy. Instead, the focus was on demilitarization and democratization. Japan successfully improved upon the weaknesses of the Meiji Constitution and established the foundation for contestation and representation. Economically, priority was placed on getting inflation under control and fostering growth. Japan pursued these goals through state intervention, a strategy that left a legacy on government–business relations that continues to influence how capitalism functions in Japan.

The geopolitical environment influenced the postwar settlement in Japan. In particular, the outbreak of the Korean War influenced the United States' plan for economic development in Japan. Stabilizing the economy became a priority as a means to shore up democracy. The Korean War also jump-started domestic industrial production in Japan.

The Cold War forced a reconsideration of the security arrangements in the postwar era. The U.S.–Japan Security Treaty drew Japan into the U.S.-led world order for good or ill. While most agree that Japan benefitted economically from this arrangement in the long run, it is important to note that Japan's participation at least initially was not completely voluntary.

Remarkably, the postwar Constitution has never been amended. For the most part, this stability reflects the cross-cutting interests of the left and the right in Japan. The left supported social reforms and balked at international involvement. In contrast, the right favored industrial development. These interests ended up balancing one another out. As a result, the Constitution remained unaltered.

References

Dower, J. W. (1999) *Embracing Defeat: Japan in the Wake of World War II*, New York: W. W. Norton & Company.

Reischauer, E. O. (1990) *Japan: The Story of a Nation*, 4th edn, New York: McGraw Hill Publishing Company.

Samuels, R. J. (2003) *Machiavelli's Children: Leaders and their Legacies in Italy and Japan*, Ithaca, NY: Cornell University Press.

4　The postwar political system[1]

This chapter considers the institutions of Japanese democracy. Institutions can be conceived as "the rules of the game" that establish the incentives and constraints that political actors respond to. The relevant political actors include politicians, political parties, and voters. The question at hand is the extent to which Japanese political institutions promote the key values of democracy. This chapter argues that while not perfect, Japan's political system is a democracy.

Democracy is a contested term with many definitions – both narrow and broad. In many ways, the more comprehensive the definition is, the more difficult it is for any country to meet the various criteria. Most scholars agree, however, at the most basic level a democracy encompasses contestation, representation, and participation. It also includes the provision of civil liberties and civil rights. Finally, many scholars also include the stable alternation of power, especially for newly constituted democracies. The following sections will explore how the rules that inform the parliament, the prime ministership, the cabinet, elections, the bureaucracy, the courts, and the localities influence democracy. The conclusion will assess the strengths and weakness of Japanese democracy in isolation as well in comparison to two other established parliamentary democracies – Great Britain and Germany.

The Diet

According to Japan's Constitution, sovereignty rests with the Japanese people and is secured through the election of representatives to the National Diet, the Japanese legislative body. Article 41 of the Constitution maintains that the Diet "shall be the highest organ of state power, and shall be the sole law-making organ of the State."

The Diet is modeled on the British parliamentary system. It contains two chambers – the lower house or House of Representatives and the upper house or House of Councilors. Members are elected to the lower house for a maximum four-year term. At any point, the prime minister can dissolve the lower house. As a result, members of the lower house more frequently serve for less than four years in any given term. Members of the upper house are elected for six-year terms with half the members elected every three years.

The lower house is the more powerful legislative chamber. Both houses must pass legislation in identical form for it to become law except in three important areas. The lower house has ultimate control of the passage of the budget, the ratification of treaties, and the selection of the prime minister. It is possible for different parties to control the lower house and the upper house, a situation referred as a "twisted Diet." Twisted

Diets have become more and more common since the JSP took control of the upper house in 1989. A party that wins a majority in the lower house still has incentives to form a coalition if it does not have a majority in the upper house in order to smooth the passage of legislation. Opposition party control of the upper house has increased the importance of this chamber given its ability to block regular legislation outside the budget and treaties.

Similar to other parliamentary systems, most legislation that is considered in the Diet is proposed by the cabinet. The cabinet in turn relies on the information and expertise of the bureaucracy to draft actual bills.

The prime minister

The majority party or coalition elects the prime minister from the lower house of the Diet. During the period of LDP dominance (1955–1993), the LDP party president was also the prime minister. The prime minister is only granted a limited number of formal powers in the Constitution: the prime minister is the head of the cabinet, has the power to appoint and dismiss cabinet ministers, is granted the support of the Cabinet Secretariat, and has the power to dissolve the lower house of the Diet and call for new elections.

Due to the limited scope of formal powers, many have argued that Japanese prime ministers are weak. Some classify the Japanese prime minister's leadership as reactive arguing that prime ministers simply respond to items already on the policy agenda, instead of adding their own initiatives (Hayao 1993). Prime ministers, however, do have informal powers at their discretion, including the prime minister's support base in the party, popularity, influence over the bureaucracy, ties to the opposition parties, and experience (Shinoda 2000: 89–90). These informal powers vary based on the individual occupying the office, but such informal powers allow for greater variation in the amount of influence a prime minister can have. Recent studies of the prime minister illustrate that individual leadership can make a difference in the policymaking process (Gaunder 2007; Samuels 2003a, 2003b; Shinoda 2003).

Cabinet reforms have increased the potential influence the prime minister can have in the policymaking process. The Cabinet Law reforms decreased the size of the cabinet in hopes of facilitating the ease of unified decision making. In addition, these revisions gave the prime minister the power to initiate his own policies at cabinet meetings (Shinoda 2003). Finally, the Cabinet Secretariat was given more resources, especially in terms of personnel, to assist the prime minister in drafting legislation.

As we shall see in Chapter 11, which discusses prime ministerial leadership in greater detail, the reforms highlighted above significantly influenced the relative power of various actors and institutions in Japan. Prime Minister Koizumi used these new powers to great advantage in his pursuit of both the anti-terrorism legislation in 2001 and postal reform in 2005 (Shinoda 2003; Gaunder 2007).

The electoral system

The lower and upper houses of the Japanese Diet were governed by different electoral rules under the 1955 system. The electoral system for the lower house under the 1955 system was a multiple-member district system with a single-nontransferable vote (MMD/SNTV). This system supported multipartyism with one dominant party, the

LDP. Both scholars and practitioners alike also argued it fostered money politics and political corruption (Nyblade and Reed 2008; Ozawa 1994; Reed and Thies 2001: 156).

The number of seats in the lower house as well as the number of electoral districts fluctuated under the MMD/SNTV electoral system, which was in place from 1947 to 1993. In 1993 when the last election under this system took place, the lower house contained 511 seats. Candidates ran for election in 129 electoral districts with 2–6 candidates elected in each district. Voters in turn only cast one vote even though multiple candidates were elected from their districts.

In order to win a majority under this system a party needed to win two seats per district on average, creating a moderate bias toward larger parties with extensive financial and/or organizational resources. Throughout the period between 1955 and 1993, the LDP ran multiple candidates across districts. The JSP did not have the resources to run multiple candidates in every district and thus were not able to challenge the LDP majority. As a result, in the first decades after World War II, the electoral system created a "one and a half party system." As the JSP weakened and new parties emerged, a one-party predominant system emerged.

Indeed, despite this bias toward larger parties, the system also supported the existence of small parties that had concentrated niche support. Especially in the larger districts with 5–6 seats, candidates only needed to receive a small portion of the vote to come in fifth or sixth place and win one seat. Thus, for larger parties the decision was how many candidates to run in each district while for smaller parties the decision was whether to run any candidates at all.

The SNTV component of the electoral system made it more difficult for parties to run the "right" number of candidates and divide the vote equally among them. Both over-nomination and under-nomination were quite common as parties struggled to maximize support at the district level (Baker and Scheiner 2004; Cox and Rosenbluth, 1994, 1996; McCubbins and Rosenbluth 1995; Reed 2009). Personal support organizations (kōenkai) served as one way to distinguish candidates. The LDP also attempted to present candidates running in the same district as policy experts from a particular policy tribe (zoku) in such areas as construction and agriculture. These zoku politicians cultivated relationships with bureaucrats and special interest groups in their field to bring favorable legislation or projects to their constituents (George Mulgan 2006). Neither of these strategies guaranteed equal division of support for LDP candidates in a particular district, though.

The MMD/SNTV electoral system provided distinct incentives and constraints to parties, politicians, and voters. Since large parties needed to win two seats on average in every electoral district to secure a majority, this electoral system promoted intra-party competition in addition to inter-party competition. As in other parliamentary systems, political parties maintained strict discipline on parliamentary votes; voting down party lines was the norm. As a result, politicians from the same party running in the same district were unable to distinguish themselves based on policy. Instead, these politicians were forced to compete for the personal vote through both patronage and pork barrel politics. Patronage is the exchange of favors by the politicians for support (votes or money) from a constituent. Favors might include college or job recommendations, assistance with a bureaucratic matter, or business connections. Pork barrel politics refers to government support for projects in your home district. Construction projects are the best example of pork. Cultivating kōenkai through patronage politics in particular put great pressure on politicians to raise large sums of money. Pork barrel politics allowed politicians to claim credit for specific projects brought to the district. Pork barrel politics also led to many backroom deals between special interest groups and politicians, which often involved illegal monetary transactions.

Politicians reformed the lower house electoral system in 1994. The rhetoric at the time suggested that at least one goal of the revisions was to reduce the incentives for money politics and corruption. Revisions to the Public Office Election Law replaced the MMD/SNTV system with a combined single-member district (SMD) and proportional representation (PR) system. Initially, this system called for 300 SMD and 200 PR seats. In 2000, the number of PR seats was reduced to 180. In 2013, the number of SMD seats was reduced to 295. As a result, there are currently 475 seats in the lower house. The PR representatives are selected from 11 regional blocs. The voters cast two votes – one for an individual candidate in the SMD and one for a political party on the PR list. As we shall see in Chapter 5, the split of the LDP in 1993 followed by electoral reform in 1994 sparked party realignment that has been reinitiated on a smaller scale by a DPJ split in 2012.

The upper house had two sets of electoral rules during the 1955 system. From 1946 to 1983, 100 of the 252 members of this chamber were selected using a nationwide MMD/SNTV system. The remaining seats were allocated through multiple-member district contests in prefectures. This system favored candidates with high name recognition. In 1983, the Diet revised the electoral law replacing the nationwide MMD/SNTV system with a closed party PR list. These revisions were meant to make the contests more party-centered; however, these revisions increased competition for party ranking on the list. In 2000, the PR component of the electoral system was further changed to an open list system, which allows voters to select either a party or individual candidate in the PR ballot. Historically, upper house elections have been more issue based, allowing opposition parties to gain some traction against the LDP during periods when its popularity was low.

Political parties

The Japanese party system has responded to the incentives and constraints of the electoral system and the changes that have been made in the postwar period. It also has functioned in an environment that moved from minimally regulated political funding to more oversight and transparency. Meanwhile, the ways parties can campaign have always been highly restricted, making it more difficult for newcomers to enter the political arena.

The Japanese party system has moved from a one and a half party system in the 1950–1960s to a one-party predominant system with multipartyism from the 1970s through electoral reform in the 1990s. Since electoral reform, the party system has tended toward two large parties that perform strongly in the SMDs and a handful of smaller parties that compete in PR. The one and a half party system emerged after party mergers on the right and left, creating the LDP and JSP in 1955. The Socialists were briefly in government prior to these mergers controlling the prime ministership from 1947 to 1948. After these mergers, however, the JSP never captured enough support nor were they able to run enough candidates to gain an outright majority in parliament. Instead, during this period the Socialists served as a vocal minority, which often turned to disruptive tactics on the Diet floor in an attempt to have its voice heard (Krauss 1984).

In the 1960s several forces converged to support the creation of new parties to fill the ideological space, which separated the Socialists and the Communists on the left and the LDP on the right. The JSP split over ideological issues with the Democratic Socialist Party (DSP) emerging as a new party in 1960. The Kōmeitō or Clean Government Party (CGP) in turn was created as the political arm of a Buddhist lay organization (the Sōka Gakkai) in 1964. The emergence and success of these smaller parties is at least partially related to the electoral system discussed earlier, as it allows candidates from smaller parties with strong niche support to be elected.

Although other small parties existed under the 1955 system, five parties received consistent representation. These parties included the LDP, the JSP, the DSP, the Kōmeitō, and the Japan Communist Party (JCP). Since electoral reform, additional parties have entered the landscape and many others have disappeared like the DSP or been minimalized like the JSP. The main parties in the current party system include the LDP, the Democratic Party of Japan (renamed the Democratic Party in 2016), the Kōmeitō, and the JCP. A few smaller parties also remain. This section briefly outlines each party's ideology and policy positions, support base, and organization. Chapter 5 explores the party system in much greater detail.

The Liberal Democratic Party (LDP) is the conservative party in Japan. The party is less ideologically driven than other parties in Japan. The LDP, however, was considered the party of rapid economic growth during this period and consistently supported policies that promoted growth. The support base of the LDP during the 1955 system consisted of farmers and rural communities, industry, small business, construction, and the self-employed. Initially, farmers represented the core conservative base of the party. Rapid economic growth, however, also meant increased urbanization. The LDP ensured the continued influence of rural districts through malapportionment.

Many observers of Japanese politics likened the LDP to a political machine (Johnson 1986; Schlesinger 1997). This characterization reflects the party's propensity to exchange particularistic favors, pork barrel projects, and favorable government regulation for votes or money depending on the supporters it was wooing. At the district level, individual politicians created kōenkai (personal support organizations). These kōenkai functioned as individual-level political machines by providing patronage and pork to constituents in return for votes (Curtis 1971). Kōenkai were institutional responses to the incentives and constraints of the MMD/SNTV electoral system under which members of the same party had to compete against each other.

Factions were another institutional response to electoral incentives. In the early postwar period anywhere from seven to twelve factions existed (Masumi 1995: 456–457). Since the 1970s, the LDP has contained five to six factions. These factions have not been ideologically based. Instead, factions within the LDP have focused on raising and distributing funds to support candidates for office in return for the faction member's support in the party presidential election. Factions have also served as an important mechanism for distributing party and Diet positions. In general, factions receive representation within the party and the cabinet in proportion to their numerical strength.

Under the 1955 system, the Japan Socialist Party (JSP), renamed the Social Democratic Party of Japan (SDPJ) in 1996, was the progressive party on the left with strong ties to public sector labor unions. It supported protecting the so-called Peace Constitution and disbanding the U.S.–Japan Security Treaty. The JSP did little to adjust its platform in response to economic, political, and societal changes in the decades following the Occupation. As a result, the public began to regard many of its policies as extreme and unrealistic. Plagued by factional struggles the party failed to achieve any type of policy coherence (Stockwin 2000).

The JSP's main support came from public service labor unions (Sōhyō), but it received support from small business, professionals, intellectuals, and farmers as well. The party never expanded its support in metropolitan areas. Overall, its connection to unions limited its broader appeal.

The JSP lacked effective organization, particularly at the local level where voter mobilization is crucial. Its organizational structure also depended on the voter support of unions, which became increasingly less viable sources for votes, although the reorganization of the national union movement into a new consolidated federation referred to as Rengō in the early 1990s did improve the organizational capacity of the unions (Stockwin 1994: 27).

Structurally, the JSP was divided into numerous factional groupings based originally both on personal ties and ideology, although these groupings became more fluid over time (Stockwin 2000: 239). The differing priorities of factions and the inability to reach a consensus on party direction inhibited the party's ability to appeal to voters, especially in the 1990s.

The Democratic Socialist Party (DSP) formed in 1960 when the right wing of the JSP broke away from the party. It occupied a space more in the middle of the political spectrum and was committed to moving beyond exclusive worker support and creating a broader base. It supported welfare state policies, and its main support came from the private sector labor unions (Dōmei). It never commanded broad public support receiving anywhere between 4 and 7 percent of the vote. The DSP dissolved in 1994. Former members of this party joined the Democratic Party of Japan during party realignment.

The Kōmeitō or the Clean Government Party (CGP) emerged in 1964 as the political arm of the Buddhist lay organization, the Sōka Gakkai. Under the 1955 system, it promoted so-called "Buddhist Democracy" and supported value-oriented policies. Its name reflected the party's desire to promote "cleaner," less corrupt politics. It emerged in response to the LDP and its continuous money politics scandals. It supported both world peace and humanitarian socialism. In particular, it supported progressive taxes and the nationalization of key industries. It was the most hated party in Japan given its exclusive nature. Many also voiced concerns over the threat Buddhist Democracy potentially posed to the principle of the separation of church and state (Hrebenar 2000).

Despite this, the Kōmeitō had a very stable support base in the Buddhist lay organization. Under the 1955 system, the party attracted both low income and lower educated voters. It also received strong support from women, youth, and the underclass. The party is highly organized, especially in terms of voter mobilization. The party consistently received niche support under the MMD/SNTV system, and it tended to do better when overall voter turnout was low because its supporters always voted (Hrebenar 2000: 187). Since electoral reform, it has assumed a frequent position in LDP coalitions serving in LDP coalitions in 1999–2009 and 2012–present. The Kōmeitō is a desirable coalition partner due to its ability to mobilize its supporters to vote for the LDP in the SMD contests in lower house elections.

The Japan Communist Party (JCP) was the most ideological party under the 1955 system. It was the party on the extreme left informed by Marxist-Leninism. It more closely resembled Communist parties in Europe than elsewhere. It moderated its position over the years, especially with its acceptance of parliamentary democracy. It was a party dedicated to the preservation and expansion of freedoms and supported welfare and environmental policies (Berton 2000).

Under the 1955 system, the JCP received support from a limited number of labor unions where its members held leadership positions. Instead, its support came from women and youth affiliate organizations as well as doctors and lawyers, nontraditional supporters of Communist parties. It raised funds through its newspaper, *Akahata*. This income made it more independent. In fact, unlike other parties it did not have to rely on outside interest groups for monetary support. While claiming to adhere to the principles of democratic centralism, in practice, the party has been dominated by strong leadership at the top.

In 1993 the LDP split over the issue of political reform ushering in an era of political realignment that appears to be ongoing. The first several years following electoral reform were marked with new parties, party splits, and party mergers. The system stabilized from 2000 to 2012 with the Democratic Party of Japan becoming the second large party in the system. The DPJ won the 2009 lower house election but was devastated in the following 2012 lower house election due in part to its poor performance in office as well as party splits.

In 2000, the DPJ emerged as the largest new party after electoral reform. It is a centrist party. Its emergence as one of the two major parties in Japan narrowed the political spectrum, especially in the SMD contests. The DPJ's founding members came from both the left and the right. With over 15 years of experience in electoral politics, though, its membership now contains a majority of politicians elected only as DPJ politicians. This trend has strengthened its cohesiveness. Still, many of its senior members began their political careers in other parties.

The party's support is strongest in urban areas, but it owed its victory in the 2009 lower house election to increased rural support. It was elected with promises to enact more welfare-state-oriented policies, most notably a child allowance to provide incentives for couples to have children. In foreign policy, it only supports the involvement of Japan's self-defense forces in UN operations and has also voiced a desire to redefine Japan's relationship with the United States while increasing Japan's connections to Asia. While in office it failed to achieve many policy goals and struggled in its response to the triple disaster (earthquake, tsunami, and nuclear incident) in 2011. Prior to the 2012 lower house election, two groups broke away from the DPJ. It performed poorly in the 2012 and 2014 lower house and 2013 and 2016 upper house elections, causing many to speculate that the system is once again experiencing a party realignment.

The bureaucracy

The bureaucracy in Japan is often considered to be one of the most powerful in the world. The prominent position of the bureaucracy in Japan predates the Occupation. The bureaucracy played a significant role in policymaking, the provision of services, and information gathering beginning in the Meiji period (1868–1911). In the postwar period the bureaucracy maintained a position of influence when other institutions were significantly purged of officials seen as responsible for wartime activities. The bureaucrats were given responsibility for carrying out Occupation reforms and continued to play a large role in policymaking after the U.S.'s departure.

The bureaucracy is responsible for policymaking, information gathering and dissemination, and the implementation of the government policy. Of particular significance is the large role the bureaucracy has played in creating and implementing the annual national budgets.

The bureaucracy is an elite institution in Japan. Civil servants are chosen by national exam. Only the best and the brightest pass the category I exam which feeds the most elite bureaucratic track. In general, there are two categories of bureaucrats – the general civil service track and the senior bureaucrat track. Members in the senior bureaucrat track are small in number in comparison to those on the regular civil servant track. Those on the senior bureaucrat track come from only the most prestigious universities, with most drawn from the University of Tokyo's Law Department. This pedigree along with the long historical tradition and actual influence in policymaking heighten the social prestige of this career.

Under the 1955 system of LDP dominance there were twenty-two bureaucratic ministries. The most powerful of these were the Ministry of International Trade and Industry (MITI) and the Ministry of Finance (MOF). MITI and MOF drew their power from their influence over industrial and monetary policy during the era of high growth. MITI was in charge of industrial policy during the high growth period. Industrial policy refers to a set of policies that rewards growth sectors of the economy by providing favorable regulations such as tax credits, subsidies, etc. The bureaucracy had few carrots and sticks to carry out its industrial policy. Instead, it relied heavily on the practice of administrative guidance. The bureaucracy exercised administrative guidance by suggesting certain directions to the business sector. Analysts disagree over the extent to which MITI's industrial policy and administrative guidance was effective in promoting growth (Haley 1987; Johnson 1982). However, most agree that the bureaucracy in general and MITI in particular played a larger role in the economy than ministries in other countries. During high growth the U.S. criticized MITI for granting Japanese industries unfair advantage over foreign competitors.

The MOF performs the functions of various U.S. bureaucratic agencies and governmental bodies including the security and exchange commission and the U.S. treasury. MITI and MOF often fought turf battles for regulatory control.

After administrative reforms in the 1990s, the number of bureaucratic ministries was reduced significantly to ten. MITI turned into the Ministry of Economy, Trade and Industry (METI). The MOF remains but its focus is on budget making, not financial regulation and enforcement as in the past. The administrative reforms were carried following a period when the MOF had been highly discredited for its inability to deal with the banking crisis in the late 1990s. The MOF's financial functions were given to a new agency, the Financial Services Agency (Grimes 2001: 207–208). Currently, there are eleven ministries.

One practice that increased the ties between government and business was amakudari, which literally translates "descent from heaven." This practice refers to when senior bureaucrats retire in their early 50s and parachute into businesses, financial institutions, and even government organizations. Both the supply and demand side drives this practice. On the supply side, a large number of bureaucrats retire young due to the traditions of the institution itself. When a new vice minister is appointed all bureaucrats in the cohort must retire so that the vice minister is the most senior member in this ministry. This forced retirement called for a need for employment outside the civil service (Curtis n.d.). The demand side is related to what businesses, financial institutions, and government organizations get in return for the retired bureaucrat – namely connections to government officials in charge of policies and resources that these institutions benefit from. While some see this practice as contributing to government corruption, others see it as critical for the type of government–business coordination that drove high growth in Japan.

Bureaucrats have traditionally been seen as above corruption. In the 1990s, however, bureaucrats were implicated in a broad range of corrupt activities. These corruption scandals along with the MOF's inability to deal with the financial crisis led to significant administrative reform including the streamlining mentioned earlier.

When the DPJ came to office in 2009, it tried to further limit the power of the bureaucracy. These efforts largely failed. In particular, the importance of bureaucratic expertise was apparent in the disarray in the government's response following the triple disaster in 2011.

The courts

Japan has a unitary court system. That is, there are no independent prefectural level courts similar to the dual court system structure in the U.S., which has an independent state judiciary system. The court system in Japan draws heavily on the German tradition. The courts since the Meiji era have seen the law as a mechanism to maintain order in society more than as a way to protect human rights (Matsui 2011). Japan follows a civil law tradition with deference to parliament. Overall, the courts are respected and autonomous, and judges are highly trusted (Haley 2002).

The Constitution places full judicial power in the Supreme Court and lower courts (Article 76). There are four levels of courts. The summary courts occupy the first level. These courts decide civil matters involving small monetary claims of no more than 900,000-yen and criminal cases subject to minimal punishments. The second level includes the district courts and the family courts. The next level is composed of the eight high courts that are appellate courts. The top level is the Supreme Court (Haley 2002).

The Supreme Court is predominantly an appellate court that is granted the power of judicial review in Article 81 of the Constitution. This power allows the court to review the constitutionality of legal statues passed by the Diet. The Supreme Court consists of a chief justice recommended by the cabinet and appointed by the Emperor and 14 associate justices appointed by the cabinet. The justices must be at least 40 years old and must retire by age 70. Appointments to the Supreme Court are shielded from partisan influence by an established pattern of promotion that draws from the most prestigious professional legal organizations. A politician has never been appointed to the Supreme Court (Haley 2002).

The Supreme Court is generally considered to be a conservative institution. It is reluctant to accept cases that involve issues of constitutionality. It also avoids cases that raise controversial political issues. Civil cases can be appealed to the Supreme Court only in instances that are shown to involve a constitutional violation or a misinterpretation of the Constitution by a lower court (Matsui 2011: 1380). Criminal cases can be appealed to the Supreme Court when a lower court has violated or misinterpreted the Constitution or violated Supreme Court precedent (Matsui 2011: 1381). The Supreme Court has limited original jurisdiction. Most cases are heard by one of the three petty benches made up of five judges. Constitutional matters are brought before the full court.

There are many reasons the court is seen as conservative. First, there are several barriers to having a case heard by the Supreme Court. It has a very stringent standing requirement, which has prevented individuals from filing cases against administrative actions that might not be constitutional. Legal standing refers to your ability to pursue the case. In order to have standing in regulatory cases a party must have "a legal right or interest protected by a statue passed by the Diet" (Matsui 2011: 1383). Individuals rarely meet this standard. Individuals have been denied standing in several cases involving Article 9, the renunciation of war clause of the Constitution. For example, individuals tried and failed to have sending minesweepers to the Gulf declared unconstitutional in 1991 (Matsui 2011: 1385). Second, the Court has been reluctant to intervene on political questions. In the 1950s, the Court refused to rule on the constitutionality of the U.S.–Japan Security Treaty and the presence of U.S. military bases in Japan, claiming that this was a political issue with national defense implications. Lower courts have followed this "political question doctrine" to avoid hearing cases related to constitutionality of the SDF in particular (Matsui 2011: 1387). The root cause of this conservative, noninterventionist approach is contested with scholars putting forth a variety of reasons including cultural, historical, institutional, and strategic ones (Matsui 2011: 1400–1416).

The Supreme Court has issued some significant unconstitutional rulings, but in many instances it has not acted beyond the declaration of unconstitutionality. For example, in two separate reapportionment cases the Court ruled the apportionment provisions in the Public Office Election Law unconstitutional, but in both cases the Court did not invalidate the election results due to this malapportionment as requested by the plaintiffs (Matsui 2011: 1391).

While the courts have high integrity, they have low institutional capacity. As a result, the law plays a more limited role in Japanese society. An exam process determines the number of lawyers, and the government determines the success rate. Until recently, professional law schools did not exist in Japan. Instead, law is the most popular undergraduate major. Very few students who study law in college practice it due to the high standards of the national exam. After passing the exam, applicants spend two years in training with the Legal Training and Research Institute (LTRI). During this training students are tracked into certain fields. All students must sit for a second exam at the end of this process. The limited institutional capacity of the courts means that pursuing a case is time consuming and costly. As a result, many disputes are often settled through arbitration with local notables (Haley 1978).

In the last two decades several reforms to broaden participation in the court system have been enacted. These reforms include the creation of professional law schools, the introduction of a lay assessor system, and the passage of information disclosure provisions. Currently, though, law schools have a low pass rate on the national exam and face strong incentives to teach for the exam. Since the pass rate is still controlled by LTRI and the government, the pipeline of lawyers remains highly regulated (Marshall 2011). The lay assessor system was introduced to increase the legitimacy of the criminal justice system by broadening participation. Lay assessors are like jurors who hear evidence for a single case and then deliberate with three judges. A guilty ruling requires the support of one judge and a majority of the panel. Currently, cases eligible to be heard in this system are limited, sitting at around 4 percent of criminal cases, mainly felonies (Marshall 2011). These reforms fail to address the fact that the criminal justice system in Japan does not focus on the procedural rights of the accused. No plea-bargaining is permitted, and prosecutors face strong incentives to secure confessions (Marshall 2011). Finally, the information disclosure law has opened an avenue for more information for citizens wishing to question administrative actions and decisions. It was passed in 1999 and has been used in some instances but not broadly (Marshall 2011).

Local governments

In Japan, local government plays an important role in fostering representative democracy as well as providing welfare state functions. This discussion of local government provides an overview of the organization of local government in Japan. It then considers the effects of institutional rules in facilitating and constraining the role of local governments in politics. Finally, recent reforms are examined.

Japan is a unitary system. In unitary systems, regional and local governments are much more dependent on the national government for policy guidance and financial support. Articles 92–95 of the Constitution outline the powers of the local government. Ensuring local autonomy was of particular concern in the immediate postwar period. Local autonomy, however, has been constrained by institutional rules and informal norms that have governed central–local relations in the postwar period.

Japan has a three-tiered unitary system, which includes the national government, prefectures, and municipalities. Japan has 47 prefectures. Prefectures are regional divisions (similar in structure to the states in the U.S. but not as powerful). Each prefecture elects a governor and a unicameral prefectural assembly. Municipalities are divided into three categories based on population – cities, towns, and villages. Cities are the largest municipalities. Cities must have a population of more than 50,000 people, and 60 percent of this population must be urban. Municipalities elect a mayor and a unicameral assembly. The unicameral prefectural and local assemblies were seen as an important check on executive power. Prefectures oversee broader initiatives involving transportation, communication, safety, disaster response and relief, etc. Prefectures also facilitate the coordination among municipalities. Municipalities are administrative agents in charge of providing public services.

Historically, local autonomy has been constrained by at least two prominent institutional features. Specifically, local governments had limited authority and financial resources. Until recent reforms, local governments were consumed with policy implementation. The national government used so-called agency-delegated functions to induce governors and/or mayors to implement policies and carry out tasks delegated by central bureaucratic ministries. In addition, local governments relied on the national government for financial resources. Local taxes were uniformly capped. The only way a locality could increase its tax rate was to request permission from the central government through the Ministry of Home Affairs.

These constraints combined with incentives from the MMD/SNTV electoral system for the lower house of the National Diet encouraged clientelism. Local politicians would often lobby the national government for funding or pork. In return for the provision of favors, Diet members would ask for electoral support. Networks of local politicians became crucial for the LDP politicians for mobilizing voters at election time.

A large number of local elections occur in the same time frame. The national unified local elections occur every four years in the spring. During this time about 30 percent of the localities elect prefectural and local assembly members. The number of localities participating in the unified local elections has declined over time due in part to municipal mergers (Saito and Yamada 2011: 106).

Local governments were not completely "captured" by the national government though. Samuels argues that local governments are more appropriately seen as interest groups lobbying the national government (Samuels 1983: 123). Others note that local governments often used mostly informal tools and powers to influence policy outcomes in a variety of areas including business promotion, industrial regulation, and welfare provision (Kitayama 2001). For example, in the 1960s local governments often took initiatives to regulate large industries in their jurisdiction even when they did not have regulatory authority. Yokohama was a forerunner in this process, convincing large companies to sign agreements to limit pollution at lower levels than regulated by the national government. The Socialist mayor of Yokoyama threatened to mobilize the unions against these companies if they did not sign the pollution control agreements (Kitayama 2001: 8). This type of informal administrative guidance did not always work, especially when the problem involved a large number of entities. Nevertheless, there are several examples of local initiatives eventually being adopted by the national government (Reed 1986). In addition, local governments often worked together to lobby the ministries for needed assistance. Lobbying did become a key aspect of local politics in Japan.

A push for decentralization in central–local relations began in the early 1990s in Japan. Many called for decentralization as necessary given Japan's economic maturity and the more global environment it functioned in. Others hoped to shift the focus from Tokyo to other areas. Decentralization was also seen as a way to deal with Japan's aging, low fertility society (Ikawa 2008: 12). This push for decentralization gained momentum after the LDP split in 1993. Decentralization was a central policy goal for Prime Minister Hosokawa who led the anti-LDP coalition. Hosokawa had been a prefectural governor and saw decentralization as an important task in reforming central–local relations. After several years of research and activity, the Diet enacted a comprehensive Omnibus Decentralization Act in 1999. This Act changed over 400 laws that involved central–local relations. It clarified the roles of central and local governments, granting localities sixty-four new functions. In particular, municipalities gained greater control over city planning and the provision of certain welfare services such as the child allowance program. This legislation also abolished the agency-delegated functions system, which allowed ministries to give local governments direct orders (Furukawa 2003). The ministries are still capable of controlling localities but not through fiat. Now they must rely on legislation (Kanai 2007: 4).

The Koizumi administration extended decentralization efforts through its so-called "Tri-ad reforms." The Tri-ad reforms focused on the financial connection between the central and local governments. These reforms called for (1) a decrease in subsidies for public services from the national government to local governments, (2) an increase in the tax authority of localities, and (3) a reduction in local allocation tax grants – unspecified grants given from the national government to localities (Saito and Yamada 2011).

The Koizumi administration also aggressively pursued municipal mergers of localities with a population under 10,000 people. The mergers in Japan were not forced as in Sweden. Instead, the mergers were encouraged through financial incentives. The changes to the subsidy and local allocation tax (LAT) grant system provided incentives to municipalities to merge as their access to funds became more limited. More explicitly, the government allowed newly merged entities to put forward local bonds for ten years to raise additional monies for public works and infrastructure for the newly consolidated municipality. The government pledged to pay 70 percent of the principal of the bond and interest through tax allocations (Kohara 2007: 9). As part of this process, the number of municipalities has declined significantly from 3,232 in 1999 to 1,820 in 2006 (Kohara 2007: 8).

One goal of the mergers was to reduce the financial burden of the central government. If municipalities merged, it would cut the central government's tax allocation, especially since small localities received very generous funding (Kohara 2007: 9).

Mergers did have some unintended consequences. In particular, mergers decreased the number of local politicians. The decline in local politicians negatively impacted the LDP political machine that had relied on local politicians to mobilize voters (Saito and Yamada 2011: 112; Kohara 2007: 10).

Japan in comparative perspective

One way to assess the strength of Japanese political institutions is to compare them to the institutions in other parliamentary democracies. This section compares Japan to Great Britain and Germany. Japan modeled many of its institutions against Britain's Westminster parliamentary democracy. The Westminster system is often the measure against which the Japanese assess their own democracy. The German system poses an interesting comparison due to its common experience as a loser of World War II that was occupied by the Allies. While democracy might look different in Japan due to the modes of operation on the ground, the institutions of democracy are informed by the same principles found in Great Britain, Germany, and other Western democracies. These principles include contestation, representation, and the provision of certain civil liberties and rights. Japan's democracy is not perfect, but it is comparable to other democracies.

Great Britain

In Great Britain, the parliament and the cabinet have more power than comparable institutions in Japan. The British system is governed by the principle of parliamentary sovereignty, which holds that other branches of government cannot overturn an act of parliament. This principle is a legacy of parliament's battle with the monarchy in the English Civil Wars (1642–1651). Parliament won this battle and as a result was able to institutionalize its strength as the institutions of political liberalism were being established. The cabinet is selected from members of parliament who are in the majority party or coalition. In theory, the prime minister is the first among equals and collective decision making is the norm aspired to. If the prime minister loses the support of the majority party/coalition, the prime minister must reshuffle the cabinet. The prime minister is also subject to votes of no confidence. In practice, the prime minister has attained more institutional resources and as a result has been able to act more independently in directing policy than originally conceived in theory.

The British parliament, like the Japanese Diet, is bicameral, consisting of a House of Commons and the House of Lords. While the House of Commons is more powerful than either chamber in the Japanese Diet, the House of Lords is not as strong as its equivalent in Japan, the upper house. In Britain, the members of the House of Lords are appointed; they are not elected. Moreover, the House of Lords only serves as a consulting body; it does not have veto power. The Japanese upper house is an elected body and has played an increasingly important role as a check on the lower house and governing party/coalition. A twisted Diet, where a different party controls the two houses of parliament, has become more common. Opposition parties have used their control of the upper house to block controversial legislation, including Prime Minister Koizumi's first attempt to pass postal system reform.

Members of the House of Commons are elected in a single-member district/first past the post system. Historically, this has led to a two-party system with two major parties – the Conservatives or Tories and the Labour Party. The single-member district system has resulted in a stable system with one majority party ruling the government until the unusual 2010 election, which resulted in a Hung Parliament – a situation when no party receives a majority in the House of Commons. This occurrence brought the Conservatives to government in coalition with the Liberal Democrats. Single-member districts tend toward two parties at the district level but not necessarily nationally. Increasingly a set of smaller parties has gained support in certain districts. This is especially true in Wales, Scotland, and Northern Ireland. Nevertheless, minority voices have more difficulty being heard in SMD systems. The Liberal Democrats' support is more spread out than that of the regional parties and would benefit from a PR system. Indeed, electoral reform is one of the major policies supported by the Liberal Democrats. Still, since the 1980s center parties have gained in strength despite the single-member district electoral system.

The bureaucracy in Britain is not as strong as in Japan. Its main role is in policy implementation. Civil servants also play an important role in the creation of cabinet initiatives, but the bureaucracy has not displayed as much independent initiative in devising policy as seen in Japan, especially in the realm of industrial policy during Japan's high growth era. In Britain, policy advisers to the prime minister have grown in importance and influence. In Japan, efforts to curb the bureaucracy's power have been premised on the need to make Japan a true Westminster system.

The judiciary is not as strong in Britain compared to in other European countries and Japan. Britain does not have a written Constitution. This combined with the principle of parliamentary sovereignty prevents the courts from exercising the power of judicial review.

The British system, like the Japanese system is a unitary system. No powers are reserved for localities. Prime Minister Blair did oversee some devolution of power to the district nations of Wales, Scotland, and Northern Island. Decentralization has not been as far reaching as in Japan.

Germany

Like Britain and Japan, the legislative and executive branches are fused in Germany. The parliament is bicameral. The Bundestag is the more powerful lower house of parliament. It has control over the budget and selects the chancellor from the ruling coalition. The chancellor is the chief executive and quite similar to the prime minister in Britain and Japan, although perhaps slightly more powerful. In Germany, the chancellor oversees the majority party and has many tools to ensure party discipline. The Bundestrat is the upper house and is the body that represents the federal states, the Lander. It has a strong administrative role as it is in charge of overseeing the implementation of regulations in the federal states.

Unlike Great Britain and Japan, the German system is a federal system. Federal systems reserve certain powers for the states or in Germany's case the Lander. While both Germany and Japan are losers of World War II with fascist pasts, German political institutions guard more heavily against the potential for central power. Federalism is one of the institutional features that prevents over-centralization by granting significant power to the sixteen Lander.

A related goal of the German postwar Constitution was to guard against extremist parties and promote more stability in government. Both the 5 percent hurdle and the constructive vote of no confidence speak to these goals. The 5 percent hurdle holds that a party must receive at least 5 percent of the party vote for the Bundestag to receive any seats in parliament. The constructive vote of no confidence makes it more difficult to overturn sitting governments. Those voting against the government must also agree on a successor – a much higher bar for a vote of no confidence.

The electoral system for the Bundestag is known as a personalized PR system. Its goal is to maximize the strengths of both SMD and PR electoral systems and minimize their weakness. Under this electoral system, a voter casts two votes – one for a party in PR and one for a candidate in an SMD. The total number of seats a party receives is determined by the percentage received in the PR portion. The first seats, however, are allocated to the party candidates who have won in their single-member districts. This combined system ensures a close connection to a district through the SMD vote. This "personalizes" the representatives for the district. The PR system allows for minority voices to be heard. Japan's new combined electoral system is similar to the German system. The main difference is that the SMD and PR votes are completely separate. Individuals win their SMD seat outright and parties are allowed a portion of the 180 PR seats in proportion to the party vote received. Japan's combined system is less proportional but still allows for more minority voices to be heard in comparison to Britain's pure SMD system.

Germany has two major parties. The Christian Democratic Union (CDU) is the conservative party on the right that has dominated postwar politics. The CDU has not been in power as long as the LDP, but it has been in power more than any other party in the postwar period and overseen much of Germany's economic growth as well as unification. The Social Democratic Party (SPD) is the party of democratic socialism with strong connections to labor. Smaller parties include the Greens, the Free Democrats, and the former Communist party.

The bureaucracy in Germany is also an elite institution fed by prestigious university graduates. It has not played a similar role in economic development as the Japanese bureaucracy. Both Germany and Japan have been classified as coordinated market economies. This classification indicates a more structured approach to economic development. In Germany, this structure has come more from associations for labor and business, not the bureaucracy like in Japan.

The judiciary in Germany is more powerful than both the British and Japanese judiciaries. In fact, the German Constitutional Court is probably the most powerful court in Europe. It holds the power of judicial review, but it is also able to administer the law, not just arbitrate it. For example, if the Constitutional Court declares a parliamentary law unconstitutional, it can provide new text for the law in its decision. Unlike the Japanese court, and to a lesser extent the U.S. court, the German court does not avoid political decisions. It is seen more as an institution capable of driving social change.

As should be clear from these comparisons the Japanese system firmly sits in the realm of parliamentary democracies. In some instances its institutions are "stronger"; in others its institutions are "weaker" or less effective. But in all cases, its institutions are constructed to promote the goals of democracy including contestation, representation, and the provision and protection of civil liberties and civil rights.

Conclusion

This chapter has illustrated the strengths and weaknesses of Japanese democracy. Japan's Constitution clearly established democratic institutions and values in the postwar period. Some argue that these institutions and values were imposed by the Allied Occupation and thus were foreign and not fully embraced. Japan's democratic history extends beyond the postwar period, however. As we have seen, Japan became a modern state with the Meiji Restoration and while the Meiji Constitution suffered from many ambiguities it also provided the foundation for the creation of political parties and the voice for political opposition. Taishō democracy featured party competition as well as the involvement of politicians in government. Japan drew on many of its previous democratic institutions when crafting its postwar institutions. These institutions were not simply borrowed. Japan had experience with many of them.

Japan's Constitution clearly invests sovereignty with the people. All adult citizens exercise their sovereignty through free and fair elections to the National Diet and the prefectural and local assemblies. Elections are competitive with at least five active political parties contesting for seats throughout most of the postwar period. Interest groups have a voice in policymaking. In fact, most conceive policymaking by politicians and bureaucrats as being driven by interest groups. An active independent press exists, and citizens have become more active in civil society over time.

Japanese democracy has fallen short in some regards in the areas of contestation, representation, and participation. Prior to electoral reform in 1994, electoral districts were severely malapportioned, greatly over-representing the LDP's core constituencies in rural areas. The close relationship among interest groups, business, and politicians, especially in the dominant LDP, often has resulted in political corruption. Social movements are often co-opted by the state, and as we shall see in Chapter 10, civil society is highly regulated.

The postwar regime has been remarkably stable with the LDP in government for most of the postwar period. Critics note that this stability has been negative, claiming that Japan under the LDP verged on "soft authoritarianism" (Johnson 1987). Citizens returned the LDP to government in free and fair elections partially because they believed it was the only party competent to rule and oversee economic growth. The LDP also responded to citizen requests in what has been labeled a "crisis and compensation" manner (Calder 1988).

Japan's Constitution grants citizens an array of civil liberties and civil rights. It even includes an equal rights provision for women. Japan's institutions do not completely ensure equality. Discrimination against outcasts, foreigners (especially Koreans), and women exists. Equality also looks somewhat different in a country where exams are used as entry criteria in most realms of education and employment and a seniority norm governs promotions. Nevertheless, during the high growth era Japan had one of the most equal distributions of wealth among industrialized democracy. As discussed in Chapter 8, though, wealth inequalities have emerged since the prolonged economic slowdown that began in the 1990s; politicians are still grappling with ways to address these inequalities.

Finally, as the comparisons to Great Britain and Germany illustrate there is no such thing as a perfect democracy. The ideal democracy does not exist. Each country's institutions have strengths and flaws. For example, the judiciary is more powerful in Germany than in Great Britain and Japan. This circumstance has positive and negative implications. On the positive side, the German court can act as a significant check on legislative and executive power. On the negative side, though, judges are not elected officials yet still are given great power. Moreover, the court's pursuit of political issues can be both positive and negative. Getting too far ahead of public sentiment can lead to instability. Avoiding political issues, as the Japanese courts do, however, can result in ongoing inequities. The perfect balance is hard to find with courts as with other political institutions considered in this chapter. Nevertheless, all three countries sit firmly in the category of parliamentary democracy.

Note

1 The discussion of the Diet, prime minister, electoral system, and political parties is a revised version of portions of Gaunder (2011).

References

Baker, A. and Scheiner, E. (2004) "Adaptive Parties: Party Strategic Capacity Under Japanese SNTV," *Electoral Studies*, 23: 251–278.

Berton, P. (2000) "Japanese Communist Party: The 'Lovable' Party," in R. J. Hrebenar (ed.) *Japan's New Party System*, 3rd edn, Boulder, CO: Westview Press.

Calder, K. E. (1988) *Crisis and Compensation: Public Policy and Political Stability in Japan, 1949–1986*, Princeton, NJ: Princeton University Press.

Cox, G. W. and Rosenbluth, F. (1994) "Reducing Nomination Errors Factional Competition and Party Strategy in Japan," *Electoral Studies*, 13: 4–16.

Cox, G. W. and Rosenbluth, F. (1996) "Factional Competition for the Party Endorsement: The Case of Japan's Liberal Democratic Party," *British Journal of Political Science*, 26: 259–269.

Curtis, G. L. (1971) *Election Campaigning Japanese Style*, New York: Columbia University Press.

Curtis, G. L. (n.d.) "The Government of Modern Japan: The Japanese Bureaucracy." Available online at http://afe.easia.columbia.edu/at/jp_bureau/govtjb09.html (accessed 17 June 2016).

Furukawa, S. (2003) "Decentralization in Japan," in S. Furukawa and T. Menju (eds) *Japan's Road to Pluralism: Transforming Local Communities in the Global Era*, Tokyo: Japan Center for International Exchange.

Gaunder, A. (2007) *Political Reform in Japan: Leadership Looming Large*, London: Routledge.

Gaunder, A. (2011) "The Institutional Landscape of Japanese Politics," in A. Gaunder (ed.) *The Routledge Handbook of Japanese Politics*, London: Routledge.

George Mulgan, A. (2006) *Power and Pork: A Japanese Political Life*, Canberra: ANU E Press and Asia Pacific Press.

Grimes, W. W. (2001) *Unmaking the Japanese Miracle: Macroeconomic Politics, 1985–2000*, Ithaca, NY: Cornell University Press.

Haley, J. O. (1978) "The Myth of the Reluctant Litigant," *Journal of Japanese Studies*, 4: 359–390.

Haley, J. O. (1987) "Governance by Negotiation: A Reappraisal of Bureaucratic Power in Japan," *The Journal of Japanese Studies*, 13: 343–357.

Haley, J. O. (2002) "The Japanese Judiciary: Maintaining Integrity, Autonomy and the Public Trust," paper given at "Law in Japan: At the Turning Point," Nagashima, Ohno & Tsunematsu and the University of Washington Asian Law Center, Seattle, Washington, August 22–24.

Hayao, K. (1993) *The Japanese Prime Minister and Public Policy*, Pittsburgh, PA: University of Pittsburgh Press.

Hrebenar, R. J. (2000) *Japan's New Party System*, 3rd edn, Boulder, CO: Westview Press.

Ikawa, H. (2008) "15 Years of Decentralization Reform in Japan," National Graduate Institute for Policy Study. March. Available online at www3.grips.ac.jp/~coslog/ en/activity/01/03/index.html (7 August 2013).

Johnson, C. (1982) *MITI and the Japanese Miracle: The Growth of Industrial Policy, 1925–1975*, Stanford, CA: Stanford University Press.

Johnson, C. (1986) "Tanaka Kakuei, Structural Corruption, and the Advent of Machine Politics in Japan," *Journal of Japanese Studies*, 12: 1–28.

Johnson, C. (1987) "Political Institutions and Economic Performance: The Government-Business Relationship in Japan, South Korea and Taiwan," in F. C. Deyo (ed.) *The Political Economy of the New Asian Industrialism*, Ithaca, NY: Cornell University Press.

Kanai, T. (2007) "Vectors of Change in Japan's Political and Fiscal Decentralization," *Social Science Japan*, 37: 3–6.

Kitayama, T. (2001) *Local Government Policy Initiatives in Japan*, Washington, DC: The World Bank Institute.

Kohara, T. (2007) "The Great Heisei Consolidation: A Critical Review," *Social Science Japan*, 37: 7–11.

Krauss, E. S. (1984) "Conflict in the Diet: Toward Conflict Management in Parliamentary Politics," in E. S. Krauss, T. P. Rohlen, and P. G. Steinhoff (eds) *Conflict in Japan*, Honolulu: University of Hawaii Press.

Marshall, J. D. (2011) "Democratizing the Law in Japan," in A. Gaunder (ed.) *The Routledge Handbook of Japanese Politics*, London: Routledge.

Masumi, J. (1995) *Contemporary Politics in Japan*, trans. L. E. Carlile, Berkeley: University of California Press.

Matsui, S. (2011) "Why is the Japanese Court So Conservative?" *Washington University Law Review*, 88: 1375–1423.

McCubbins, M. D. and Rosenbluth, F. (1995) "Party Provision for Personal Politics: Dividing the Vote in Japan," in P. F. Cowhey and M. D. McCubbins (eds) *Structure and Policy in Japan and the United States*, Cambridge: Cambridge University Press.

Nyblade, B. and Reed, S. R. (2008) "Who Cheats? Who Loots? Political Competition and Corruption in Japan, 1947–1993," *American Journal of Political Science*, 52: 926–941.

Ozawa, I. (1994) *Blueprint for a New Japan: The Rethinking of a Nation*, trans. L. Rubinfien, Tokyo: Kodansha International.

Reed, S. R. (1986) *Japanese Prefectures and Policymaking*, Pittsburgh: University of Pittsburgh Press.

Reed, S. R. (2009) "Party Strategy or Candidate Strategy: How Does the LDP Run the Right Number of Candidates in Multiple Member Districts?" *Party Politics*, 15: 295–314.

Reed, S. R. and Thies, M. F. (2001) "The Causes of Electoral Reform in Japan," in M. S. Shugart and M. P. Wattenberg (eds) *Mixed-Member Electoral Systems: The Best of Both Worlds?* Oxford: Oxford University Press.

Saito, J. and Yamada, Y. (2011) "Local Government in Japan," in A. Gaunder (ed.) *The Routledge Handbook of Japanese Politics*, London: Routledge.

Samuels, R. J. (1983) *The Politics of Regional Policy in Japan*, Princeton, NJ: Princeton University Press.

Samuels, R. J. (2003a) *Machiavelli's Children: Leaders and Their Legacies in Italy and Japan*, Ithaca: Cornell University Press.

Samuels, R. J. (2003b) "Leadership and Political Change in Japan: The Case of the Second Rincho," *Journal of Japanese Studies*, 29: 1–31.

Schlesinger, J. M. (1997) *Shadow Shoguns: The Rise and Fall of Japan's Postwar Political Machine*, New York: Simon and Schuster.

Shinoda, T. (2000) *Leading Japan: The Role of the Prime Minister*, Westport, CT: Praeger.

Shinoda, T. (2003) "Koizumi's Top-Down Leadership in the Anti-Terrorist Legislation: The Impact of Political Institutional Changes," *SAIS Review*, 23: 19–34.

Stockwin, J. A. A. (1994) "On Trying to Move Mountains: The Political Career of Doi Takako," *Japan Forum*, 6: 21–34.

Stockwin, J. A. A. (2000) "The Social Democratic Party (Formerly Japan Socialist Party): A Turbulent Odyssey," in R. J. Hrebenar (ed.) *Japan's New Party System*, 3rd edn, Boulder, CO: Westview Press.

5 Political parties[1]

The Japanese party system has experienced both periods of stability and flux during the postwar period. A large number of parties emerged following the end of World War II, some new and some revived from the prewar period. The system stabilized in 1955 when the left Socialists and the right Socialists merged to form the Japan Socialist Party (JSP) on the left, and the Liberal Party and the Democratic Party joined to form the Liberal Democratic Party (LDP) on the right. Initially, observers anticipated that these two parties would challenge each other along the progressive and conservative spectrum with intermittent changes in power. The JSP, however, did not have the resources or organizational strength to support multiple candidates in every district, a strategy that was necessary to get a majority in the lower house. As a result, a one and a half party system emerged with the JSP serving as the strongest opposition force but unable to unseat the LDP.

In the mid-1960s several smaller, minor parties emerged in the center of the ideological spectrum. Some parties came into existence due to party splits like the Democratic Socialist Party (DSP) and the New Liberal Club (NLC); others like the Kōmeitō were new and emerged in response to new social forces associated with economic growth. The LDP continued to dominate throughout this period because none of the new parties gained momentum. Moreover, the opposition parties remained divided and unable to mount a coalition challenge to the LDP.

The LDP's overall support declined during the 1960s and 1970s, partially due to demographic shifts related to economic growth. Japan became more urban and less rural, but neither the LDP nor the JSP were able to respond to this shift and increase their strength. The LDP, however, managed to stay in power due to opposition weakness and fragmentation. The LDP rebounded in the early and mid-1980s, but began to fall apart due to a variety of factors including scandal and corruption in the late 1980s, unpopular policies, and the end of the Cold War.

In 1993, the LDP split on the issue of political reform, ushering in a period of party realignment. While a grand coalition of eight opposition parties were able to take control of government following the split, this anti-LDP coalition was not able to stay in power for a full year. The anti-LDP coalition did successfully push forward electoral system and political funding reform, although the final vote occurred once the LDP returned to power. These reforms significantly changed the incentives and constraints faced by politicians, parties, and voters in elections.

The LDP found itself back in power in coalition with the JSP ten months after its split. The LDP then re-established its dominance with one significant difference – it no longer ruled as a single dominant party; instead, it ruled in coalition from 1994 to 2009.

By the mid-2000s, the party system appeared to have stabilized with the Democratic Party of Japan (DPJ) emerging as the new challenger to the LDP. Following a strong performance in the upper house elections in 2007 and frustration with the LDP's inability to deal with Japan's economic woes, the DPJ won a landslide victory in the 2009 lower house election and took control of the government. Many observers believed that this election marked the beginning of two-party alternation. The DPJ, however, proved ineffective in office. It was weakened by leadership struggles, policy indecisiveness, and ineffective attempts to reduce the power and influence of the bureaucracy. The DPJ's response to the triple disaster (the earthquake, tsunami, and nuclear crisis in Fukushima) in 2011 further inhibited the party's ability to lead. By the time the DPJ dissolved the lower house for a new election in 2012, it was already 74 members weaker due to internal splits. It then suffered dramatic defeats in the 2012 lower house and 2013 upper house elections. It only slightly recovered in the 2014 lower house election, winning 73 seats as opposed to 57 in 2012. Recent elections indicate the party system has returned to a period of flux and party realignment. Instead of two parties vying for seats in the SMD portion of the electoral system for the lower house, once again new parties have entered the contests effectively splitting the anti-LDP vote.

This chapter explores the ideology, organization, and support bases of the major political parties in the 1955 system of LDP dominance and the post-1993 system of party realignment. It addresses why the LDP was able to hold on to power for most of the postwar period. It also considers the challenges faced by opposition parties.

The LDP

The LDP is a classic catch-all party. Since its inception, it has been a large party that reached out to cross-cutting interests. The number and types of interest groups that the party courted increased over time. The core support base of the LDP during its dominant reign (1955–1993) consisted of farmers and rural communities, industry, corporations, small business, construction, the postal lobby, and the self-employed. Despite its broad support base, the LDP struggled with weak party identification and low levels of party membership.

The LDP has been classified as a political machine. A political machine represents an exchange relationship between politicians and voters. Political machines were a prevalent feature of local politics in large metropolitan areas in the U.S. in the late 1800s and early 1900s – the most well known being Tammany Hall in New York City. Tammany Hall provided social welfare services to poor, predominantly Irish Americans in return for votes. In general, the goal of the machine was to cement loyalty from voters, mainly immigrants, by providing favors including jobs or necessities like fuel. The machines were headed by a political boss who held a local or state position and used the spoils of office to reward supporters. Machines were strictly hierarchical with party bosses, ward bosses, and precinct captains who were responsible for getting the vote out on election day. Over time, these machines became plagued by corruption and many developed close connections to gangsters and the underworld. Due to corruption and the development of social welfare services through President Roosevelt's New Deal, the power of political machines waned with most machines disappearing by the 1960s (Gosnell 1968).

The Japanese version of a political machine features political parties and/or individual politicians exchanging favors or policies for votes or money. At the party level, the

LDP accepted money from constituents, mainly businesses and interest groups, in return for favorable policies and regulations. At the individual level, LDP politicians created kōenkai (personal support organizations) to provide patronage and pork to constituents in return for votes (Curtis 1971). Patronage is the exchange of votes for favors. Individual politicians can provide access to the bureaucracy, introductions to employers, or assistance in getting into a school in return for a constituent's vote. In Japan, patronage often focuses on a group of supporters. Kōenkai sponsored trips to hot springs, cooking classes, or the like at very little cost to the supporter. The goal is to create a positive feeling toward the politician. Pork is a government budget appropriation for a project that brings revenue and jobs to your constituency such as a bridge, a museum, or most famously in the case of the first national "boss" of the LDP machine, Tanaka Kakuei, a bullet train station in your district. Patronage and pork distributed through an individual politician's kōenkai have promoted weak party identification. Voters who often see themselves as supporters of the individual, not the LDP as a whole emerged, however, precisely because the LDP only provided the party label and seed money to the candidate; candidates were responsible for building their own support. Observing this, Curtis described the LDP as a "franchised party" (Curtis 1988: 143). Kōenkai are difficult for all new politicians to build as they require connections and money. Those outside the old boys' network, such as women, were not part of the LDP's machine and faced great obstacles in electioneering.

The LDP's clientelism has not been completely exclusionary. Its desire to "catch" as many groups as possible has made it more open to consider the interests of groups outside its social coalition. Interest groups with closer ties to the LDP exert greater influence than outsiders, but overall the LDP was inclusive and flexible during its period of dominance (Muramatsu and Krauss 1990). Indeed, the LDP has represented many cross-cutting interests, including big and small businesses, productive and non-productive sectors, and rural and urban constituencies. It has favored interests that provide votes and/or money, such as construction.

Political parties care about office, votes, and policy (Müller and Strøm 1999). While all three have been important to the LDP, it has clearly prioritized office (Reed 2011). Being in power was crucial for the maintenance of the LDP machine as the party needed the resources available to the governing party to provide patronage and pork to its constituents.

The LDP is a decentralized party with a bottom-up decision-making process. The key organizational features of the LDP – factions and the Policy Affairs Research Council (PARC) – promote this decentralization. While anywhere from seven to twelve factions existed in its early years, the number of factions stabilized to five to six by the 1970s. These factions are not ideologically based. Instead, factions within the LDP focus on raising and distributing funds to support candidates for office in return for the faction member's support in the party presidential election. Factions have also served as an important mechanism for distributing party and Diet positions. In general, factions receive representation within the party and the cabinet in proportion to their numerical strength (Kohno 1997). Factions have been the main institution for maintaining internal balance. The LDP has always feared internal split. Factional balancing in appointments to party and Diet positions promotes cohesion.

The PARC is the other structure within the LDP that organizes interests. It parallels the Diet committee structure and served as the main forum for policy debate under the 1955 system of LDP dominance. During LDP dominance, this body was responsible for national policy formulation. The chairs and vice chairs of the PARC divisions wielded considerable power as policy gatekeepers. However, the PARC also afforded backbenchers influence, something that contributed to the fragmented policymaking in the LDP (Krauss and Pekkanen 2011). According to Krauss and Pekkanen, "PARC performed important socialization, training, and career-structuring functions for both the party and government. And in these roles and functions it was an almost uniquely powerful party organ among the parties of parliamentary democracies in the industrialized countries" (Krauss and Pekkanen 2011: 158).

Participation on the PARC committees provided opportunities for credit claiming and fundraising as politicians could pursue the interests of their district and key interest groups. Indeed, the PARC committees and positions cultivated so-called zoku (policy tribe) politicians who were experts in certain areas with strong connections to the relevant ministries and interest groups in this area (Krauss and Pekkanen 2011). The inordinate influence of party backbenchers through the Policy Affairs Research Council and zoku politicians defies the norms of Westminster systems (George Mulgan 2011c).

The Westminster model refers to parliamentary systems that are cabinet dominated. The Westminster model emerged in the United Kingdom but can be found in other parliamentary democracies such as Canada, Australia, New Zealand, and several other former British colonies. Westminster systems are highly centralized. In the "pure" Westminster systems, executive power is concentrated in a dominant political party and decisions are made by the cabinet (Liphart 1999). The LDP's decentralized approach to governing made its period of dominance far from the Westminster model.

A large part of the reason the LDP was able to stay in office for so long had to do with its ability to adjust its positions in the wake of social and economic change. As a catch-all party it continued to expand its social coalition. It also pursued a "crisis and compensation" strategy (Calder 1988). The crisis and compensation logic suggests that the LDP would act in times of crisis and appease those affected through favorable policy shifts. One example of crisis and compensation is the LDP's response to the high-profile pollution cases in the 1970s. While these suits were initially addressed by the courts, the LDP eventually co-opted this agenda and passed important industry regulations and standards in the so-called Pollution Diet in the 1970s. The Ministry of the Environment was also established.

The LDP was able to adapt its policy agenda to fit the changing needs of Japan as it developed and then reached maturity. In the 1950s and 1960s, the LDP promoted rapid growth; in the 1970s the LDP focused on fiscal restraint and balancing the budget; in the 1980s the LDP carried out administrative reform; in the 1990s the LDP oversaw electoral reform and further administrative reforms. The LDP, however, struggled from the 1990s to address the challenges of economic stagnation. Prime Minister Koizumi saw modest success with his passage of postal system reform and the reform of the Fiscal Investment and Loan Program (FILP), but the economy remains troubled.

Under the SNTV electoral system, candidate nomination in the LDP was a bottom-up process with the Electoral Strategy Committee considering recommendations from the local branch offices. The Electoral Strategy Committee passed its recommendation along to the Executive Council (Shiratori 1988: 172–173). Factional balancing was a major decision rule in determining official endorsements. After incumbents, second generation politicians or candidates who could demonstrate strong support in a given district were given priority (Woodall 1996: 108).

Under both the old and new electoral systems, local party branch offices, factions, and kōenkai have played a key role in the recruitment and nomination process. The LDP often recruits bureaucrats, local and prefectural assembly members, or political assistants to politicians. In the 2014 lower house election, the LDP won 291 seats with 25 women representatives and 266 male representatives.

The JSP

The JSP was the second largest party in the 1955 system and the LDP's main competitor. It was a progressive party on the left, but it was ultimately constrained by its strict adherence to radical Marxism. It formed when the left Socialist party and the right Socialist party merged in 1955. Ultimately, however, the left and right wings of the party could not work together. The party split in the 1960s with the less radical Marxists forming the Democratic Socialist Party and taking the support of the private sector labor unions with them.

The JSP, like the LDP, was not a metropolitan party. Its main support came from public sector labor unions. To a lesser extent, it also received support from small business, professionals, intellectual communities, and farmers. In the 1980s, the party attempted to expand its support from labor to citizens, but Doi Takako, the leader at that time, met resistance from other party members. The party halted these efforts when Doi resigned.

Ideologically, the JSP's rhetoric was steeped in Marxism. This adherence to Marxism made the JSP distinct from Western Social Democratic parties and ultimately led to the defection of the right wing of the party to create the DSP in 1960 (Stockwin 2000, 212). Despite its rhetoric, its main platform included a strict interpretation of and adherence to Article 9 of the Constitution. It also opposed the U.S.–Japan Security treaty. The JSP felt that the U.S.–Japan Security Treaty locked Japan into the U.S.-led Cold War world order. The treaty called on both countries to act in each other's defense if attacked, establishing the basis for the continued presence of U.S. military bases on Japanese soil. The provisions were problematic given Article 9 of the Japanese Constitution which forbids Japan from maintaining armed forces. The JSP boycotted the lower house on the day of the vote in 1960. Large protests by students and union activists ensued following the bill's passage. Prime Minister Kishi was forced to resign. Despite the JSP's opposition, the U.S.–Japan Security Treaty remains intact today. By the end of the Cold War, the JSP's strong stance only resonated with a very small portion of the electorate.

The JSP suffered from factionalization and weak organization. The factional groupings in the JSP originally were based both on personal ties and ideology, although these groupings became more fluid over time (Stockwin 2000: 239). The differing priorities of factions and the inability to reach a consensus on party direction inhibited the party's ability to appeal to voters, especially in the 1990s. For example, in 1992 the JSP had 26 different "groupings," not all necessarily factions that fell into three categories: left, center, and right (Stockwin 2000: 237). The significance of the factional divisions became clear when the party system was thrown into flux in the early 1990s. Party leaders on the right pledged JSP participation in the anti-LDP coalition in 1993; a year later party leaders on the left forged a JSP alliance with the LDP. These divisions prevented the party from flourishing when a new electoral system was adopted in 1994.

The JSP also lacked effective organization, particularly at the local level where voter mobilization is crucial. Its organizational structure depended on the voter support of unions, which became increasingly less viable sources for votes. Unions also stood as obstacles to the broadening of support. The privatization efforts in the 1980s decreased the power of unions and led to the formation of the union federation, Rengō, which actually fielded its own candidates in the early 1990s.

The JSP often performed better at the prefectural and local levels. The party won several governorships during the 1970s when environmental issues hit center stage. Opposition parties as a whole won even more seats and leadership positions at the local level through coalition. These parties were not able to cooperate nationally, but locally they found greater common ground. According to Stephen Johnson, cooperation emerged at the local level because the organizational interests of parties "were easier to reconcile" (2000: 140).

Doi Takako is probably the most famous JSP politician. She is the first female party leader. She was selected as party leader in 1986. She began her career as a constitutional scholar. She was also involved in citizens' movements and women's rights. She was an effective speaker known for her straight talk and often appeared on TV variety shows. She was a controversial choice as party head, but the entire party benefitted from her strong electioneering skills. She managed to capitalize on LDP weaknesses in the 1989 upper house election. Just prior to this election, the LDP found itself embroiled in the Recruit stocks-for-favors scandal. It also had just passed a very controversial 3 percent national consumption tax. An LDP sex scandal involving Prime Minister Uno, the prime minister who replaced Takeshita who resigned to take responsibility for the Recruit scandal, also broke before the election. In the wake of strong anti-LDP sentiment, Doi chose to support twelve female newcomers in the 1989 upper house election. Most of the women were housewife activists. These women emphasized traditional gender characteristics such being "clean" (Ogai 2001: 209). To the surprise of many, ten of the twelve candidates won, ushering in the largest number of women in the upper house. The JSP had a solid performance in the 1990 lower house election but struggled to find quality candidates to field in every district. Given that parties have to win at least two seats in every district to gain a majority in the lower house, the JSP never had a chance of capitalizing on the momentum of the Madonna boom and winning the majority in the lower house, a stated party goal. It simply did not have the candidates.[2]

The tide changed abruptly for the JSP with the outbreak of the first Gulf War. The JSP staunchly and visibly protested attempts to expand Japan's involvement. Prime Minister Kaifu proposed a Peacekeeping Operations (PKO) bill, at least partially in response to pressure from the U.S. for Japan to move beyond checkbook diplomacy. This bill would allow Japanese self-defense forces to participate in UN peacekeeping operations. The JSP opposed this bill because it felt the bill violated Article 9 of the Constitution. Opinion polls taken at the time, however, revealed that the public no longer saw a need for such an isolationalist stance. The JSP paid for its inability to adjust to changing public attitudes in the 1993 lower house election, losing nearly half its seats. This defeat was even more remarkable given that the LDP split just prior to the election, making it just as vulnerable as it had been in the 1989 upper house election. After the JSP's leader Murayama served a brief stint as prime minister in an LDP/JSP coalition in 1994, the JSP pretty much disappeared as a player in post-electoral reform politics.

The JCP

Unlike the LDP, the Japan Communist Party (JCP) is an ideologically driven party. It is the party on the extreme left informed by Marxist-Leninism. As Japan experienced dramatic economic growth, the JCP came to resemble Communist parties in Europe as it moderated its position over the years. Like Communist parties in Europe, it accepted parliamentary democracy and was not solely a representative of the working class. Instead, it supported a variety of groups whose interests were compatible with those of the working class. It was a party dedicated to the preservation and expansion of freedoms and supported welfare and environmental policies (Berton 2000).

Under the 1955 system, the JCP received support from a limited number of labor unions where its members held leadership positions. Its main support came from women and youth affiliate organizations as well as doctors and lawyers, nontraditional supporters of Communist parties. It raised funds through its newspaper, *Akahata*. This income made it more independent. In fact, unlike other parties it did not have to rely on outside interest groups for monetary support. While claiming to adhere to the principles of democratic centralism, in practice, the party has been dominated by strong leadership at the top.

As a rule, the JCP ran candidates in every multiple-member district in the SNTV system. Its goal was not to maximize seats but to educate the electorate. Initially, after reform it supported candidates in both SMD and PR districts. It then moved to a focus on PR. Since 2012, however, it has switched to supporting candidates in SMDs without dual listing (Gaunder 2016; Martin Murphy 2013).

The emergence of center parties

Over time, smaller opposition parties emerged to fill in the space between the LDP and the JSP. The Democratic Socialist Party and the New Liberal Club emerged as splits from the JSP and the LDP, respectively. The Kōmeitō was created in response to the new social forces that economic growth ushered in.

As discussed in greater detail in Chapter 6, the MMD/SNTV electoral system provided these smaller new parties both opportunities and constraints. Given that each district elected two to six representatives, parties did not have to win a majority of the vote to gain a seat. Instead, in the larger districts a politician could win a seat with as little as a fifth or sixth of the vote. This circumstance allowed small parties to win seats where niche support was strong. None of the new parties that entered the scene in the 1960s and 1970s, however, had a message that resonated with a large portion of the population, preventing all the new parties from challenging the LDP. Most of these center parties also did not have the resources or organizational support to mount a true challenge to the LDP. As we shall see in the case of the Kōmeitō, while it had strong organizational support, it was constrained by its ideology.

The LDP's vote share declined consistently during its period of dominance due in large part to the emergence of new parties. Its vote share dropped six percentage points when the Kōmeitō contested its first election in 1967, and it dropped five percentage points when the NLC broke from the LDP and ran independently in 1976. The largest drop in vote share occurred when the LDP split in 1993. In this election, the LDP's vote share was only 36.6 percent.[3] The ideology and support base of the DSP, New Liberal Club, and Kōmeitō are briefly discussed below.

The DSP

The DSP split from the JSP in 1960. The right and left wings of the JSP remained after the party merged in 1955. Different internal groups disagreed on whether the JSP should be a class- or mass-based party and how strong the party's position on national security should be. Most of the politicians who split to form the DSP were from the right wing of the JSP. This wing of the party was more moderate. It actually supported the U.S.–Japan Security Treaty. As its name indicates, it advocated social democracy and supported many welfare-type provisions. These were not the only moderate members of the JSP though, and as a result the JSP continued to debate what kind of party it should be even after the departure of these rightist elements.

The DSP also struggled to distinguish itself from the JSP. Its main support came from Dōmei – private sector labor unions. It could not claim to be the sole party of social democracy; it had to share this distinction with the JSP. It did claim to be staunchly anti-Communist in contrast to the JSP. This distinction alone was not enough to attract significant support.

The Kōmeitō

The Kōmeitō emerged in 1964. Its name literally translates into Clean Government Party. This name was chosen to distinguish the party from the LDP which often found itself embroiled in scandals related to money politics. The Kōmeitō is known for its close ties with the Sōka Gakkai, a Buddhist religious sect. Initially, there was a direct connection between the religious organization and the party, but due to a high-profile scandal involving a Sōka Gakkai leader in the 1970s, the party officially declared its independence from the Buddhist sect. This declaration was more for show, however, as the party's candidates and monetary support continued to come from the Sōka Gakkai.

The Kōmeitō is a religious-based party, not a class-based party like the JSP and the DSP. It calls for Buddhist democracy and emphasizes peace, the environment, and welfare programs. More recently, it has advocated for the rights of foreigners. Many Japanese are wary of the party due to its close connection to the Sōka Gakkai, claiming it violates the postwar norms of separation of church and state.

Indeed, the party's support predominantly comes from members of the Buddhist sect. It is an urban party that serves constituents that have not benefitted from economic growth, including nonunionized workers, small business owners, and the poor and uneducated. Although it has tried to expand its support, it has failed to appeal to voters outside the Buddhist sect. In fact, the party is often referred to as the most hated party in Japan due to the public's wariness of its connection to religion (Hrebenar 2000). Its supporters are very loyal, though, ensuring the party stable support throughout the postwar period.

Due to its religious foundations, it is difficult to place the Kōmeitō on the left/right ideological spectrum. Initially the party's stance on security was more similar to that of the JSP. Its position on security has waffled over time. At times, it called for preserving the status quo of the U.S.–Japan Security Treaty due to the dictates of the Cold War; other times, however, it advocated for ending the Security Treaty. In general, its religious connections make the party more conservative, if not right wing. By the 1970s the Kōmeitō appeared closer to the DSP and the LDP than the JSP (Curtis 1988: 26). As we shall see, in the post-1994 electoral reform environment, the Kōmeitō has been the LDP's most frequent coalition partner.

The New Liberal Club[4]

The New Liberal Club (NLC) emerged when seven junior members of the LDP left the party over the issue of party reform. Kōno Yōhei, a third term heredity politician, led the new party. These members left the LDP on the heels of the Lockheed scandal in which former Prime Minister Tanaka was accused of accepting bribes from the U.S. company to broker contracts for Lockheed with a Japanese airline company. The LDP defectors were disillusioned by the pervasiveness of money politics within the party and hoped that their exit would force the issue of party reform. The NLC politicians essentially demanded party reform in exchange for their re-entry into the party.

Initially, the NLC saw modest success with 17 of its 25 candidates elected in the 1976 lower house election. By leaving the party, the NLC was able to deny the LDP a majority in the lower house, forcing it to scramble for the support of independent candidates following the 1976 and 1979 elections and to officially ask the NLC for its support after the 1983 election.

The NLC, however, could not agree on a clear vision for the party, something that prevented it from forming alliances with other political parties. Some members saw the creation of the party as a temporary strategy to incite reform in the LDP; others hoped the NLC would change into a viable opposition party that attracted enough politicians to deny the LDP an outright majority. In the end, the NLC failed to distinguish itself from the LDP, especially with its decision to join the LDP in government following the 1983 election (Curtis 1988: 32). The NLC did receive a cabinet position as part of its coalition agreement. By 1986, though, the NLC's numbers had shrunk considerably, and it had not achieved any of its major goals. Conceding defeat, the few remaining members of the party rejoined the LDP only having had a marginal influence on the party in their ten years outside the party.

One-party dominant regimes in comparative perspective

Outside observers have often questioned whether LDP dominance in the 1955 system was democratic. Some have actually gone so far as to label the LDP's rule soft authoritarian (Johnson 1987). There are many ways to measure democracy; these critics are emphasizing the importance of party alternation in the democratic process. For new democracies party alternation is connected to regime stability, the question being is the regime strong enough to withstand the peaceful transition to power.

Japan meets the standards of democracy under LDP dominance. The LDP was elected in free and fair elections where voters were given the choice of several viable parties. The LDP also adjusted its positions in response to voter demands.

Why then was the LDP able to hold on to power for 38 uninterrupted years? The answer rests with several of its political institutions as well as voting behavior. As discussed in Chapter 6, Japan's electoral system, its political funding regime, and its campaign regulations all favored large parties with significant resources. Voters also associated the LDP with economic growth and prosperity. For much of the postwar period, the LDP was the only party the public felt competent to govern. It was closely associated with democracy and regime legitimacy. In the context of the Cold War, voters were quite wary of the parties of the left. As we have seen, the parties of the center could not expand beyond very particular niche support.

The undemocratic nature of LDP dominance is even more easily refuted when Japan is placed in comparative perspective. Parliamentary systems lend themselves to long periods of rule by a single party or coalition of parties. The executive and legislative branches are fused in parliamentary systems. As a result, gridlock is attenuated; divided government is not possible. Without divided government, parties can more effectively pursue their agendas. Gridlock can emerge if a different party controls the weaker house of parliament, but in general fewer obstacles are present.

Several other democratic regimes, including Sweden, Italy, Germany, and Israel, have experienced long periods of rule by a single party or with a dominant party in coalition with smaller parties (Pempel 1990). Critics are much less likely to question the democratic credentials of these predominantly Western democracies. Democracy does look somewhat different in Japan, but Japan certainly meets the minimum standards of democracy.

The LDP's form of dominance did have some unique characteristics. As we have seen, the LDP built a political machine with strong ties to interest groups. These interest groups were rewarded with the spoils of office. As a catch-all party, the LDP's approach to interest groups was inclusive. Some interest groups were more important than others, but the LDP remained open to establishing ties with a variety of groups as long as they could provide money and/or votes in return.

Italy and Germany also experienced long periods of rule by conservative parties following World War II. The Christian Democrats (DC) dominated Italian politics from 1945 to 1992 with a member of the DC serving as prime minister consecutively from 1946 to 1981. The DC, like the LDP, formed close ties to diverse and often conflicting groups in Italian society, including the constituents in both the private and state sector and representatives from unions and labor. These ties often resulted in corrupt activities. The DC, unlike the LDP, was not able to transcend its corrupt activities. A series of scandals in the late 1980s followed by electoral reform led to a party split and the eventual demise of the once dominant DC.[5]

The CDU also has dominated German politics in the postwar period, albeit usually in coalition with smaller parties. The CDU is a corporatist catch-all party (Wiliarty 2010). Unlike traditional catch-all parties, the CDU mobilizes its membership, providing representation and voice for various groups in its internal decision-making bodies. This inclusiveness has allowed the CDU to better respond to societal change and the demands that have accompanied it (Wiliarty 2010).

One-party dominant regimes have not been exclusively conservative. Both Sweden and Israel have had dominant parties of the left. The Social Democratic Party (SDP) in Sweden has a strong working class base. It also garnered rural support. Over time, like other dominant parties, the SDP found it necessary to broaden its policy positions to attract additional groups. Specifically, it began to target white collar wage earners with its pension policies. After a period in opposition, the SDP returned to government from 1994 to 2006 promising more jobs and fiscal responsibility (Pempel 1990). In Israel, Mapai/Labor dominated the scene for 30 years from the late 1940s to the late 1970s. This party established its strong hold by courting the immigrant population. Labor has only managed brief stints in government since the late 1970s as the conservatives have gained more legitimacy (Pempel 1990).

These comparative examples illustrate that the dominance of a single party or large party in coalition is not as uncommon as often perceived when looking at one country in isolation. Many of these countries and parties have suffered from corruption, something that access to government resources and largess fosters, or at least makes more possible.

1993: the party system in crisis

Both outside observers and LDP politicians saw internal split as one of the largest threats to the LDP's dominance under the 1955 system. The party devised several institutional mechanisms to guard against internal splits. Factions were an institutional response to the electoral system which called for members of the same party to run against one another in order for a party to win an average of two seats in each district. LDP factions never ran more than one member in each district. Instead, factions competed against one another. To keep the peace after the elections, the party used a "balancing norm" to distribute Diet and party posts (Kohno 1997). Factions received positions roughly in proportion to their strength within the party. This balancing helped but did not prevent the emergence of disgruntled groups within the party.

The NLC's break in the 1970s was the first example of a high-profile party split. The NLC's leader, Kōno Yōhei, was a heredity politician who commanded significant media attention. Kōno and his followers represented a significant cleavage in the party – junior versus senior politicians. Posts are distributed based on seniority. Junior members had to wait until their fifth or sixth election before receiving a significant appointment. Part of the reason the members of the NLC left was that they were frustrated by the limited voice of junior politicians. Kōno, however, was only able to convince six members to leave with him. Life outside the LDP was not easy. Only politicians with secure seats and strong kōenkai could be convinced to take this risk.

The second major split in the LDP occurred in 1993 and threw the party system into disarray. While this split was prompted by many similar concerns expressed by the NLC – frustration with corruption, calls for reform, and the junior–senior divide – it was much larger.

The path to the LDP split began in 1988 with the outbreak of the Recruit stock-for-favors scandal. This scandal involved a part-time employment magazine bribing several LDP politicians for favorable regulations. The LDP responded to the scandal, by forcing Prime Minister Takeshita, who had been implicated in the scandal, to resign. He was replaced by Uno Sōsuke. Just weeks after taking office, Uno was implicated in a sex scandal with the exposure of an affair with a geisha. Uno resigned and was replaced by Kaifu, a "clean" politician from a smaller faction. These personnel changes were too little, too late for the 1989 upper house election. The LDP lost its majority in the upper house for the first time since 1955. Although senior members were often implicated in scandals, junior members often bore the brunt of the public's discontent in elections because these politicians had less secure seats.

The LDP also initiated several unpopular policies prior to the 1989 election, including a 3 percent national consumption tax and agricultural reform that included opening several protected markets. While the LDP kept its majority in the 1990 lower house election, it continued to flounder.

The end of the Cold War also had at least an indirect impact on the party system. One reason that the LDP was able to stay in government for so long is that the public viewed it as the only party competent to govern. The LDP also received support from the West as the party capable of safeguarding democracy. The end of the Cold War opened up more space for parties to compete.

The LDP had barely recovered from the Recruit scandal and the sex scandal when the Sagawa Kyubin scandal broke in 1992. This scandal involved a delivery company bribing LDP politicians for favors. It implicated several top LDP politicians, including former Prime Minister Takeshita and LDP kingmaker and shadow shogun Kanemaru Shin. The public's tolerance for LDP excesses was waning as the country was just beginning to feel the effects of the economic woes caused by the bursting of the housing bubble. The image of prosecutors emerging from Kanemaru's office with a shopping cart full of gold bars outraged many. This outrage intensified when Kanemaru only received a small fine for his misdeeds; he was not even expelled from the party (Gaunder 2007: 99).

Two separate groups of reformers within the LDP used the issue of political reform to bolt the party in the midst of this scandal. One group was made up of several second generation politicians who had relatively safe seats. Another group consisted of members of the LDP with close connections to the shadow shogun in training, Ozawa Ichirō. These groups ran separately in the 1993 lower house election as the Sakigake (the Harbinger Party) and the Shinseitō (the New Renewal Party), respectively. They grudgingly put aside their differences to form an anti-LDP coalition following the election. This coalition included strange bedfellows including the Kōmeitō, JSP, DSP, the Japan New Party (see next section), the two LDP splinter groups, and a few smaller parties.

What allowed these groups to leave and why were they initially more successful than the NLC? The leaders were able to leave due to seniority, safe seats, and monetary resources. Many of the members of the Sakigake party were heredity politicians with safe seats and strong kōenkai. These members, however, rejected the Ozawa-style of money politics and wanted to establish a different image for their party. The members of the Shinseitō all had strong connections to Ozawa. Many of the senior members of the Shinseitō entered the Diet in the same election as Ozawa and were part of his cohort. The junior members of the Shinseitō had received electoral assistance from Ozawa in his role as secretary general. Many outsiders saw Ozawa as an opportunist using reform as a chance to wield more power after he lost the battle for head of the largest faction in the LDP (Gaunder 2007)

No matter what his motives were, though, Ozawa had money, strong political connections to opposition parties, and a vision for reforming the party system (Gaunder 2007). Ozawa's financial resources allowed him to convince junior members to follow him out of the party. His connections to opposition parties allowed him to build the anti-LDP coalition. His vision for reform garnered support from within and outside the party. His vision was found in his book *Blueprint for a New Japan*. He argued that electoral system reform was essential to remedy the money politics of a one-party dominant regime. He called for a single-member district system, claiming that it would push Japan to become a two-party system with party alternation. The ability to "throw the rascals out" would make political parties more responsible to the public. It would also allow Japan to become a "normal" country that could take a larger role in international politics, one of Ozawa's ultimate goals (Ozawa 1994). Ozawa's other major goal was to be the head of the second party that would emerge and contend for power against the LDP.

The creation of the anti-LDP coalition in 1993 and the passage of electoral system reform in 1994 marked initial success for Ozawa and his vision. Ozawa's dictatorial leadership style, however, eventually undermined the anti-LDP coalition, causing the JSP to abandon the coalition. After a short-lived minority coalition led by Ozawa's front person, Hata Tsutomu, the LDP found itself back in government a short 10 months after its split, albeit in a very odd coalition with its former opponent, the JSP.

Party realignment

It is important to note that the LDP lost the 1993 lower house election due to an internal party split. Very few of the remaining LDP members actually lost their seats in the 1993 election. The JSP was the party that suffered the greatest losses in the 1993 election, nearly halving its strength. As discussed earlier, the JSP experienced voter backlash due to its antiquated ideology, something that became apparent in debate over the PKO bill. Several new parties emerged to fill the vacuum created by the LDP split. In addition to the two splinter parties, a new outside party entered the arena. The Japan New Party was created by Kumamoto prefectural governor Hosokawa Morihiro. Hosokawa was a former member of the Diet. His party emerged out of frustration with the status quo – money politics and corruption. It called for broader political reform, not just electoral reform but administrative reform as well. The Japan New Party won four seats in the 1992 upper house election, including one for Hosokawa. With its recent entrance onto the national scene the Japan New Party was poised to capitalize on the LDP split over corruption and reform. The Japan New Party won 35 seats in the 1993 lower house election. Recognizing the importance of this new force, Ozawa convinced Hosokawa to lead the anti-LDP coalition.

As with several parties created in the wake of the LDP split, the Japan New Party's life was short-lived. It was only in existence between 1992 and 1994. In 1994 it dismantled and joined the Shinshintō (the New Frontier Party). The New Frontier Party was Ozawa's second attempt at creating a party strong enough to challenge the LDP. It included members from the Shinseitō, the Kōmeitō, the Japan New Party, the DSP, and Rengō. Like the anti-LDP coalition it struggled to find cohesion given that it contained members with diverse ideological predispositions ranging from social democracy to neoliberalism. Ozawa headed the party from 1995 to 1997 when it disintegrated.

Clearly, the LDP split prompted a period of political realignment. Political realignment occurs when parties change in strength or in this case when new parties emerge to compete for a position in the ideological space. During the period from 1993 to 1998, especially, it was not uncommon for a politician to switch parties once or even several times. Books were published that simply tracked the changes in politicians' party affiliations during this time. The system began to stabilize with the formation of the Democratic Party of Japan in 1998. It further settled when Ozawa's Liberal Party (the party he created after the New Frontier Party) merged with the DPJ in 2003.

The LDP's response: coalition government

After its split in 1993, the LDP realized that if it was going to find its way back into power it would need to form a coalition with other parties. It initiated its first coalition in 1994, just ten months after its split. To the surprise of many, the LDP forged an agreement with the JSP and Sakigake. Both the JSP and Sakigake had left the anti-LDP coalition due to Ozawa's unwillingness to make significant compromises. The LDP convinced the parties to join it to replace Hata's weak minority coalition in 1994.

As part of the agreement the sitting JSP leader, Murayama, would become prime minister, and each party would be granted a number of cabinet positions proportional to the party's strength in the Diet. The position of prime minister turned out to come at a high price for the JSP. The party found its leader hostage to the will of the LDP-dominated cabinet. Moreover, both the LDP and the JSP made significant compromises to enter the conservative–progressive grand coalition. The JSP reversed its stance on foreign and defense policies as well as some domestic issues. The JSP declared the SDF constitutional, pronounced its support of the U.S.–Japan Security Treaty, and recognized the legitimacy of the national anthem and national flag. It also changed its position to support the development of nuclear power and to support the consumption tax (Curtis 1999: 198). In return, the LDP agreed to maintain the status quo on its defense policy (i.e., not to push for the revision of the Constitution). While the JSP struggled with its limited leverage, it was more incorporated in this coalition than it had been in the anti-LDP coalition. The LDP devised a policy coordination council to discuss and agree on policy, a stark contrast to Ozawa's top-down decision-making style (see Curtis 1999: 200–201). This council became less important after the JSP and Sakigake suffered large defeats in the 1996 lower house election. This coalition, how-ever, would become the first of many coalition governments as coalitions became the norm under the new electoral system.

The new electoral system certainly contributed to coalition government. Before a strong opposition threat to the LDP emerged from party realignment, no party won a clear majority in the lower house preventing single party rule. In the 2000s, the reinvigorated LDP under Koizumi did regain majorities in the lower house, but it continued to rule in coalition. The main reason for continued coalition government in these circumstances was the more common occurrence of a twisted Diet. A twisted Diet refers to divided parliamentary government – when the lower and upper houses of the Diet are controlled by different par-ties. Since both houses of the Diet must pass most legislation, achieving a majority in both houses became critical. Coalition governments also emerged due to electoral cooperation.

The LDP has ruled in coalition with several different parties in the post-electoral reform era. It began in coalition with the Socialists and Sakigake. This coalition ended in 1997. By 1999, the LDP again was searching for an alliance. This time it chose Ozawa's new party, the Liberal Party. Ozawa desired to create a conservative–conservative connection, but many members of the LDP were not happy with the agreement. This coalition failed to create an outright majority in the upper house, but it weakened the unity of the opposition. The Kōmeitō initially was unwilling to join a coalition; it was still recovering from its experience in the New Renewal party. It did join the LDP-Liberal coalition in late 1999. By 2003, the LDP and Kōmeitō had discovered that their parties were the most suited to form a stable alliance. They remained in a two-party coalition from 2003 to 2009 and re-formed a coalition after the 2012 lower house election (Stockwin 2011).

The LDP-Kōmeitō coalition governments have both electoral and governing dimen-sions. Electorally the Kōmeitō agreed to have its party supporters vote for LDP can-didates in single-member districts. In return, LDP supporters were supposed to vote for the Kōmeitō in the PR vote. The LDP got more from this agreement than the Kōmeitō for several reasons. First, the Kōmeitō is a highly organized party; its members turn out at election time and vote as instructed. The LDP is much less well organized and its sup-porters are more connected to individuals than the party. It also was a harder sell to convince LDP supporters to vote for the "most hated party in Japan," the Kōmeitō. Nevertheless, the Kōmeitō accepted the unequal results for access to government.

On the policy front, the Kōmeitō also has received fewer benefits than the LDP. The LDP certainly achieved a greater ease in the passage of its policies when both parties held the majority in the lower and upper houses.

The emergence of the DPJ: its rise and split

The DPJ was initially constituted as the Democratic Party in 1996. It became the Democratic Party of Japan (DPJ) in 1998. It was originally an amalgam of former members of the LDP, the JSP, and other smaller parties. In its early years, it performed strongest in urban areas, but over time it expanded its support to all but the most rural areas. Its supporters are varied, but it is strongest with unions, citizens' groups, and the wealthy and well educated in suburban areas and capital cities outside of metropolitan areas (Weiner 2011: 93; Hyde 2009: 130).

Unlike the JSP, the DPJ is not a progressive party of the left. It began as a center left party (due in part to the contingent of former JSP members and its connections with Rengō). Over time, in response in part to the incentives of the SMD portion of the new lower house electoral system to appeal to the median voter, it has moved more to the center (Kabashima and Steel 2006; Koellner 2011; Miura, Lee, and Weiner 2005). While DPJ politicians have become more cohesive ideologically over time, it has still struggled to find quality candidates for all districts (Weiner 2011).

The DPJ does not have a strong ideological commitment to any particular issue. Instead, like many new parties before it, the DPJ has struggled to distinguish itself from the LDP and establish its credentials as a center left or centrist party. It has tweaked its stance on issues for electoral expediency and often defined its position in reaction to the LDP's position.

One of the major institutional innovations of the DPJ was the creation of any party manifesto as a campaigning tool. The DPJ issued its first party manifesto in the 2003 election. Its manifesto outlined the party's position on the key issues in the election. This tool was so effective that the LDP found it necessary to issue its own manifesto in response in the following election. The LDP, even more than the DPJ, struggles to summarize its positions in one document. This fact is probably related to the catch-all nature of the LDP.

The DPJ saw a gradual increase in support from 1998 to 2007, experiencing more difficulties during Prime Minister Koizumi's tenure in office. The DPJ initially saw greater success in the upper house. When Koizumi became prime minister in 2001, though, he co-opted many of the DPJ's policy positions. Koizumi presented himself as an anti-LDP crusader within the party. His goal was to change the LDP and get rid of many of its "sacred cows." His message resonated with the public, and the DPJ could not establish a counter message of reform while he was in office. The DPJ suffered a devastating defeat in the 2005 lower house election when Koizumi dissolved the lower house after members of his own party failed to support postal reform, the centerpiece of his reform efforts. He kicked out postal rebels and mobilized tremendous support around a fairly complicated policy issue by simplifying the narrative into those for or against change.

The DPJ regained momentum after Koizumi's departure in 2006. The LDP was unable to find a suitable replacement. Instead, it appointed three different prime ministers in three years. The public showed its disenchantment with the LDP in the 2007 upper house and 2009 lower house elections, granting the DPJ large victories. When the DPJ won a landside election in the 2009 lower house election, it took over the reins of government. Many observers felt that this marked the beginning of true party rotation in Japan.

While the DPJ manifestos proved effective electioneering tools, they did not remedy the DPJ's ideological difficulties. The lack of ideological cohesiveness was even more apparent when the DPJ entered government. The DPJ's stance on policies, such as the consumption tax and nuclear power, changed with each prime minister switch (Schoppa 2012).

One of the main goals of the DPJ upon entering government was to increase the power of politicians vis-à-vis the bureaucracy, something that ultimately limited the party's effectiveness. It carried out several policies to decrease the power of the bureaucracy, including cancelling the administrative vice minister meeting, banning press conferences for bureaucrats, and abolishing subcommittee meetings with bureaucrats (Shinoda 2012). The DPJ created internal party organs to take on the responsibilities of policy formation and coordination. These organs included the Government Revitalization Unit (GRU) and the National Strategy Office (NSO). While the GRU had some success, the NSO was never fully established. The GRU was in charge of reviewing 2010 budgetary requests from the national, prefectural, and local levels with the goal of cutting spending and increasing coordination as warranted. While the GRU did not meet its goal of cutting 3 trillion yen from the budget, the transparent process resulted in significant cuts and garnered initial praise from the public. The NSO's role was ambiguous and the institution was never fully developed or utilized. Its purview was limited to economic policies, but it was never fully staffed. The shortcomings in these reforms, especially the attempts to bypass the bureaucracy, became apparent during the triple disaster where government coordination suffered (Shinoda 2012). Overall, DPJ party reorganization upon taking office focused on Westminsterizing Japan, not on expanding support with key constituents like women or citizens' movements (George Mulgan 2011c).

The DPJ has struggled with weak leadership and factionalization since its inception. Factions in the DPJ are both ideological and leader centered. DPJ politicians can be a member of more than one group. The factions are most active during presidential elections. When Ozawa was implicated in the funding scandal in 2009, his group was the largest with around 120 members (Koellner 2011: 32).

The internal leadership struggle that emerged once the DPJ took control of the government might have been its complete undoing. Ozawa was the main force behind the internal disagreements. Ozawa centralized power in the Secretary General's office, which he led under Prime Minister Hatoyama. When Kan became prime minister he locked Ozawa out of positions of influence. Ozawa ran against Kan in the party presidential election in 2010 in an attempt to regain power. Ozawa lost mostly due to grassroots support for Kan. Kan officially suspended Ozawa from the party in February 2011 as mandated by Ozawa's indictment for alleged violations of the Political Funds Control Law. This suspension prevented Ozawa from participating in any official party functions, including running for party president. Ozawa stayed in the party in part because the prospects for success outside the party were low. Initially, Ozawa believed his best hopes for a comeback were from within the DPJ (George Mulgan 2011a). Ozawa attempted to play "shadow shogun" in the next DPJ party presidential election (George Mulgan 2011b). After Noda was elected, he tried to reunify the party and repair its widening pro- and anti-Ozawa split by appointing two Ozawa group members to key positions. Ozawa was not satisfied, though, and chose disagreements over the consumption tax as a policy difference to justify a party split. Ozawa was only able to convince 40 lower house and 17 upper house members to leave with him.

Due to its poor performance in office and a series of internal splits, the DPJ suffered a devastating defeat in 2012. The DPJ's strength in the lower house was reduced from 308 seats in 2009 to 57 seats in 2012. It only recovered slightly in the 2014 lower house election, receiving 73 seats. Table 5.1 illustrates the party composition in the lower house following the 2014 lower house election. In 2016, the DPJ joined with the Japan

Table 5.1 Current composition of the lower house (as of July 14, 2016)

Liberal Democratic Party (LDP)	289
Democratic Party (Minshintō) and Mushozoku Club	96
Kōmeitō	35
Japanese Communist Party	21
Initiatives from Osaka (Osaka ishin no kai)	14
The People's Life Party and Taro Yamamoto and Friends	2
Social Democratic Party	2
Independents	14
Vacancies	2
Total	475

Source: www.shugiin.go.jp/internet/itdb_english.nsf/html/statics/english/strength.htm.

Innovation Party to form a new party referred to as the Democratic Party in English and the Minshintō in Japanese. After its formation in July 2016 it held 98 seats in lower house and 60 seats in the upper house.

Conclusion

To the surprise of many Japan scholars, the Japanese party system appears to be experiencing party realignment again. In 2009, observers were heralding the beginning of two-party alternation, something that has been virtually absent from postwar politics in Japan. In the 2009 lower house election, for the first time almost all single-member districts only had two candidates on the ballot – one from the LDP and one from the DPJ. Smaller parties chose to contend only in the PR portion of the lower house electoral system. This was how the system was supposed to work after reform.

The DPJ's implosion was not anticipated. Early on, gaffes, blunders, and foreign policy failures were seen as rookie mistakes. But, the DPJ's failure to see its agenda realized, its disorganization, and its leadership infighting became its undoing. The triple disaster only compounded problems that were already readily apparent.

The DPJ's decision to join forces with the Japan Innovation Party to form the Democratic Party indicates that party realignment continues. The Democratic Party is now the largest opposition party; however, it is not clear that the consolidation will strengthen the party's organization and leadership. Even after the Democratic Party formed, the LDP with its coalition partner, the Kōmeitō, still held a majority in both houses. At the time of this writing in 2016, expectations are high for Prime Minister Abe and his economic reform agenda given the absence of a twisted Diet.

Notes

1 This chapter expands the overview of political parties in Gaunder (2011). The discussion of the LDP draws on Gaunder (2011) and Wiliarty and Gaunder (2014); portions of the discussion of the JSP come from Gaunder (2015); the discussion of the DPJ builds on Gaunder (2012).
2 See Gaunder (2009) for a discussion of Doi Takako's leadership.
3 Vote share is considered by dividing a party's total number of votes by the total number of people who voted in the election. Vote share for these elections was calculated using election

data provided by the Statistics Bureau and Statistical Training Institute (www.stat.go.jp/data/chouki/27.htm). See Gaunder (2007).
4 This section draws on Gaunder (2007: 107–114).
5 The DC was replaced by the Popular Party and the Christian Democratic Center which would later form part of Berlusconi's *Forza Italia!*

References

Berton, P. (2000) "Japanese Communist Party: The 'Loveable' Party," in R. J. Hrebenar (ed.) *Japan's New Party System*, 3rd edn, Boulder, CO: Westview Press.

Calder, K. E. (1988) *Crisis and Compensation: Public Policy and Political Stability in Japan, 1949–1986*, Princeton, NJ: Princeton University Press.

Curtis, G. L. (1971) *Election Campaigning Japanese Style*, New York: Columbia University Press.

Curtis, G. L. (1988) *The Japanese Way of Politics*, New York: Columbia University Press.

Curtis, G. L. (1999) *The Logic of Japanese Politics: Leaders, Institutions, and the Limits of Change*, New York: Columbia University Press.

Gaunder, A. (2007) *Political Reform in Japan: Leadership Looming Large*, London: Routledge.

Gaunder, A. (2009) "Women Running for National Office in Japan: Are Koizumi's Female 'Children' a Short-term Anomaly or a Lasting Phenomenon?" in S. Reed, K. M. McElwain, and K. Shimizu (eds) *Political Change in Japan: Electoral Behavior, Party Realignment, and the Koizumi Reforms*, Washington, DC: Brookings Institution.

Gaunder, A. (2011) "The Institutional Landscape of Japanese Politics," in A. Gaunder (ed.) *The Routledge Handbook of Japanese Politics*, London: Routledge.

Gaunder, A. (2012) "The DPJ and Women: The Limited Impact of the 2009 Alternation of Power on Policy and Governance," *Journal of East Asian Studies*, 12: 441–466.

Gaunder, A. (2015) "Quota Nonadoption in Japan: The Role of the Women's Movement and the Opposition," *Politics and Gender*, 11: 176–186.

Gaunder, A. (2016) "Women and the 2014 Lower House Election," in R. J. Pekkanen, S. R. Reed, and E. Scheiner (eds) *Japan Decides, 2014: The Japanese General Election*, London: Palgrave Macmillan.

George Mulgan, A. (2011a) "Why Japan's Ichiro Ozawa stays in the DPJ," *East Asia Forum*, July 15. Available online at www.eastasiaforum.org/2011/07/15/why-japan-s-ichiro-ozawa-stays-in-the-dpj/ (accessed 17 June 2013).

George Mulgan, A. (2011b) "The Return of Japan's Shadow Shogun Ichiro Ozawa?" *East Asia Forum*, August 23. Available online at www.eastasiaforum.org/2011/08/23/the-return-of-japan-s-shadow-shogun-ichiro-ozawa/ (accessed 17 June 2013).

George Mulgan, A. (2011c) "The Politics of Economic Reform," in A. Gaunder (ed.) *The Routledge Handbook of Japanese Politics*, London: Routledge.

Gosnell, H. (1968) *Machine Politics: Chicago Model*, 2nd edn, Chicago, IL: University of Chicago Press.

Hrebenar, R. J. (2000) "The Komeito: Party of 'Buddhist Democracy'," in R. J. Hrebenar (ed.) *Japan's New Party System*, 3rd edn, Boulder, CO: Westview Press.

Hyde, S. (2009) *The Transformation of the Japanese Left*, London: Routledge.

Johnson, C. (1987) "Political Institutions and Economic Performance: The Government-Business Relationship in Japan, South Korea and Taiwan," in F. C. Deyo (ed.) *The Political Economy of the New Asian Industrialism*, Ithaca, NY: Cornell University Press.

Johnson, S. (2000) *Opposition Politics in Japan: Strategies Under One-Party Dominant Regime*, London: Routledge.

Kabashima, I. and Steel, G. (2006) "How the LDP Survives," *Japan Echo* (June), 7–15.

Koellner, P. (2011) "The Democratic Party of Japan: Development, Organization and Programmatic Profile," in A. Gaunder (ed.) *The Routledge Handbook of Japanese Politics*, London: Routledge.

Kohno, M. (1997) *Japan's Postwar Party Politics*, Princeton, NJ: Princeton University Press.

Krauss, E. S. and Pekkanen, R. (2011) *The Rise and Fall of Japan's LDP: Party Organizations as Institutions*, New York and Ithaca, NY: Cornell University Press.

Liphart, A. (1999) *Patterns of Democracy: Government Forms and Performance in Thirty-six Countries*, New Haven, CT: Yale University Press.

Martin Murphy, S. (2013) "Women Candidates and Political Parties in Election 2012," in R. J. Pekkanen, S. R. Reed, and E. Scheiner (eds) *Japan Decides 2012: The Japanese General Election*, London: Palgrave Macmillan.

Miura, M., Lee, K. Y., and Weiner, R. (2005) "Who Are the DPJ?: Policy Positioning and Recruitment Strategy," *Asian Perspective*, 29: 49–77.

Müller, W. C. and Strøm, K. (1999) *Policy, Office or Votes?* Cambridge: Cambridge University Press.

Muramatsu, M. and Krauss, E. S. (1990) "The Dominant Party and Social Coalitions in Japan," in T. J. Pempel (ed.) *Uncommon Democracies: The One Party Dominant Regimes*, Ithaca, NY: Cornell University Press.

Ogai, T. (2001) "Japanese Women and Political Institutions: Why are Women Politically Underrepresented?" *PS: Political Science and Politics*, 34: 207–210.

Ozawa, I. (1994) *Blueprint for a New Japan: The Rethinking of a Nation*, trans. L. Rubinfien, Tokyo: Kodansha International.

Pempel, T. J. (1990) *Uncommon Democracies: The One Party Dominant Regimes*, Ithaca, NY: Cornell University Press.

Reed, S. R. (2011) "The Liberal Democratic Party of Japan: Development, Organization and Programmatic Profile," in A. Gaunder (ed.) *The Routledge Handbook of Japanese Politics*, London: Routledge.

Schoppa, L. (2012) "Japan Chair Platform: A Vote Against the DPJ, Not in Favor of the LDP," *Center for Strategic and International Studies Newsletter*. Available online at www.csis.org/analysis/japan-chair-platform-vote-against-dpj-not-favor-ldp (accessed 1 July 2016).

Shinoda, T. (2012) "Japan's Failed Experiment: The DPJ and Institutional Changes for Political Leadership," *Asian Survey*, 52: 799–821.

Shiratori, R. (1988) "Japan: Localism, Factionalism and Personalism," in M. Gallagher (ed.) *Candidate Selection in Comparative Perspective*, London: Sage Publications.

Stockwin, J. A. A. (2000) "The Social Democratic Party (Formerly Japan Socialist Party): A Turbulent Odyssey," in R. J. Hrebenar (ed.) *Japan's New Party System*, 3rd edn, Boulder, CO: Westview Press.

Stockwin, J. A. A. (2011) "The Rationale for Coalition Government," in A. Gaunder (ed.) *The Routledge Handbook of Japanese Politics*, London: Routledge.

Weiner, R. J. (2011) "The Evolution of the DPJ: Two Steps Forward, One Step Back," in L. J. Schoppa (ed.) *The Evolution of Japan's Party System: Politics and Policy in an Era of Institutional Change*, Toronto: University of Toronto Press.

Wiliarty, S. E. (2010) *The CDU and the Politics of Gender in Germany: Bringing Women to the Party*, New York: Cambridge University Press.

Wiliarty, S. E. and Gaunder, A. (2014) "Conservative Female Candidates in Germany and Japan: Supply and Demand," in K. Celis and S. Childs (eds) *Gender, Conservatism, and Political Representation*, Colchester: ECPR Press.

Woodall, B. (1996) *Japan Under Construction: Corruption, Politics and Public Works*, Berkeley: University of California Press.

6 Elections and electioneering[1]

Elections are important because they are the mechanism that allows citizens to exercise their sovereignty and select government representatives. Free and fair elections with stable transitions in power are seen as the cornerstone of democracy because they foster contestation, participation, and stability.

Democracies, however, have chosen a variety of electoral system rules to select representatives. The type of electoral system selected matters because electoral rules can influence the character and stability of democracy. Electoral rules affect the role of parties, access of minority voices, and the amount and kind of corruption. In general, electoral system rules provide cues to politicians, parties, and voters and thereby influence behavior and outcomes.

Electoral system rules are not the only relevant regulations that influence elections. A country's political funding regime as well as campaigning laws are also important. Political funding laws regulate access, voice, and influence. The amount of transparency and the ability of the government to monitor compliance and exact penalties for non-compliance vary from country to country. As we shall see in the case of Japan, detailed campaigning laws do not necessarily result in "cleaner" elections as the over-regulation and weak monitoring and penalties often provide politicians incentives to carry out illegal activities underground. The media and civil society can potentially play important roles in information dissemination, especially acting in a watchdog function, something that has not really been the case in Japan.

This chapter concludes by placing Japan in comparative perspective. Taiwan is one of the few other democracies to use a single-nontransferable vote (SNTV) electoral system, a cornerstone of Japan's old lower house electoral system. A look at Taiwan allows us to explore some similarities and differences that these electoral system rules produced in different context. Like Japan, Italy also enacted electoral reforms in the 1990s. This chapter will compare the motivations for and the effects of reform in Japan and Italy.

The electoral system

The lower house

The electoral system for the Japanese lower house has received a large amount of scholarly attention for a variety of reasons. The lower house is the more powerful house; it controls the budget and selects the prime minister. The first electoral system in place during the 1955 system which used a single-nontransferable vote (SNTV) in multiple-member districts (MMD) was also rather unique, drawing much interest. The SNTV/MMD system was also seen as the source of money politics and corruption in Japan. Electoral system reform in Japan provided social scientists a natural experiment to test the effects of rule changes on the behavior of politicians, parties, and voters, drawing even more attention.

The lower house used an SNTV/MMD electoral system from 1947 to 1993. In the last election for the lower house there were 511 seats and 129 districts with two to six candidates elected per district based on population. Voters cast a vote for one candidate. This system provided a moderate bias to large parties. In order to win an outright majority in the lower house, a party had to win at least two seats per district on average. Running multiple candidates required monetary resources and/or organization. The LDP was the only party capable of doing this. Running multiple candidates, however, meant that members of the same party were competing against one another. Since the LDP voted down party lines, candidates were not able to compete on policy. Instead, they competed on favors and pork. LDP factions only ran one candidate at most per district. And LDP politicians had incentives to specialize in particular issue areas such as construction and agriculture. These specialists were referred to as *zoku* politicians. *Zoku* literally translates into policy tribe. The high level of intra-party competition also increased the pressure to raise large sums of money, increasing the amount of corruption.

Despite the bias toward large parties, the system was moderately proportionate. In particular, the medium-sized districts allowed for the emergence of new parties. The larger the multiple-member district, the smaller the threshold for victory. For example, in a six-person district, a candidate could win with less than one-sixth of the vote. As a result, smaller parties could often gain one seat in a district with strong niche support. All parties strived to figure out the right number of candidates to run in any given district. There was no advantage to a party to come in first place, especially if there was enough support to be divided into support for two seats. The LDP, in particular, struggled to divide support evenly. Factions and *zoku* specializations were two ways to divide support, but factional affiliation was not always apparent to the voter. Voters in turn had incentives to support the candidate who met their own special interest. The focus was on the candidate, not the party.

Table 6.1 illustrates how the main parties performed in the 1955 system under the SNTV/MMD rules. As discussed in Chapter 4 and Chapter 5, the party system began as a one and a half party system. The LDP was the only party able to effectively respond to the incentives and constraints of the SNTV/MMD system, which favored parties with strong organization and/or monetary resources. In the 1960s, smaller niche parties including the Kōmeitō and the Democratic Socialist Party entered the scene and whittled support away from other parties, especially weakening the JSP. Smaller parties tended to do better in larger districts where the threshold to win a seat was lower or in regions where their voters were concentrated. With a greater number of smaller parties dividing support, the LDP became the dominant party.

A new electoral system for the lower house was implemented in 1994. The new system is a combined SMD/PR system. Originally, 300 seats were SMD and 200 seats were PR. Currently, there are 295 SMD seats and 180 PR seats, bringing the total number of seats to 475 seats. Voters cast two votes – one for a candidate for an SMD seat and one for a party for the PR seats. Politicians who run in SMDs can also appear on the PR party list. This rule provides incentives for politicians to take on difficult

Table 6.1 Party seat representation in the lower house under the SNTV/MMD system

	1958	1960	1963	1967	1969	1972	1976	1979	1980	1983	1986	1990	1993
LDP	287	296	283	277	288	271	249	248	284	250	300	275	223
JSP	166	145	144	140	90	118	123	107	107	112	85	136	70
Kōmeitō	n/a	n/a	n/a	25	47	29	55	57	33	58	56	45	51
JCP	1	3	5	5	14	38	17	39	29	26	26	14	15
DSP	n/a	17	23	30	31	19	29	35	32	38	26	16	15

Source: www.stat.go.jp/data/chouki/zuhyou/27-08-a.xls 衆議院議員総選挙の党派別当選者数及び得票数.

challenges in SMDs, especially if they are promised a high PR ranking. Some party list rankings are linked to overall performance in the SMD contests, with the candidates who have stronger performances, despite losing, receiving higher PR rankings. This is known as the best loser provision.

The combined system is similar to the German system of personalized PR, although not as proportional. In Germany's Bundestag half of the seats are allocated by single-member district and half are determined by PR party list. A party's total number of seats is determined by the PR vote. The first seats are distributed to the candidates who won their SMD contest. In Japan, the SMD and PR votes are separate. Politicians win seats in SMD outright. Parties receive a percentage of the 180 seats based on the percentage vote received in the PR portion of the ballot.

The combined system was a compromise between large parties and small parties. Larger parties, especially the LDP, favored a pure SMD system. In SMD systems, a politician must win a majority or plurality of the vote. This system favors larger parties with resources and organization. PR systems allow for representation of minor, smaller parties since the number of seats allocated corresponds to the percentage of vote each party receives. The anti-LDP coalition government led by Hosokawa initiated reform, but it failed to pass the upper house. As a result, the LDP was able to influence its final content to secure the final passage of the bill.

Combined systems have become more popular in the last several decades. In general, combined systems are appealing because they attempt to combine the strengths of SMD and PR and minimize their weaknesses. For example, SMD systems are appealing because they allow for accountability and provide a strong connection between representatives and their constituents. An SMD system also promotes stability because this system supports fewer parties, especially in countries with few regional, ethnic, religious, or racial cleavages, such as Japan. The major weakness of SMD systems is that they are disproportional and waste votes. If your party loses, it does not receive a seat and all those votes are "wasted." This diminishes minority voices. Adding a PR element to the electoral system helps correct this weakness since PR systems represent more voices. Votes are more closely matched with seat allocations in PR systems. Pure PR systems can be unstable if several parties receive support. Coalition governments are usually necessary in a PR system because it is less likely for a party to receive a majority of the seats. The SMD element, however, provides pressure to reduce the number of parties.

Electoral reform is significant for several reasons. Changing the "rules of the game" governing elections can potentially influence several variables, including the number and size of parties in the system, minority representation, the amount of inter- and intra-party competition, voter turnout, and the amount of particularism (Grofman, Lee, and Woodall 1999: 1–2).

In Japan, the combined system reduced intra-party competition, one of the major goals of reforms. Candidates from the same party no longer compete against each other at the district level. There still remains a lot of competition for nomination to open districts as well as PR ranking. The effect of reform on scandal and corruption has been more difficult to determine, partially because corruption by definition goes on beneath the surface. In general, the number of scandals that emerged after electoral reform declined, but with time and as politicians adjusted to the new electoral system and political funding regulations more scandals have emerged.

Table 6.2 illustrates the performance of the LDP, DPJ, Kōmeitō, JCP, and Social Democratic Party (formerly named the JSP) under the new electoral rules. The Kōmeitō's electoral performance has been the most stable. This outcome reflects the party's strong organization and its ability to mobilize voters. The party has won fewer seats under the new rules and is only competitive in the PR portion, which only has 180 seats. The LDP and DPJ were the only parties to compete for SMD seats in the 2009 election. The SMD districts favor larger parties with resources to run candidates in every district. The DPJ has struggled to maintain this momentum following splits from the party in 2012. In general, however, elections have become more nationalized (McElwain 2012), party leaders are more important in elections (Krauss and Nyblade 2005), party popularity has been the greatest indicator of candidate success (Reed, Scheiner, and Thies 2012), and the electoral swings have been more volatile (Christensen 2011).

LDP party dynamics have changed in response to the new incentives and constraints of the MMD/SNTV electoral system passed in 1994. Specifically, the reform influenced electioneering, party organization, and policymaking.

Under the new electoral system, the party has more control over the nomination of candidates. Under the old electoral system, factions nominated their own candidates and provided significant financial backing. Candidates who did not receive party or factional support ran as independents and appealed to the party for affiliation after successfully winning a seat. Under the new electoral system, factions fight to receive party endorsement when open seats become available in the single-member constituencies because such openings provide an opportunity for a faction to increase its overall strength in the LDP (Park 2001: 438). The factions of the LDP president and secretary general often are able to recruit more potential candidates because these candidates realize these officials have greater weight in deciding party endorsements (Park 2001: 438). Candidates who receive LDP endorsement, however, have an incentive to keep their factional affiliation a secret during the election so as to secure more votes (Koellner 2004: 94). Under the new funding rules, factions cannot receive monetary donations. This provision has also weakened their ability to exert influence in elections.

Many predicted that kōenkai would disappear under the new electoral rules, but these organizations remain. Those who predicted the kōenkai would fade failed to realize that SMD systems also reward institutions that cultivate the personal vote. The district size increased under the new electoral system so these support organizations now must mobilize voters over a larger area. But, unlike party branches, which have traditionally been weak, kōenkai are strong, established, vote-getting institutions. Under both the old and new electoral systems, voters tend to see themselves as supporters of individual politicians as opposed to the LDP (Krauss and Pekkanen 2011: 91).

Table 6.2 Party seat representation in the lower house under the post-1994 electoral system

	1996	2000	2003	2005	2009	2012	2014
LDP	239	233	237	296	119	294	291
DPJ	52	127	177	113	308	57	73
Kōmeitō	n/a	31	34	31	21	31	35
JCP	26	20	9	9	9	8	21
SDP	15	19	6	7	7	2	2

Source: www.electionresources.org/jp/.

LDP party organization was also affected by electoral reform. Factions have become weaker since reform, mainly in their electoral functions. Factions, however, still play an important role in party and government appointments (Krauss and Pekkanen 2011: 132). In general, factional balancing and seniority govern these appointments. The LDP continues to fear internal splits. Due to the connections to appointments, factions still can promote a politician's advancement in the party.

The PARC remains an important arena for policymaking, although it has been partially weakened by the dictates of coalition government. Moreover, the SMD portion of the electoral system provides greater incentives for politicians to become generalist as opposed to specialists (i.e., zoku politicians). LDP members may now serve on as many PARC committees as they wish. These committees provide opportunities to educate politicians and can also serve to advance them in the party (Krauss and Pekkanen 2011: 193).

Electoral reform did not completely change factions, kōenkai, and the PARC because these institutions perform important non-electoral functions (Krauss and Pekkanen 2011). These institutions also influence party organization and policymaking. These functions have ensured their survival, albeit at different levels of importance and strength.

The upper house

The upper house is the less powerful body in the Diet. Its electoral system has received less scholarly attention. Nevertheless, the rules provided certain incentives to politicians, parties, and voters, something that becomes clear when the first set of electoral system rules is compared to the subsequent revisions. Historically, upper house elections have been more issue based, allowing opposition parties to gain some traction against the LDP during periods when its popularity was low.

The upper house has used two sets of electoral rules during the 1955 system. This body began with 250 seats. This number was increased to 252 seats because two seats were added when Okinawa was returned in 1972. Currently, the upper house has 242 seats. Members serve six-year terms and half of the body is re-elected every three years. Initially, the upper house employed a nationwide MMD/SNTV system for 100 seats. The remaining seats were determined through multiple-member district contests in prefectures. This system was in effect from 1946 to 1983. This system favored candidates with high name recognition.

In 1983, the Diet revised the electoral law implementing a closed party proportional representation list in place of the nationwide MMD/SNTV system. The goal of this revision was to create party-centered elections. The closed PR list, however, increased competition within parties for higher PR rankings. The LDP, for example, decided to rank its candidates based on fundraising and party membership recruitment.

In 2000, the PR component of the electoral system was further changed to an open list system, which allows voters to select either a party or individual candidate in the PR ballot. Under the current electoral system, 96 of the members are elected via the open party PR list and 146 of the members are elected from multiple-member prefectural districts using a single-nontransferable vote. Elections occur every three years with half of the 242 seats contested in each election (48 PR seats and 73 SNTV prefectural seats). The effects of the SNTV system in the upper house have been more muted than they were under the lower house MMD/SNTV system. In fact, 27 of the 47 prefectures only elect one member to the upper house per election cycle, allowing these districts to function as single-member districts. As a result, parties only nominate one candidate eliminating intra-party competition.

The political funding regime

Under the 1955 system, the political funding regime was plagued with ambiguities and provided many incentives for subversion. Prior to the first major revision to the Political Funds Control Law (PFCL) in 1975, political contributions were not heavily regulated. The revisions to the PFCL passed in 1975 created an upper limit on contributions from corporations in an attempt to increase the "voice" of individual contributors. This legislation, however, contained a major loophole. While the amount of corporate and individual contributions was restricted, the number of political organizations that could receive donations was not. As a result, the new regulation provided incentives for politicians to create more political organizations to receive donations (see Gaunder 2007).

Politicians employed creative methods to raise funds. One of the most common means of fundraising was a political funding party where corporate representatives and supporters purchased tickets to attend. Other politicians resorted to more illegal forms of fundraising including accepting cash under the table or accepting pre-floatation stocks. The pressure to raise funds along with the weak regulations certainly influenced the fact that one national-level political funding scandal emerged virtually every year in Japan during this period (Murobushi 1988).

The Diet passed political funding reform in conjunction with the revisions to the electoral system in 1994. The initial revisions to the Political Funds Control Law allowed each politician to maintain one fundraising organization with the maximum corporate contribution being 500,000 yen per company. In 2000, however, a complete ban on corporate contributions to individual politicians went into effect; however, corporations can still contribute to the party branch. The political reform package also introduced party subsidies at 250 yen per capita (Carlson 2007: 10). Reapportionment was indirectly addressed with the creation of new electoral districts to accommodate the SMD system.

Many politicians asserted that the changes to the Political Funds Control Law in 1994 followed by the ban on corporate contributions in 2000 would weaken the incentives for pork barrel politics that have driven the relations among special interests, bureaucrats, and zoku politicians. During the postwar era, however, most of these special interests have been a source of both money and votes. Not surprisingly, perhaps, pork in exchange for votes remains a staple in Japanese politics despite reform. The official annual income of individual politicians has declined since reform, which might indicate that the pressure for election funds has declined due to the reform (Carlson 2011). The new rules certainly have influenced the decline in contributions. The disclosure requirement is stronger, requiring disclosure for smaller contributions. And obviously the ban on corporate contributions has influenced the decline. Subsidies are still an important source of funds for individuals, but these funds are filtered through and distributed by parties. Even though the goal of party subsidies was to make elections and fundraising more party focused, evidence exists to suggest that fundraising remains candidate centered (Carlson 2011).

The revisions to the Political Funds Control law, especially the party subsidies, also sought to even the playing field. Here again, the law has only had a minimal impact. The LDP continues to be the strongest fundraiser. It raised three times as much as the

DPJ in 1998–2008 and twice as much as the DPJ in 2008–2011. The LDP also outspends all parties in elections (Carlson 2011).

Another anticipated effect of political funding as well as electoral reform was the reduction of money politics and corruption. While the number of corruption cases that came to the surface in the form of scandal did initially decline when the laws were implemented, both new and old forms of money politics have emerged in response to these regulations.

Campaigning

In contrast to the political funding regime under the 1955 system, the restrictions on campaigning were exhaustively detailed. While the lower house electoral system and the political funding regime underwent major reforms in the 1990s, these campaigning restrictions remain largely intact. In particular, publicity is highly restricted, providing high barriers to entry for newcomers who need to increase name recognition. Candidates are given a limited number of television and radio appearances, and the content and length of these appeals are highly regulated (Christensen 1998). Candidates also are only allotted a certain number of handbills and posters. Door-to-door canvassing is prohibited during the official election period. Finally, the Internet is a medium that the government has struggled to accommodate in relation to campaigns (Ducke 2007; Freeman 2003). Until 2013, candidates were required to freeze their websites on the day that the official election campaign period began. Internet campaigning is now legal.

The state provides many of the resources for candidates including the posters, handbills, and sound trucks, but it does not have the tools and resources to monitor the compliance of politicians. As a result, candidates have incentives to exploit loopholes and ambiguities in these regulations. Much campaigning is forced "underground" and several candidates simply conduct restricted activities during the unofficial election period. Many candidates exploit the distinction between political activities that are allowed at all times and election activities that are highly restricted during the official campaign period. A politician can engage in a political activity to promote the public's understanding of politics and partisan issues as opposed to an election activity by not mentioning the election or asking for votes (Curtis 1988: 165). This distinction allows politicians broader leeway in how they interact with constituents. It also provides incentives for politicians to build personal support organizations (Christensen 1998). The campaign activities of parties also are regulated. Parties can promote the party as a whole during the election period, but parties must refrain from endorsing individual candidates (see Gaunder 2007).

The influence of the voter

Individual voters in Japan historically have been characterized as being less engaged in politics than in other democracies. Participation is comparatively high hovering between 60 and 75 percent in lower house elections throughout the postwar period. Voter turnout hit an all-time low in the 2014 lower house "snap" election with only 52 percent turnout (IDEA n.d.). Voting, however, is the most passive form of participation. In general, individuals feel their influence on politics is low. Citizens consider politicians unresponsive and believe politics is complicated (Martin 2011). Women in particular see politics as distant from their lives (LeBlanc 1999).

Voter influence has been most effective through organized interest group participation. Not all interest groups have had success or even access to politicians. In general, groups connected to economic growth have had a greater impact on politics and elections. Industrial groups effectively formed connections with zoku politicians and bureaucrats. Citizens' groups and consumer groups faced more barriers to access and influence, though (Martin 2011). Some argue that recent elections and alternations in power provide voters with evidence that by acting collectively they are able to influence outcomes (Martin 2011).

Several shifts in the institutional environment have altered incentives for voters. The collapse of the bubble economy has made it more difficult to maintain the strong connections among politicians, bureaucrats, and interest groups. Globalization has also increased the pressure to liberalize economic policies providing fewer opportunities for clientelism. The shift in the power balance between the national and local government has also changed the dynamics of local politics. Decentralization has broken down the strong connection between national and local politicians. Unlike in the past, local politicians and groups have fewer incentives to mobilize the vote for national politicians (Martin 2011: 86–87). Several trends provide more opportunities for voters to influence politics including anti-establishment citizens' movements in local politics, the expansion of nonprofit organizations, and the emergence of new social movements on both the left and the right (Martin 2011: 87).

The role of the media

In democracies, the media play several different roles in politics in general and in elections in particular. These roles include: information dissemination and education, agenda setting, and watchdog functions. Critics also note that high levels of media coverage, especially television coverage, can exacerbate feelings of political alienation (Saito 2008: 102).

Newspapers and television play different roles in Japan. Newspapers tend to play the roles of education and agenda setting; there is not a strong tradition of investigative journalism and the watchdog function is weak in Japan (Krauss 2000: 272–273). Instead, newspapers pride themselves on neutrality. Newspaper coverage is very uniform, partially due to this neutrality norm but also because of the reporters' club system (kisha kurabu) (Krauss 2000: 270). Reporters' clubs are exclusive and foster a close relationship between reporters and politicians. Reporters are assigned to certain politicians and the clubs can expel reporters who do not conform to the written rules governing reporting. These clubs can lead to close relationships and therefore result in less critical coverage.

Scholars who focus on reporters' clubs classify the media as "servant." In this view, reporters have been co-opted by politicians. In exchange for access, reporters present the news in accordance with the wishes of politicians (Feldman 2005: 179–180). Others emphasize additional functions of the media including that of "trickster." The trickster image does not deny the dependence of the media on the state and politicians but claims that the media "provides release," "evaluates," "horrifies," "induces reflection," and "bonds" within these constraints (Pharr 1996: 27). Campaign coverage conceivably falls within this "trickster" function.

Television coverage has increased in importance since the 1990s with the emergence of interpretative news. Prior to this point, television news had been led by NHK, a publicly owned news station that tended to support the conservative rule of the LDP. It, like newspapers, focused on more descriptive coverage that provided information and education (Saito and Takeshita 2008).

A candidate's use of the media is highly regulated in Japan. During the official campaign period, each candidate receives four appearances on television of 4.5 minutes, which are paid for by the government. Moreover, if a candidate is covered in the television news it is required that both a picture of the candidate and the opponent(s) be included (Krauss 2000, 285; Curtis 1988). While these regulations emphasize equality, they also make it difficult to create a campaign narrative, especially for candidates with limited name recognition or experience. Political parties face fewer regulations. Parties have unlimited use of the media to promote policies but cannot promote individual politicians.

While the official methods of campaign advertising are limited in Japan, other methods exist for increasing a candidate's name recognition. The media begin covering elections for the lower house from the point of the dissolution of the Diet. Increasingly candidates have used television interviews and opinion-based news programs like Asahi TV's Sunday Project to receive coverage and increase their exposure throughout the campaign period without technically violating the campaign regulations (Krauss 2000: 291). Participating on these types of news program can have a large impact on candidate evaluations. Taniguchi found that "the more frequently an LDP representative appears in the mass media, the higher evaluations they tend to receive from their constituents" (Taniguchi 2007: 157).

Both newspapers and television media conduct their own opinion polls throughout the campaign period. Newspapers in particular focus on election prediction polls (Saito and Takeshita 2008). Since the 1990s, television has played an increasing role in news coverage in general and election coverage in particular. This coverage extends until the end of the brief official campaign period, lasting about a month in total. Unlike newspapers, which are more issue oriented, the television media focus more on strategic aspects of the election, so-called "horse race coverage" (Saito and Takeshita 2008: 392).

Election coverage can be "stereotyped and sensational," especially in the case of women running for national office (McLaren 2008: 124). When women enter an election in large numbers the tendency has been to label them. For example, in 1989 when Doi Takako, the first female head of a political party, backed twelve Socialist women candidates in the 1989 upper house election the move was dubbed the "Madonna strategy." Similarly, LDP prime minister Koizumi Junichirō hand-picked several glamorous, successful career women to act as so-called "assassins" in districts where postal rebels were running. Postal rebels were members of the LDP who had voted against postal reform and subsequently been kicked out of the party by Prime Minister Koizumi prior to the 2005 lower house election. The women running against the postal rebels were not the only assassins, but they received a large amount of media attention. Finally, in the 2009 lower house election, the 26 first-term Democratic Party of Japan (DPJ) women politicians were called "Ozawa's girls," referencing the president of the DPJ who supported their nomination. These labels reflect party strategy that treats women as symbols of change (Gaunder 2009). McLaren explains, "The relationship between political women and the media in Japan is a case of all or nothing: they receive either sensationalized coverage or are completely ignored" (McLaren 2005: 31). The media also exacerbate cultural stereotypes by representing women in politics as unnatural (McLaren 2005; 2008). Such framing contributes to the outsider status of women.

Finally, the increase of soft news and infotainment as a way to campaign has heightened the importance of party leaders. Parties now seek out more telegenic leaders to enhance their competitiveness (Taniguchi 2007: 162). The public image of prime ministers in particular has become more important. Krauss and Nyblade (2005) note that since television increased in importance in the 1980s, the role for prime ministers in electioneering has also increased. This campaigning role became even more important with the 1994 electoral reforms that provided incentives for parties to compete on policy as opposed to personal favors. Other factors have accentuated the need for a popular prime minister to woo voters including the decreasing vote share of the LDP and the increasing number of floating voters (Krauss and Nyblade 2005).

Japan in comparative perspective

SNTV in Japan and Taiwan

Japan is not the only country to use an SNTV electoral system. Both Korea and Taiwan also adopted this system for a time. Given their common experience as Japanese colonies, this is not completely surprising. Some have argued that SNTV is an ideal system for developmental states because it provides the stable rule by a party that promotes growth (Lin 2006: 119). It is certainly a rare set of electoral rules. Jordan, Afghanistan, Vanuatu, and Pitcairn Island also have experience with it for national elections (Lin 2006: 119). Korea only used an SNTV system under authoritarian regimes prior to its transition to democracy from 1973 to 1988. Taiwan used SNTV both before and after its transition to democracy. It, like Japan, also eventually implemented electoral reform and moved to a combined system with some significant differences in chamber size and the threshold for smaller parties. A comparison with Taiwan illustrates some similar effects of electoral systems as well as some significant differences most likely influenced by different political and cultural contexts.

Taiwan has a long history with SNTV. It first used the system under Japanese colonial rule. It also used this system during authoritarian rule to help ensure the Kuomintang's (KMT) dominance and promote growth as well as clientelism. SNTV was used under "transitional" democracy in Taiwan from 1992 to 2004 (Grofman, Lee, and Woodall 1999: 11); reform was being debated during most of this period. This system did have a small PR element with 36 of the 161 seats being selected by PR; the rest were selected by SNTV. SNTV in Taiwan also promoted elections based on personalism, one-party dominance, and a tendency toward corruption.

Taiwan began its transition to democracy in the 1990s and the KMT nearly lost to the opposition Democratic Progressive Party (DPP) in 1994. From this point on, the country began a debate on electoral reform. The KMT like the LDP struggled to maintain clientelistic favors and particularistic transfers when economic growth slowed. As the dominant parties struggled and weakened, the opportunity for reform emerged (Lin 2006: 120). In Japan, scandal and corruption opened the window for reform; in Taiwan, it was the public's frustration with an "inefficient and chaotic national legislature" (Lin 2006: 120).

Like in Japan, different parties had different positions on reform. The DPP initially favored the German combined system of personalized PR. Its position shifted as it gained in strength, particularly after it secured the presidency in 2000 and 2004. The KMT was in favor of the Japanese combined system with a strong SMD portion. Smaller parties favored proposals that were more proportional.

In the end, Taiwan implemented a combined system similar to Japan's but considerably smaller. Interestingly enough, just as in the Japanese case, reform only passed after the KMT had lost its legislative majority. In Taiwan, the Legislative Yuan was reduced from 225 to 113 seats, a priority of a smaller party, the Taiwan Solidarity Union (TSU). Voters cast two ballots: one for a candidate in an SMD and one for a party. Seventy-three seats are determined by SMD; 34 are closed list PR (with half of these seats reserved for women). Six additional seats are reserved for indigenous populations in two multiple-member districts.

At least two intervening factors influenced electoral system rules for the legislative body in Taiwan. First, it is a presidential system, not a parliamentary one. A presidential system can influence the importance of party, policy, and the nature of campaigning. Second, there is a much stronger social cleavage in Taiwan that surrounds the unique issue of independence from China.

Since electoral reform, both countries have moved toward a two-party system. This move occurred much faster in Taiwan with the KMT and DPP remaining the strongest parties (Jou 2009: 760). Most of the smaller parties that have emerged have been splinters from these parties. Still, the People First Party (PFP) and TSU did win some seats in 2012. In Japan, the movement to a two-party system has been much slower. The DPJ did take control in 2009 but appears to have fallen apart after a weak performance in office, throwing the system back into party realignment. The combined system in both countries has provided incentives for smaller parties to run candidates in SMDs in an attempt to raise their PR vote even though the smaller party has no chance to win in an SMD. This tendency is less strong in Taiwan and had begun to fade in Japan in the 2009 election. This tendency might be less strong in Taiwan because its system does not support dual candidacy, and it also does not have regional PR blocs, only one national bloc (Jou 2009: 765).

Electoral reform in Japan and Italy

Like Japan, Italy also implemented electoral reform in the 1990s. Both countries had very different electoral systems prior to reform. Italy had a PR system with preferential voting while Japan had an SNTV/MMD system. Both countries adopted a type combined SMD/PR system after reform, although the details and rules governing the combined systems varied.

Electoral reform in Italy in 1993 affected both the Lower Chamber and the Senate. Under reform, the Lower Chamber had 630 seats distributed among 26 multiple-member districts. These districts were further divided into single-member districts that elected 75 percent of the seats. The remaining 25 percent of the seats are allocated via PR. SMD candidates are required to run on at least one PR list. PR candidates can only be list candidates. All parties face a 4 percent hurdle; that is, each party must receive at least 4 percent of the vote to receive seats. As in the reformed lower house in Japan, voters are given two ballots – one for an SMD candidate and one for a party. The rules for the Senate are more complicated. There are 20 regional constituencies with 232 SMDs and 83 PR seats. Voters cast one ballot for the SMD candidate and the PR seats are allocated using a "best loser" provision (Giannetti and Grofman 2011: 5–6). The best loser provision allocates PR seats to the politicians who lost in single-member districts but received the highest amount of votes. In 2005, Italy abandoned the SMD portion of the combined system for the Lower Chamber and returned to a closed list

PR system with bonus seats. The new mechanism ensures that a coalition or party list gets about 54 percent of the vote. If this bar is not met, then a seat bonus is given to the party or coalition list with the highest vote percentage to ensure a majority (Giannetti and Grofman 2011: 6).

The contexts for reform were quite similar. The goals of reform shared some similarities and differences. Both Japan and Italy had strong conservative parties that dominated postwar politics. As we have seen, the LDP enjoyed single party rule from 1955 to 1993 in Japan. Similarly, the Christian Democratic Party (DC) in Italy ruled in multiparty coalitions in Italy from 1948 to 1992. Both countries also experienced frequent outbreaks of corruption scandals and high levels of public dissatisfaction. Reformers focused on the electoral system because it could be connected to the perceived lack of accountability, the dominance of the LDP and the DC, clientelism, and corruption (Giannetti and Grofman 2011: 3). One of the goals for reform in Japan was to shift the focus of elections from individual politicians to political parties. In Italy, the goal of reform was to decrease party fragmentation and increase stability. In both countries, reform did result in major party restructuring. In Japan, the system appeared to be stabilizing on two-party competition until the 2012 lower house and 2013 upper house elections that devastated the DPJ that split prior to the elections. In Italy, the DC split and broke into many small pieces. Over time, two political blocs have emerged. One of the blocs actually pushed through the second electoral reform for the Lower Chamber.

Generalizing a reason for these similar undertakings is not easy or straightforward. Indeed, the reasons for reform are many, varied, and contested in both countries. Both Japan and Italy had high levels of voter alienation most often expressed as political inefficacy. The accountability of politicians was weak and cases of corruption were rampant (Sakamoto 1999: 434). In both countries, politicians and/or citizens pointed to the electoral system as being partially responsible for these outcomes. The Italian PR system with preferential voting provided incentives for members of the same party to compete against one another (like Japan's MMD/SNTV). It also contributed to unstable coalition governments as well as corruption.

Politicians initiated reform in Japan. In Italy, reform occurred following a national referendum process. Japan does not have the legal basis for national referenda. Certainly, politicians in Japan felt pressure from the public for some kind of political reform following the outbreak of several scandals, but the public was not specifically demanding electoral reform; politicians proposed electoral reform as a solution (Sakamoto 1999; Gaunder 2007). In Italy, the referendum process is initiated by popular demand, and politicians are obligated to follow successful referenda with legislation. In Italy, sitting politicians favored preserving the status quo, not implementing electoral reform. The referendum process forced their hands and resulted in change.

Conclusion

Electoral system, political funding, and campaigning regulations are significant because they provide the incentives and constraints that influence the behavior of parties, politicians, and voters. Changes to these rules often have unintended consequences as politicians and parties search for loopholes that will facilitate re-election.

Japan is one of several countries to experiment with electoral reform. Both the reasons for and the effects of electoral system reform vary. Nevertheless, comparative politics embraces studies of these cases to broaden our understanding of the impact of electoral system reform in various contexts.

Note

1 Portions of this chapter draw on Gaunder (2007, 2011).

References

Carlson, M. (2007) *Money Politics in Japan: New Rules, Old Practices*, Boulder, CO: Lynne Rienner Publishers.

Carlson, M. (2011) "Money in Japanese Politics: Regulation and Reform," in A. Gaunder (ed.) *The Routledge Handbook of Japanese Politics*, London: Routledge.

Christensen, R. (1998) "The Effect of Electoral Reforms on Campaign Practices in Japan: Putting New Wine in Old Bottles," *Asian Survey*, 38: 986–1004.

Christensen, R. (2011) "Election Systems and Campaign Rules," in A. Gaunder (ed.) *The Routledge Handbook of Japanese Politics*, London: Routledge.

Curtis, C. L. (1988) *The Japanese Way of Politics*, New York: Columbia University Press.

Ducke, I. (2007) *Civil Society and the Internet in Japan*, London: Routledge.

Feldman, O. (2005) *Talking Politics in Japan Today*, Brighton: Sussex Academic Press.

Freeman, L. A. (2003) "Mobilizing and Demobilizing the Japanese Public Sphere: Mass Media and the Internet in Japan," in F. J. Schwartz and S. J. Pharr (eds) *The State of Civil Society in Japan*, Cambridge: Cambridge University Press.

Gaunder, A. (2007) *Political Reform in Japan: Leadership Looming Large*, London: Routledge.

Gaunder, A. (2009) "From Madonnas to Assassins: The Changing Image of Japanese Politicians," paper presented at the Southwest Conference on Asian Studies Meeting, Austin, Texas, October 16–17.

Gaunder, A. (2011) "The Institutional Landscape of Japanese Politics," in A. Gaunder (ed.) *The Routledge Handbook of Japanese Politics*, London: Routledge.

Giannetti, D. and Grofman, B. (2011) "Introduction: Long-run Consequences of Electoral Rules Change: Comparing Italy and Japan," in D. Giannetti and B. Grofman (eds) *A Natural Experiment on Electoral Law Reform: Evaluating the Long Run Consequences of 1990s Electoral Reform in Italy and Japan*, New York: Springer.

Grofman, B., Lee, Sung-Chull, and Woodall, B. (1999) *Elections in Japan, Korea, and Taiwan under the Single Non-Transferable Vote: The Comparative Study of an Embedded Institution*, Ann Arbor: University of Michigan Press.

IDEA (n.d.) "Voter Turnout Data for Japan." Available online at www.idea.int/vt/countryview.cfm?id=114 (accessed 5 July 2016).

Jou, W. (2009) "Electoral Reform and Party System Development in Japan and Taiwan: A Comparative Study," *Asian Survey*, 49: 759–785.

Koellner, P. (2004) "Factionalism in Japanese Political Parties Revisited or How Do Factions in the LDP and the DPJ Differ?" *Japan Forum*, 16: 87–109.

Krauss, E. S. (2000) "Japan: News and Politics in a Media-Saturated Democracy," in R. Gunther and A. Mughan (eds) *Democracy and the Media: A Comparative Perspective*, New York: Cambridge University Press.

Krauss, E. S. and Nyblade, B. (2005) "'Presidentialization' in Japan? The Prime Minister, Media and Elections in Japan," *British Journal of Political Science*, 35: 357–368.

Krauss, E. S. and Pekkanen, R. J. (2011) *The Rise and Fall of Japan's LDP: Political Party Organization as Historical Institutions*, Ithaca, NY: Cornell University Press.

LeBlanc, R. M. (1999) *Bicycle Citizens: The Political World of the Japanese Housewife*, Berkeley: University of Berkeley Press.

Lin, Jih-wen (2006) "The Politics of Reform in Japan and Taiwan," *Journal of Democracy*, 17: 118–131.

Martin, S. (2011) "The Influence of Voters," in A. Gaunder (ed.) *The Routledge Handbook of Japanese Politics*, London: Routledge.

McElwain, K. M. (2012) "The Nationalization of Japanese Elections," *Journal of East Asian Studies*, 12: 323–350.

McLaren, S. (2005) "Makiko, Madonnas and Political Melodramas: Researching Women, Media and Elections in Japan," *Ritsumeikan Social Sciences Review*, 41: 31–51.

McLaren, S. (2008) "Democratainment, Gender and Power in Japanese and Australian Election Night Television Programs," *The Journal and Proceedings of GALE*, 1: 123–134.

Murobushi, T. (1988) *Jitsuroku Nihon Oshokushi (An Authentic Account of the History of Corruption in Japan)*, Tokyo: Chikuma Shobō.

Park, C. H. (2001) "Factional Dynamics in Japan's LDP Since Political Reform: Continuity and Change," *Asian Survey*, 41: 428–461.

Pharr, S. J. (1996) "Media as Trickster in Japan: A Comparative Perspective," in S. J. Pharr and E. S. Krauss (eds) *Media and Politics in Japan*, Honolulu: University of Hawaii Press.

Reed, S. R., Scheiner, E., and Thies, M. F. (2012) "The End of LDP Dominance and the Rise of Party-Oriented Politics in Japan," *Journal of Japanese Studies*, 38: 353–376.

Saito, S. (2008) "Television and Political Alienation: Does Television News Induce Political Cynicism and Inefficacy in Japan?" *International Journal of Japanese Sociology*, 17: 101–113.

Saito, S. and Takeshita, T. (2008) "The Media Coverage of Election Campaigns and Its Effects in Japan," in J. Stromback and L. L. Kaid (eds) *The Handbook of Election News Coverage Around the World*, London: Routledge.

Sakamoto, T. (1999) "Explaining Electoral Reform: Japan versus Italy and New Zealand," *Party Politics*, 5: 419–438.

Taniguchi, M. (2007) "Changing Media, Changing Politics in Japan," *Japanese Journal of Political Science*, 8: 147–166.

7 The economic miracle

At the end of the U.S. Occupation Japan's economy was getting back on its feet. The Dodge Line had gotten inflation under control, and the Korean War had jump-started industrial production. By the mid-1950s, Japan found itself in an environment conducive to growth. In fact, Japan's growth rates from the mid-1950s to the early 1970s stood around 10 percent, prompting many outside observers to deem it a "miracle." This chapter explores what the "miracle" looked like and considers several potential reasons for rapid economic growth. Most agree that at least initially Japan overcame the obstacles of late development through state-led growth characterized by industrial policy championed by its elite bureaucracy. The relationship among bureaucrats, politicians, and business, however, changed over the course of the postwar period with politicians and vested interests gaining greater sway. The legacies of the way Japan developed are clearly marked in the ongoing influence of the bureaucracy and the relationships that characterize Japan's variety of capitalism.

Japanese growth did not come without its costs. Domestically, Japan felt the environmental costs of growth with several high-profile pollution cases forcing the conservative LDP to heighten industrial regulations. Urbanization also had a set of costs including high housing costs and less available labor in rural areas for farming and fishing. Finally, Japan's growth increasingly drew criticism from Western countries that felt Japan's protection of domestic markets long exceeded the time needed for it to catch up. After Japan became the second largest economy and experienced annual trade surpluses, it received more pressure from the West to liberalize its markets.

Japan's attempts to liberalize, though, have been inhibited by legacies of economic development. Specifically, the close connections between business, politicians, and bureaucrats have hampered reform. As we shall see in the next chapter, the arrangements that promoted growth have made reform more difficult.

The economic miracle

One point that often gets overlooked when exploring the Japanese economic miracle is the fact that Japan was a developing country from the late 1800s until World War II. Japan's growth during the five decades prior to World War II hovered around 3 percent. This growth plummeted midway through the war in 1943. Japan only returned to pre-1943 levels of industrial production by the mid-1950s (Ito 1996). Clearly, though, Japan had the foundations for growth prior to the postwar period.

The postwar environment favored economic growth. The Korean War increased demand for Japanese products and gave Japan's economy an initial boost. Moreover, the U.S.–Japan Security Treaty provided Japan with a security umbrella making it less necessary to spend funds on defense. Specifically, Japan was able to limit defense spending to about 1 percent while other developed nations tended to spend at least 3–5 percent on defense. Japan's relationship with the U.S. after the Occupation also opened up channels for trade and technology transfers. The postwar international environment in general was quite conducive to free trade, especially in comparison to the environment in the 1930s. In fact, global GDP averaged 5 percent from 1950 to 1965. This created a favorable environment for Japanese exports and also promoted cheaper access to raw materials (Nakamura 1994: 177). Japan overcame its resource problem by gaining access to cheap oil from the Persian Gulf. In addition, most companies were able to get capital from city banks that were over-loaned by the Bank of Japan (Reischauer 1990: 225–228). Japan experienced a baby boom immediately after the war, meaning that Japan eventually had a young, well-educated workforce to rely on. Labor relations were relatively tranquil. Finally, lifetime employment with seniority wages contributed to the success of certain firms by promoting loyalty and productivity.

Japan began to rebuild its economy by focusing on areas it had excelled in during the prewar period, such as textiles. Early on, Japan focused on labor-intensive products to promote industrialization. Textiles were Japan's largest export in the 1950s and early 1960s. As time passed, though, Japan began to produce more advanced products such as cameras, electronics, motorcycles, ships, and eventually automobiles and computers. As the period of rapid growth continued, Japanese company names such as Sony, Nikon, Canon, Seiko, Hitachi, Honda, Toyota, Datsun, Kawasaki, and Yamaha became more familiar in the West (Reischauer 1990: 230). This shift in products helps explain the increase in exports. Textiles require expensive raw materials; cars and electronics do not. As a result, these products were more competitive on the world market. It is important to note, however, that Japan's rapid economic growth was not export driven. Exports expanded in the 1960s, making Japan's strong economy even stronger.

The period of rapid economic growth was also characterized by a dramatic increase in the standard of living. After the U.S.–Japan Security Treaty crisis in 1960s, the Japanese government turned its focus from security to economic development. Prime Minister Kishi resigned to take responsibility for the Security Treaty crisis and Prime Minister Ikeda took office with a pledge to double a family's income in ten years. This goal was met much sooner than anticipated. The Japanese people measured their economic success through the accumulation of consumer goods. The three prized household possessions in the 1960s included a washing machine, a refrigerator, and a television set. By 1970, 98 percent of households owned a washing machine, 95 percent of households owned a refrigerator, and 67 to 70 percent of households owned a television set (Bennett and Levine 1976: 453). By the end of the 1960s Japan had become the third largest economy in the world, only trailing the United States and Soviet Union (Reischauer 1990: 245). Internationally, the extent of Japan's growth was acknowledged in 1964 with its entrance into the Organisation for Economic Co-operation and Development (OECD). The OECD promotes democracy and world trade and Japan's membership signaled its acceptance as a developed country by its peers.

The most remarkable aspect of the Japanese miracle was the speed at which the Japanese economy caught up with other developed countries. Japan began its recovery in light industries. By the 1970s though it was competitively producing automobiles, steel, and electronics. These advances continued into the 1980s when Japan challenged other countries in semiconductors, computers, telecommunications, and biotechnology.

Many argue that it caught up more rapidly due to market conforming industrial policy (Katz 1998).

Industrial policy involves both the protection and promotion of infant industries. In Japan, the bureaucracy implemented industrial policy. The main bureaucratic agency in charge of industrial policy was the Ministry of International Trade and Industry (MITI), but the Ministry of Finance (MOF) often influenced development policies as well. The MITI would choose which industries to develop and decide what mix of incentives to use to promote growth. It would also monitor competition. Industrial policy entailed the protection of domestic industries (both competitive and non-competitive ones) and the development of strategic industries. Protection involved import restrictions, such as quotas and tariffs. Foreign direct investment was also discouraged. Incentives used to promote the development of strategic industries included subsidies, tax breaks, low interest loans, credit allocation, and foreign exchange controls. While these market conforming policies worked well when industries were exposed to international competition, these policies also promoted corruption and market inefficiencies.

Industrial policy worked most effectively in the 1950s and 1960s in industries such as steel and shipbuilding. The first wave of government industrial policy was aimed at electric power, steel, shipbuilding, and coal. The Export-Import Bank of Japan and the Japan Development Bank were created to provide capital to promote exports and domestic growth, respectively. The Japan Development Bank provided low interest loans to these four priority sectors during the first part of the 1950s to promote growth (Nakamura 1994: 178–179). The Fiscal Investment and Loan Program (FILP) funded the Japan Development Bank. The FILP funneled capital from Japan's Postal Savings System into industries targeted to promote growth.

In the auto industry, industrial policy was used initially and then diminished. MITI originally protected the car industry from foreign imports. MITI only granted foreign exchange for a limited number of imports. This policy allowed Japanese auto companies to develop economies of scale, a development that takes a good amount of time. MITI only "liberalized" the auto industry when Japanese automakers were able to compete with foreign companies in 1965. In 1965, Japan switched from quotas to tariffs. The tariffs continued to make foreign cars quite expensive in Japan (Katz 1998: 111–112). Meanwhile, domestic car producers received subsidies, tax breaks, and low interest loans. These promotional policies were also extended to auto parts suppliers. While the auto industry got a jump-start from MITI's industrial policy, it eventually outgrew the need for protection and promotion. At the height of growth in the mid-1980s, Japanese auto companies exported over half of their production. In general, auto exports accounted for one fourth of all exports in the mid-1980s (Katz 1998: 113). One reason that industrial policy worked in the auto industry was that there was sufficient domestic competition to promote innovation (Katz 1998: 114). Motorcycles and electronics also benefitted from high levels of domestic competition.

Industrial policy worked less well in other industries in Japan, such as chemicals and plastics, aerospace, aircraft, and computer software. In these industries the government often pursued conflicting policies. For example, MITI's Basic Industries Bureau promoted petrochemicals, but MITI's Energy and Natural Resources Agency protected the petroleum industry, making fuel for the petrochemical industry expensive and thus reducing its overall competitiveness (Katz 1998: 114).

The protection of industries that were not subject to international competition was more problematic. Agriculture and construction received high levels of protection. The developmental state model does not adequately explain this type of protection. The developmental state model, also dubbed Japan, Inc. asserts that the bureaucracy rules while the politicians reign (Johnson 1982). Japan, Inc., is made up of politicians, bureaucrats, and business. Politicians simply provide legitimacy and stability to the system while the bureaucrats direct growth to promote the "national interest" through industrial policy and administrative guidance. Administrative guidance points to the carrots and sticks that MITI had at its disposal to promote growth in certain industries and discourage expansion in others. Agriculture and construction arguably are not part of this growth paradigm. The reason these industries received support was that farmers and construction workers were important constituents in the LDP's political machine. Farmers provided votes for the LDP in return for high agricultural prices. This type of protection for domestic industries meant higher prices for everyone. All industries would have preferred lower prices, but the LDP protected a broad range of industries. These inefficiencies were initially tolerated or less apparent due to the ever-expanding economy. The strains would have consequences once growth slowed.

While the state-led growth explanation most accurately captures Japan's economic growth in the 1950s and 1960s, this model began to change as Japan's economy developed. The bureaucracy certainly plays a larger role in Japan than in most developed democracies, but it is generally seen as one of several important actors in structuring growth, especially since the 1970s. The New Japan, Inc. school suggests that since the 1970s it makes more sense to analyze economic policy development by beginning with private interests at the business level. Politicians have incentives to respond to these interests to get votes and/or money. The bureaucracy also is part of these networks of communication, but its main role is to facilitate discussion, structure conflict, and provide information. The bureaucracy no longer has as much power and authority to direct growth as it did in the immediate postwar (Pempel 1987).

Alternative explanations for rapid growth

While the state-led growth paradigm provides insights into Japan's rapid economic growth in the 1950s and 1960s, it is not the only explanation for growth. One alternative explanation focuses on Japanese culture as the distinctive feature responsible for the miracle. The cultural explanation for growth centers on how the values and beliefs of the Japanese people shaped its postwar institutions. The values emphasized include the importance of personal relationships, especially the family, morality, loyalty, hierarchy, and cooperation – values with deep roots in the Confucian religion. These values are seen as influencing practices such as lifetime employment, tranquil labor relations, seniority wage scale, and high savings rates. Companies are viewed as paternalistic. Each company put the national interest of growth above all else, including profit.

While the cultural explanation does provide some insight into the Japanese version of capitalism, it overstates its influence. Culture does influence behavior thus explaining, for example, why conflict resolution looks different in Japan than in the United States; however, it cannot fully explain the economic miracle. For one, Confucian values influenced behavior long before Japan's economy undertook rapid economic growth. Given the continuity of culture, it is unclear why it suddenly started influencing economic development in the postwar period. Clearly, some other factors were at play.

In addition, much evidence exists to suggest that Japanese people do not cooperate at all times. A classic example is the bureaucracy's inability to get competing companies to agree on a standard videodisk format. Two different versions – beta and VHS – competed for a decade before the tension was resolved through market demand. In this case, the government tried to encourage cooperation and failed. Finally, examples of Japanese companies sacrificing profit for the national interest do not exist. The fact is that during rapid economic growth the government's interests and firms' interest often were in line. As Reed explains, if cooperation makes a company money, then the company will cooperate. If, however, competition is more profitable, then the company will compete (Reed 1993: 112).

Classic liberals provide a different explanation for growth. Classic liberals believe in freedom and the individual. Classic liberalism asserts that capitalist economies are inherently prone to growth. Adam Smith's invisible hand is the most efficient mechanism for the allocation of resources and capital. That is, the government should only protect private property and provide certain public goods. Otherwise, laissez-faire economic policies are seen as the most effective ones to promote growth. Finally, classic liberals would argue that internationally countries should pursue their comparative advantage, exporting goods most suited for growth.

Classic liberals argue that market competition was the major source behind growth in Japan. A classic liberal would be opposed to industrial policy. A liberal interpretation of growth suggests to the extent that the bureaucracy was involved in the Japanese economy it only slowed growth. Instead, Japan's growth was propelled by its high rates of saving and investment, its educated, skilled labor supply, and capital provided by banks. According to classic liberals, the private energy of firms drove growth.

While it is true that some sectors of the economy grew without the assistance of the bureaucracy and that MITI in particular did not always pick winners, it is hard to ignore the large role the bureaucracy played in economic planning, especially in the early postwar years. Given this, the classic liberal explanation is not fully persuasive.

Japanese growth in the 1970s and 1980s

As growth continued, Japanese exports thrived. While Japan ran trade deficits in the early postwar years, by the 1970s Japan began experiencing trade surpluses. In the 1980s, trade surpluses were the norm, and the source of great tensions between Japan and the West. Japan's share of world trade was only 2 percent in 1960, but in 1973 its share had increased to 9 percent (Reischauer 1990: 281).

The types of growth and protection policies pursued by the MITI produced a dual economy. Competitive export industries made up one part of the dual economy while protected noncompetitive sectors, such as agriculture, made up the other part.

As time passed, the stresses of economic growth became more apparent in Japan. One of the largest domestic problems that emerged as a byproduct of growth was pollution. In the late 1960s four high-profile pollution cases captured national attention through grassroots mobilization. All the pollution cases involved the improper disposal of industrial waste. The earliest cases of pollution were related to illnesses that occurred in Toyama prefecture. Itai itai disease emerged in this area due to cadmium poisoning in the water. Itai itai literally translates into "it hurts, it hurts" and denotes the verbal reaction of victims of the disease which could cause its victims to be bedridden. While the first cases emerged in the early nineteenth century, the disease only received national attention when 29 plaintiffs, including 9 victims and 20 family members, brought a lawsuit against Mitsui Mining. The case was settled in favor of the victims. Another high-profile pollution case involved the revelation of methyl mercury poisoning by the Chisso Corporation in Kumamoto prefecture. This poisoning gave rise to Minamata disease, denoting the fishing city where the cases emerged from eating polluted fish. This disease could result in dementia. Nearly a decade later, it also arose in Nigata prefecture from methyl mercury poisoning from the Shōwa Denko Corporation; it was labeled Nigata Minamata disease. The final high-profile pollution case involved sulfur dioxide air pollution from an oil refinery plant in Yokkaichi that led to severe asthma. In all, four lawsuits related to these pollution incidents were filed in the late 1960s. The growing attention these lawsuits brought made it more difficult for corporations and local and national governments to deny the problem. The pollution cases actually rattled the pro-growth public sentiment and placed the LDP's hold on power in jeopardy. While the LDP maintained control at the national level, it lost control of local governments to progressives in several areas (Upham 1987).

With increased public pressure and attention, the government eventually was forced to respond to this externality of growth. The so-called Pollution Diet in 1970 passed several regulatory policies to address the pollution problem. Between 1967 and 1973, the Diet passed laws that established emission standards and provided liability costs for victims (Upham 1987). It also established the environmental agency in 1971.

After the big four pollution cases were resolved, future environment concerns were addressed through channels outside the judiciary. Instead, the bureaucracy oversaw compensation for pollution injuries and the resolution of pollution disputes (Upham 1987). The government also included citizens in government planning to neutralize the influence of grassroots movements.

The Big Four Pollution cases are significant for several reasons. First, these cases brought to light the real costs of rapid economic growth. The cases also challenged the growth coalition of bureaucrats, politicians, and business – all these actors had denied or ignored the pollution charges prior to litigation. The litigation itself belies the cultural stereotype that Japanese people are conflict adverse. The pollution cases were bolstered by grassroots activism around the pollution problem. This type of social movement illustrated the vibrancy and potential effectiveness of civil society in Japan. The resolution of the pollution cases is also telling. The courts uniformly supported the victims. The government's response was to minimize the future role of the courts by establishing bureaucratic channels for future resolution. Some have argued that this action was an explicit attempt by the LDP to maintain control of social change (Upham 1987).

Another blow to Japan's rapid economic growth came with the Nixon shock followed by the oil crisis of 1973. The Nixon shock occurred in August 1971 when President Nixon announced that the dollar would no longer be tied to the gold standard. He also called for a 10 percent tariff on dutiable imports in an attempt to encourage other developed countries to revalue their exchange rates vis-à-vis the dollar. Eventually, Japan followed these incentives. Over the next two years, several revaluations occurred before the United States finally abandoned fixed exchange rates completely in 1973 establishing a floating exchange rate system with several other G-10 nations. The Nixon shock made Japanese exports more expensive and caused domestic price inflation.

The 1973 oil crisis was an international event that broke out when the Organization of Petroleum Exporting Countries (OPEC) began an export embargo on petroleum in 1973. It was followed by dramatic price hikes in petroleum prices in 1973 and 1974. In fact, the price increased fourfold during this period. The effect of the price hikes was far reaching in Japan leading to price inflation, an economic recession, and balance of payments deficits. The oil crisis exacerbated price inflation already underway due to the Nixon shock.

The oil crisis significantly slowed Japan's growth rates. While the Japanese economy recovered, it never returned to the growth rates of the 1950s and 1960s. Instead, growth resumed at about 4 percent, as opposed to 10 percent in the previous decades. The oil crisis highlighted the potential costs of Japan's reliance on others for natural resources.

Trade tensions

The strains of growth were not only present domestically but also quite apparent internationally. In particular, trade tensions increased dramatically as Japan's share of world trade increased. Trade friction, however, was present throughout the postwar period. In the prewar period Japan had received criticism for dumping cheap products, especially textiles, on the U.S. and European markets. Fears in the West that Japan would return to these practices lingered in the postwar period. In fact, most European countries refused to recognize Japan's entrance into the General Agreement on Trade and Tariffs (GATT) in 1955 with the fear of unfair trade practices upmost in their minds. Japan's entrance into the GATT, however, marked a long process of liberalization with Japan addressing tariffs, quotas, and nontariff barriers.

Trade tensions between the United States and Japan went through several phases related to Japan's path to development. Initial disputes centered on textiles and apparel in the 1960s. Given Japan's comparative advantage in textiles at this time, the U.S. asked for antidumping measures, voluntary export restraints, or exports quotas through various negotiations. Congress also threatened to impose import restrictions on Japanese products if Japan did not respond to its demands (Komiya and Itoh 1988: 194).

Trade negotiations between Japan and the U.S. intensified in the mid-1970s and 1980s as Japan's trade surplus increased. Trade talks shifted from negotiations to broad unilateral demands. These demands went beyond specific trade policies in specific sectors like textiles, steel, and autos and instead extended to a wider set of economic policy reforms, such as the yen–dollar exchange rate, macroeconomic policies, liberalization of foreign exchange controls, domestic financial deregulation, domestic industrial policy, and domestic reforms of government safety, health, and telecommunication regulations (Komiya and Itoh 1988: 212). In the 1980s, in particular, the focus shifted to nontariff barriers to trade. The emphasis was on structures and policies that limited foreign access to Japanese markets. The U.S. consistently called for Japan to increase its imports of manufactured goods and agricultural products, to remove import quotas, tariffs, and nontariff barriers, to revalue the yen exchange rate, and to relax foreign exchange controls (Komiya and Itoh 1988: 190).

Trade tensions between the U.S. and Japan tended to escalate in periods when the U.S. economy experienced low growth, rising unemployment, and increases in inflation. One of the most severe periods of tension came in the late 1980s when all these phenomena were occurring in the U.S. (Grimes 2002: 49). Increases in Japan's economy relative to the U.S.'s economy continually worried the U.S. about its relative place in the world economy. At the same time, increases in Japan's stature as an international economic superpower made it more possible for it to resist U.S. demands (Grimes 2002: 49). Nevertheless, Japan's economy was more dependent on the U.S.'s market than vice versa throughout the postwar period, giving the bilateral relationship added significance and placing the U.S. in a superior bargaining position. Specifically, U.S.–Japan trade is a larger portion of Japan's overall trade than the U.S.'s total trade with Japan for both imports and exports (Grimes 2002: 51–52). Japan's trade with Asia eventually became much larger than its trade with the U.S., but no one bilateral relationship stood out in Asia thereby allowing the U.S.–Japan bilateral relationship to continue to loom large (Grimes 2002: 52).

Tensions between Japan and the United States were particularly high in the late 1980s and early 1990s. The U.S. economy was in recession in the 1980s, and many policymakers claimed that increased access to the Japanese market was important to solve the U.S.'s economic woes. The trade tensions also coincided with the end of the Cold War. Without a military superpower as the U.S.'s other, some highly vocal revisionists began to make a case for Japan as the next major threat to the United States' economic security (van Wolferen 1989; Fallows 1989). Members of Congress staged protests at the Capitol that included taking a sledgehammer to Japanese electronics in their calls for further opening of Japanese markets. Meanwhile, Japan replaced the former USSR as the U.S.'s major threat in best-selling spy thrillers, such as Michael Crichton's *Rising Sun*. While the media in both countries exacerbated much of the tensions, the tensions were real and mostly contained to the economic arena. With the outbreak of the first Iraq war providing a new enemy, the dot com technology boom of the early 1990s, and the bursting of the economic bubble in Japan followed by a prolonged recession, economic tensions receded to the background of U.S.–Japan relations.

While the tendency was to emphasize the negative aspects of the unequal trade relationship between the two countries, both countries benefitted from the relationship in some significant ways. High saving rates in Japan provided capital to subsidize consumption and investment in the U.S. Similarly U.S. consumer demand bolstered Japanese exports (Grimes 2002: 53).

With the significant appreciation of the yen following the Plaza Accord of 1985, Japan began to increase its foreign direct investment. It also started locating production overseas, primarily in Newly Industrializing Countries (NIC), especially within ASEAN (Association of Southeast Asian Nations) countries. This trend also weakened tensions between the U.S. and Japan over time. U.S.–Japan economic relations are explored further in Chapter 12.

Legacies of Japanese rapid economic growth

Coordinated market economy

A country's path to development varies according to the institutions used to promote growth, the underlying ideology, and how underdeveloped a country was to begin with (Gerschenkron 1962). The way a country develops, in turn, can leave institutional legacies. That is, even when an institution used for growth changes or is discontinued, it still leaves an imprint on how the economy functions when the economy is a mature economy.

Scholars now recognize that countries do not go down the same path to development, and as a result varieties of capitalism have emerged. Comparing countries using the lens of varieties of capitalism illustrates the similarities and differences among developed countries. These similarities and differences emerge in relation to political institutions, financial systems, and labor relations that accompanied and promoted growth.

A model of capitalism refers to the institutions, including corporate governance, employee relations, industrial relations, vocational training and education, and inter-firm relations that influence how an economy functions. Two general models of capitalism exist: liberal market economies and coordinated market economies. The United States is a liberal market economy while Japan and Germany fall into the category of coordinated market economies. A liberal market economy is dominated by outside shareholders, short-term market relations between employee and employer, weak employer organizations and unions, private vocational training, and the use of contracting and subcontracting relationships. In contrast, coordinated market economies are dominated by long-term bank relationships and cross-shareholding, long-term market relationship between employee and employer, industry-wide collective bargaining, industry-based training, and cooperation among firms (Hall and Soskice 2001; Vogel 2001).

Japan's model of capitalism is a coordinated market economy which fosters long-term, cooperative relationships between firms and labor, between firms and banks, and between different firms. These relationships manifest themselves in the keiretsu system. The keiretsu system is a system of business relationships. The keiretsu system has its historical roots with the family-owned zaibatsu (industrial conglomerates) of the prewar period. Both vertical and horizontal keiretsu relationships exist. Vertical keiretsu connect all companies in the supply chain for particular products, linking suppliers and distributors. Major automobile companies and electronic conglomerates were organized as vertical keiretsu including Toyota, Honda, Nissan as well as Hitachi, Toshiba and Sony. Horizontal keiretsu are centered on a bank and include a trading company and various industrial groups such as steel, chemicals, and shipping. The most well-known horizontal keiretsu include Mitsui, Mitsubishi, and Sumitomo. The bureaucracy plays a critical role in protecting industry from international competition in sectoral markets and establishing and maintaining the framework for coordination in the private sector. Keiretsu were targeted as nontariff barriers. The cross-shareholding made it difficult for foreign countries to penetrate the market (Vogel 2001).

Even though both Japan and Germany fall into the category of coordinated market economy, significant differences between the ways the two economies are organized still exist, illustrating the variation that can exist within a model of capitalism. In Japan, the government organizes and guides the private sector more directly than the German government. The Bundesbank and universal banking in general played a larger role in German economic development. The German government codified much of its economic policy into legal code; the Japanese model of capitalism relies more heavily on informal networks and standard practices. Finally, Japanese labor is much weaker than labor in Germany and plays a smaller role in politics and corporate management than in Germany (Vogel 2001).

Keidanren and Nikkeiren have been two key actors in Japan's model of capitalism. Keidanren is the Federation of Economic Organizations and has been the key representative for all major firms and industries in Japan. It acts as an intermediary between the government and industry. Nikkeiren is the Japan Federation of Employers' Association. Its membership overlaps with Keidanren, but its main focus is on employment matters, especially the annual spring negotiations with labor unions in Japan.

Japan's tranquil labor relations are often seen as contributing to rapid economic growth. Labor found itself outside the system of LDP dominance in the postwar system. Instead, public sector labor unions were connected to the Japan Socialist Party (JSP) and private sector labor unions were tied to the Democratic Socialist Party (DSP). While the JSP had some strength early in the postwar period, its strength dwindled as the decades passed. Overall, labor's connections to government were weak.

Unlike in other capitalist countries, unions negotiated labor contracts annually at the spring offensive (shuntō) in Japan. Every spring national labor unions such as the railway workers and steel workers unions negotiated annual wage increases. While the spring offensive was often contentious, especially in the 1960s when labor was stronger, overall this system secured the ongoing bargain that increases in productivity would be rewarded with wage increases. Welfare provisions tended to come from companies in the form of job security instead of from the state in the form of income maintenance. During the high growth period, male workers had high job security in return for long working hours and transfers away from their families. Women, on the hand, tended to exit work either at marriage or childbirth and return to work at middle age as temporary, part-time, non-regular workers. This system gave companies incentives to invest in their male employees and flexibility to hire women as needed (Miura 2012). The problems with this gendered dual system of labor only became apparent when growth slowed and a large number of male workers fell into the temporary category (Miura 2012).

Overall, Japan has found it difficult to liberalize its economy due to the legacies of the model of capitalism it used to develop. This model is characterized by cooperation. Significantly, however, this cooperative model ties potential beneficiaries of reform to potential losers of reform. That is, organizations such as Keidanren and Nikkeiren include members in favor of liberalization as well as members opposed to it. The result has been a reform stalemate and economic stagnation (Vogel 2001).

East Asian model of growth

Japan's phenomenal postwar growth was followed by rapid economic growth in Korea and Taiwan. Many argued that these so-called "little tigers" followed the Japanese model. Korea and Taiwan were two of the four Asian Tigers to experience rapid economic growth following Japan. The other two tigers were Hong Kong and Singapore. Growth in Korea and Taiwan led many to ask whether the Japanese model of growth was in fact generalizable. Could the model be replicated with success in other countries? Were Korea and Taiwan examples that proved the viabilities of an East Asian model of growth? Japan, Korea, and Taiwan share some remarkable similarities both historically and in terms of their approaches to growth. Significant differences, however, also exist. As a result, it is best to consider growth in Korea and Taiwan as variations on a theme as opposed to replications of the Japanese experience.

Culturally and historically, Japan, Korea, and Taiwan share some striking similarities that arguably influenced their paths to development. All three countries are in the East Asian region and were deeply influenced by China in one way or another. Japan, Korea, and Taiwan are all small, crowded, relatively homogeneous countries that suffer from a dearth of natural resources. Furthermore, Japan colonized both Korea and Taiwan during its quest to create an imperial empire at the turn of the century. This colonial experience further connected these countries.

Several common institutional features also informed growth in Japan, Korea, and Taiwan. In general, conservative parties in conjunction with strong bureaucracies oversaw growth. Cooperation between the private and public sectors was overseen by pilot agencies such as MITI in Japan and the Economic Planning Board in Korea. These agencies pursued market conforming policies built on intervening in the economy based on the price mechanism. Government policies also tended to favor producers over consumers and savers over spenders. Sectors with connections to the international market received particular attention. The countries also benefitted from weak labor movements, high levels of education, and relatively equitable distributions of wealth (Johnson 1987; Gold 1986; Wade 1990).

Despite these similarities some key differences also existed. These differences call into question the notion of a single model of growth. Most significantly, Korea and Taiwan experienced growth under authoritarian rule. Japan was a democracy throughout its period of rapid economic growth. The LDP was in power for an uninterrupted period from 1955 to 1993, but it remained in power through free, open, competitive elections. In contrast, development began under the military government of Park Chung Hee in 1961 in South Korea and the authoritarian rule of the Kuomintang (KMT) in Taiwan. Korea only transitioned to democracy in 1987 due to grassroots pressure from social movements for reform that saw the election of Roh Tae-woo. Similarly, Taiwan's KMT began to introduce democratic reforms in the late 1980s: it lifted martial law and allowed an opposition party to form. This party, the Democratic Progressive Party, replaced the KMT in 2000 after competing in several election cycles. In both cases development was well underway prior to the transition to democracy.

In addition to the differences in their political environments, differences also exist in the way the governments pursued growth. Korea actually employed a more aggressive industrial policy than Japan. Industrial conglomerates known as chaebol played a more dominant role than Japanese keiretsu. Chaebol are family-owned industrial conglomerates that developed strong government connections when the military government took control in 1961. The chaebol system was modeled on the Japanese prewar zaibatsu system; however, unlike zaibatsu, chaebol did not have a main bank. Instead, chaebol relied exclusively on government funding, making the state connection even stronger than in the Japanese case. In general, Korean industrial policy focused on promoting large firms, mass production, and low wages (Wade 1990). In contrast, Taiwan had a more mixed industrial structure during its rapid economic growth period. The focus was on small firms, more specialized niches, and low wages. More than Japan and Korea, Taiwan focused on broad fiscal policy to promote growth – much more than on industrial policy (Gold 1986). All these differences call into question an East Asian model of growth.

Conclusion

When any country starts on its path to development, the major concern is how to raise the capital needed for growth. In Japan's case, the initial capital mainly came from subsidies from the government. Banks with strong connections to the government like the Japan Development Bank or city banks, which were over-loaned by the Bank of Japan, also funded growth. The Japanese economy did not rely on the stock market for capital. The government aided both domestic and internationally focused firms, but in the long run, companies with an orientation to the international market remained more productive and competitive.

This type of development differed considerably from other models and left specific legacies in Japan. Japan's model of development was state led with protectionist elements. The type of state-led growth had unique features. For example, Japan did not follow an import substitution model like several Latin American countries and India. An import substitution model protects domestic markets by placing restrictions, such as prohibitively high tariffs, to give infant industries a chance to catch up. While the Japanese government did protect certain sectors of the economy from imports, it also encouraged domestic competition within the sector. It eventually eased tariffs and quotas as the sectors became internationally competitive. Countries that have instituted strict import substitution models have been more isolationist in their approach. And as we have seen, even though development in Korea and Taiwan also was state-led, key differences still existed. All these models vary considerably from the classic liberal model of growth that emphasizes laissez-faire policies, the price mechanism, and the role of the individual. The Japanese model which Pempel labels "embedded mercantilism" protects the domestic market from imports until sectors are internationally competitive. The Japanese government kept its expenditures low and focused on maintaining a balanced budget. This model also was egalitarian in that the government protected inefficient sectors while promoting efficient export sectors (Pempel 1998).

The truly remarkable rapid economic growth period began in the 1950s and ended in the 1970s with the first major slowdown coinciding with the first oil crisis. Following the oil shocks in the 1970s, Japan's economy recovered to solid growth throughout the 1970s and 1980s. The strength of Japan's economy negatively affected Japanese–U.S. relations as the United States often put unfair trade practices at the top of any diplomatic interactions between the two countries. With the end of the Cold War, some so-called revisionists in the United States actually saw Japan as the largest potential future security threat. As we shall see in the next chapter, though, an upswing in the United States economy in the early 1990s thanks to the dot com boom combined with the decade-long recession due to the collapse of a real estate and asset bubble in Japan tempered tensions between the two countries. The question changed from what caused the Japanese miracle to why is the Japanese economy unable to recover. Japan's slow growth in the 1990s and 2000s is the subject of the next chapter.

References

Bennett, J. W. and Levine, S. B. (1976) "Industrialization and Social Deprivation: Welfare, Environment and the Postindustrial Society in Japan," in H. T. Patrick (ed.) *Japanese Industrialization and its Social Consequences*, Berkeley: University of California Press.

Fallows, J. (1989) *More Like Us: Making America Great Again*, Boston, MA: Houghton Mifflin.

Gerschenkron, A. (1962) *Economic Backwardness in Historical Perspective*, Cambridge, MA: Belknap/Harvard University Press.

Gold, T. B. (1986) *State and Society in the Taiwan Miracle*, Armonk, NY: M. E. Sharpe.

Grimes, W. W. (2002) "Economic Performance," in S. K. Vogel (ed.) *U.S.-Japan Relations in a Changing World*, Washington, DC: Brookings Institution Press.

Hall, P. A. and Soskice, D. (2001) *Varieties of Capitalism: The Institutional Foundation of Comparative Advantage*, Oxford: Oxford University Press.

Ito, T. (1996) "Japan and the Asian Economies: A 'Miracle' in Transition," *Brookings Papers on Economic Activity*, 27: 205–272.

Johnson, C. (1982) *MITI and the Japanese Miracle*, Stanford, CA: Stanford University Press.

Johnson, C. (1987) "Political Institutions and Economic Performance: The Government-Business Relationship in Japan, South Korea and Taiwan," in F. C. Deyo (ed.) *The Political Economy of the New Asian Industrialism*, Ithaca, NY: Cornell University Press.

Katz, R. (1998) *Japan, the System that Soured: The Rise and Fall of the Japanese Economic Miracle*, Armonk, NY: M. E. Sharpe.

Komiya, R. and Itoh, M. (1988) "Japan's International Trade and Trade Policy, 1955–1984," in T. Inoguchi and D. L. Okimoto (eds) *The Political Economy of Japan, Volume 2: The Changing International Context*, Stanford, CA: Stanford University Press.

Miura, M. (2012) *Welfare Through Work: Conservative Ideas, Partisan Dynamics, and Social Protection in Japan*, Ithaca, NY: Cornell University Press.

Nakamura, T. (1994) *Lectures on Modern Japanese Economic History 1926–1994*, Tokyo: International Library Foundation.

Pempel, T. J. (1987) "The Unbundling of 'Japan, Inc.': The Changing Dynamics of Japanese Policy Formation," in K. Pyle (ed.) *The Trade Crisis: How Will Japan Respond?* Seattle: Society for Japanese Studies, University of Washington.

Pempel, T. J. (1998) *Regime Shift: Comparative Dynamics of the Japanese Political Economy*, Ithaca, NY: Cornell University Press.

Reed, S. R. (1993) *Making Common Sense of Japan*, Pittsburgh, PA: Pittsburgh University Press.

Reischauer, E. O. (1990) *Japan: The Story of a Nation*, 4th edn, New York: McGraw-Hill Publishing Company.

Upham, F. K. (1987) *Law and Social Change in Postwar Japan*, Cambridge, MA: Harvard University Press.

van Wolferen, K. (1989) *The Enigma of Japanese Power: People and Politics in a Stateless Nation*, New York: Alfred A. Knopf.

Vogel, S. K. (2001) "The Crisis of German and Japanese Capitalism: Stalled on the Road to the Liberal Market Model," *Comparative Political Studies*, 34: 1103–1131.

Wade, R. (1990) *Governing the Market: Economic Theory and the Role of Government in East Asian Industrialization*, Princeton, NJ: Princeton University Press.

8   Economic slowdown

Since the 1990s Japan's economy has not been performing strongly. In the early 1990s, an asset bubble that accrued in the real estate and stock markets burst, sending the economy into a decade-long recession. The following decades have been plagued by periods of recovery subsequently undone by domestic political decisions and/or external events. Deflation, the decline in prices due to low consumer demand, along with massive increases in the government debt have only made the economic situation worse. Japan has financed its debt through the purchase of government bonds that are largely backed by domestic savings. Some worry less about Japan's debt due to the fact it has not relied on foreign financing, but the growth of its debt has now gotten the attention of both the domestic and international community.

Japan's growth patterns prior to the 1990s have made the relative stagnation that has occurred since Japan's asset bubble burst in 1990s that much more perplexing to policymakers and scholars alike. This chapter explores the causes of the asset bubble that emerged in the late 1980s and the prolonged recession that lasted throughout the 1990s. Why did the recession last so long? And why has the Japanese economy continued to perform poorly into the 2000s even though it has shown positive growth during the last decade? As with most large, complex phenomenon many different explanations have emerged to answer these questions. This chapter will review the major developments in Japan's political economy since the 1990s, paying particular attention to the legacies of the way Japan developed. This chapter will also consider attempts to reform Japan's economic system and analyze the extent to which these reforms have positively impacted Japanese growth.

The asset bubble of the late 1980s

Japan's economy from 1985 to 1990 is referred to as the "bubble economy." The bubble denotes the speculative growth in two areas – stocks and real estate. Essentially, both stock and land prices became unsustainably inflated in the 1980s. The Japanese stock index increased fivefold from 1980 to 1990. It tripled between 1985 and 1989 alone. In 1990, stock prices dropped dramatically and continued to decline throughout the 1990s, never surpassing stock price levels in the early 1980s, prior to the bubble's creation. While there were medium-term fluctuations, the major trend in the 1990s was a long-term decline in stock values.

Whereas stock prices peaked in value in 1990, land prices rose until 1991. Land prices in several urban areas more than tripled during the 1980s. Prices increased more in urban areas than in rural areas; however, the trend was more pronounced in urban areas due to greater demand.

During the bubble economy, many excesses emerged. As land prices rose dramatically, people who owned land became rich. Those who did not have land, however, had a lesser chance of acquiring land as the bubble increased. These social inequalities eventually pressured policymakers to respond to the bubble. Those who owned land in urban areas were pressured to sell it for the construction of office buildings. An excess of office buildings eventually emerged, and many stood vacant. During the bubble, the construction industry boomed and brought in legal and illegal foreign workers. During this time of excess and extravagance in the 1980s, trade tensions between Japan and the U.S. reached their height of contention.

The end of the speculative bubble in stock and real estate prices is often referred to as the bursting of the economic bubble. The bubble burst in the stock market when stock prices plummeted on the first day the stock exchange was open in 1990. The market reacted to the Bank of Japan's decision to increase interest rates from 2.5 percent to 3.25 percent. Many critics argued that the increase in interest rates was long overdue. Signs of the speculative bubble were clear in 1987 and many, including the Deputy Governor of the Bank of Japan, recommended raising interest rates. Officials were reluctant to raise interest rates, though. Many pointed to Japan's commitment in the 1985 Plaza Accord among G-5 countries to stimulate the total demand for final goods and services as a reason why interest rates could not be raised. Others argued that after stock prices dropped significantly in the U.S. on Black Monday in 1987, Japanese officials felt obligated to promote a stable dollar. These actions signaled to banks that interest rates would remain low indefinitely, encouraging risky behavior. While there is little agreement as to why Japan did not raise interest rates earlier, in retrospect most agree that the Bank of Japan raised interest rates too late and too much in 1990 (Vogel 2006: 24–25).

Explanations for the bubble economy

There are two predominant explanations for the asset bubble – a structural explanation and a policy explanation. In reality some mixture of structure and policy contributed to the bubble economy. Both explanations illuminate some of the weaknesses in the Japanese economy at the time. In fact, one could argue that the structural reasons explain risky investments by banks which prompted the beginning of the bubble while monetary policy could explain how the bubble grew so big and lasted so long.

Those who emphasize the structural causes of the bubble economy focus on bank deregulation. Through the 1970s banks were under the tight control of the Ministry of Finance (MOF). The MOF guaranteed banks a modest profit and protected banks from bankruptcy. With these assurances, banks found little incentive to innovate. This system changed in the 1980s with the introduction of more competition. In addition, corporations became less reliant on banks for loans as new avenues of capital became available to them through international markets or corporate bonds. As a result, banks began to seek other customers such as small- and medium-sized enterprises. Banks also pursued more land and property investments, such as urban office buildings or rural resorts. These new types of loans were much riskier. Banks, however, were not sufficiently regulated and thus overextended themselves (Ohno n.d.; Vogel 2006: 25–27).[1]

The policy explanation focuses on monetary policy. It suggests that the prolonged period of low interest rates created a situation where it was easy to acquire land and stocks.

The low interest rate policy initially came in response to the yen appreciation brought on by the Plaza Agreement. Officials allowed the low interest rates to persist absent signs of price inflation. The low interest rates encouraged the speculative bubble. When the Bank of Japan raised interest rates, the bubble burst (Ohno n.d.; Vogel 2006: 24–25).[2]

The lost decade – the 1990s

The decade of the 1990s is often referred to as the "lost decade." The phrase "lost decade" captures the uncertainty and transition Japan experienced in the economic, political, and social realms during this period of economic stagnation.

Economic uncertainty and transition during the lost decade

The economic conditions in the 1990s were not completely static. Japan showed signs of recovery in both the mid- and late 1990s, but each time it was thrust back into recession due to government policy or international economic conditions. The Japanese economy was particularly weak in 1992–1993 following the bursting of the bubble, in 1997–1998 after the banking crisis and the government's decision to raise the consumption tax, and in 2001 when the U.S. and global IT recession occurred. Signs of economic recovery occurred when international trade was high and was driven by Japan's stronger export industries.

For example, in 1996 Japan exhibited the highest growth among G7 countries (at 3.5 percent). In April 1997, however, the Hashimoto administration raised the consumption tax from 3 percent to 5 percent. The motivation for the consumption tax increase was to raise more funds to cover government spending. The economy immediately began to slow in response to this policy decision (Katz 1998: 232; Ohno n.d.). At the end of 1997, economic conditions worsened further with the bankruptcy of Yamaichi Securities, Japan's fourth largest brokerage firm, and Hokkaido Takushoku Bank, one of the twenty largest banks in Japan. These failures ignited a banking crisis and credit crunch.

Signs of financial weakness first emerged with the Jusen housing loan scandal in 1995–1996. Jusen was not a bank; it was a housing loan company. It had close connections to the agricultural cooperative Nōkyō, which in turn is a major supporter of the LDP. Jusen borrowed money from financial institutions to make housing loans. When the bubble burst, Jusen became a central part of many banks' nonperforming loan portfolio. Nonperforming loans include outstanding loans to borrowers in bankruptcy, loans that have been past due for over six months, or loans that have had to be restructured at lower interest rates. Japanese banks were saddled with a large amount of these non-performing assets, many attached to non-bank entities like the Jusen. The government eventually stepped in to address the Jusen problem for political reasons, especially the connection to agriculture (Leheny 2006: 32). In the end, Jusen foreshadowed many of the problems that came to a head in 1997.

The bankruptcy of Yamaichi Securities and Hokkaido Takushoku Bank truly ignited the banking crisis. The banking crisis of 1997–1998 had structural causes that dated back to rapid economic growth as well as the practices that developed during the bubble economy. Banks were not sufficiently regulated by the Ministry of Finance. Many cozy relationships emerged due to the amakudari (revolving door) practices where MOF officials retired to sit on the board of financial institutions. In the context of greater liberalization and internationalization, Japanese banks made riskier loans to small- and medium-sized companies as well as other non-bank entities (such as Jusen) in the 1980s (Lincoln 2011: 364). The recession that followed the bubble's collapse meant that many of the banks' borrowers could not repay their debt. In addition, the banks had loans that were backed by land as collateral. The significant drop in land prices made these loans nonperforming loans. Banks also held stock, and the significant drop in these assets negatively impacted their balance sheets. Banks began to lend less in an attempt to reduce their risky assets, but the reduction in lending created a credit crunch (Fujii and Kawai 2010)

In the "financial Diet" of 1998, the government finally stepped in and addressed the bad debt issue, spending trillions of Japanese yen to infuse capital into banks. It created the Financial Services Agency to oversee the regulation of banks, taking this task away from the MOF (Lincoln 2011: 364). It also oversaw the merger of weaker banks. The Bank of Japan initiated its zero interest rate policy in April 1999. Even though the Bank of Japan has since tried to raise the rate, it has been forced to keep the interest rate close to zero for fear of harming Japan's economic recovery.

The government also implemented an expansionary fiscal policy during the lost decade to stimulate growth (Posen 1998). Fiscal stimuli in the form of construction projects fit nicely with the LDP's machine politics. The LDP exchanged these types of pork barrel projects for votes and/or financial assistance throughout the postwar period. In the 1990s, though, such fiscal stimuli led to a rising national debt. When Koizumi became prime minister, he attacked the fiscal stimuli and attempted to reform the LDP from within with varying levels of success.

Political uncertainty and transition during the lost decade

Japan's political landscape also experienced a large amount of change and uncertainty during Japan's lost decade. While political scandals were part and parcel of the Japanese political landscape throughout the postwar era, the public's tolerance for the excesses of Japanese politics waned with the bursting of the economic bubble. The Sagawa Kyubin scandal broke in 1992, just as the full extent of Japan's economic woes were becoming apparent. Sagawa Kyubin was a parcel delivery company accused of bribing LDP politicians for favorable policy outcomes as well as using connections to the yakuza (the Japanese mafia) to contain right-wing activists who were bothering former Prime Minister Takeshita Noboru. The investigation of LDP kingmaker Kanemaru Shin and his connections to Sagawa Kyubin produced 500 million yen in questionable funds. Additional search warrants uncovered outrageous amounts of money in the form of cash, bonds, and gold bars. These funds were not explicitly related to Sagawa but instead seen as the fruits of the LDP's political machine. The LDP initially refused to dismiss Kanemaru, further outraging the public. Some politicians within the party used this scandal in the context of hard economic times to push for reform.

As discussed in Chapter 5, in 1993 two separate groups broke from the LDP throwing the previously stable 1955 system of LDP dominance into a period of party realignment. The initial result of the LDP split was the creation of a short-lived anti-LDP coalition that remained in power for ten months. This coalition supported electoral reform. When the LDP returned to government it invited the JSP to serve as a coalition partner, an arrangement that ended up delegitimizing the JSP and weakening its already dwindling support. The LDP only remained in office after reform by securing coalition partners. Confidence in the LDP remained low throughout the 1990s, especially following the government's weak and disorganized response to the Kobe earthquake in 1995.

Social uncertainty and transition during the lost decade and beyond

Some of the most visible changes since the bubble burst have come in the labor market. Lifetime employment is often cited as a cornerstone of the Japanese economic miracle. In reality, lifetime employment only extended to a certain segment of white-collar workers even during the economic boom. When Japan entered the prolonged recession of the 1990s, the lifetime employment system began to break down. One of the first signs of these changes came with the emergence of a new class of part-time workers labeled *friitaa* (also spelled *freeter*). Friitaa is a borrowed word combining the English word "free" and the German word "arbeiter" (worker). This label is attached to people, mainly men, between the ages of 15 and 34 who are unable to find full-time jobs. Friitaa often work part time and generally are underemployed. The category does not include students and housewives, the main sources of part-time work during Japan's rapid economic growth. This growing class of underemployed male workers is affecting society, especially in terms of marriage and birth rates.

Friitaa are stigmatized. Some people are in this category by choice, but others genuinely cannot find full-time work. By the 2000s, these workers became considered irregular workers. In 2000, the percentage of men ages 24–34 years old with irregular jobs stood at 9 percent. This figure has since increased to 18 percent by 2012. The figures are even higher for those ages 15–24 years with 28 percent in irregular jobs by 2012 (Butkiewicz 2012: 4). Irregular and temporary male workers have opened up an entirely new set of welfare provision problems in Japan (Miura 2012). Certainly men are less well off due to these shifts given that irregular jobs tend to pay 40 percent less than regular jobs. In addition, irregular jobs do not have benefits (Butkiewicz 2012: 4). Overall, the number of irregular workers has increased from 16 percent of the work force in 1985 to over one-third in 2012 (OECD 2014: 6). Friitaa make up a large part of this increase.

Several structural features have contributed to the growth of irregular regular workers. The larger forces at work are the prolonged economic recession and a series of neoliberal economic policies. Of particular note is the Labour Dispatch Law of 2004, which was passed under Koizumi and allows companies to hire a greater number of irregular workers. As a result of these forces, companies have restructured, and a smaller number of full-time jobs exist. In addition, companies have a bias for younger workers and have a negative bias towards workers who are seeking full-time employment after spending some time in part-time work. The Ministry of Health, Labor, and Welfare found a negative bias against friitaa of 40 percent (Cook 2013: 35).

Explanations for the prolonged recession

The explanation of Japan's dramatic turn from strong growth to prolonged recession is contested. Many different hypotheses exist. Some focus on structural causes while others point to policy decisions. Variation further exists within these broad schools.

Structural explanations

The structural school focuses on the features of Japan's political economy that have not facilitated growth. One predominant structural explanation claims that the policies and institutions that fostered growth are ill suited for a mature economy. In particular, this school claims that the Japanese government went from promoting winners to protecting losers. One could argue that the government did this throughout rapid economic growth – the dramatic growth just hid the inefficiencies (Katz 1998).

Others focus on the fact that the Internet technology revolution that occurred in the 1990s did not favor Japan's model of capitalism. Stable labor relations and cross-share holding favored lean production in automobiles and electronics. Lean production is also referred to as "just in time" production. It focuses on the elimination of "waste" in the production process. This efficiency model also reduces costs and production time. Stable labor relations and cross-shareholding was less well suited to the fast pace of technological innovation characteristic of information technology. As a result, Japan became less competitive (Vogel and Zysman 2002).

Another explanation emphasizes the new pressures created by globalization, especially the liberalization of the financial and trade sectors. Japan's model of growth had been focused on a relatively protected market. Liberalization challenged this model and Japan did not have a good response (Vogel 2006: 33).[3]

The main problems with these explanations are that they use the same features that are seen as promoting growth as inhibiting growth (Vogel 2006: 31).

Policy explanations

As we have seen, government policy is a potential explanation for why the bubble burst. The Bank of Japan raised interest rates and the bubble burst. In retrospect, the Bank of Japan probably raised the interest rates too fast and too much. Time lagged before it recognized this, which exacerbated the problem.

The Bank of Japan struggled to effectively use monetary policy as a mechanism to drive the economy. Interest rates were close to zero throughout the decades of stagnation – they could not be pushed much lower. Some economists, however, note that near zero interest rates can still be a positive tool when an economy is experiencing chronic deflation (Vogel 2006: 28). The other monetary policy option is to expand the money supply. With the exception of a brief period under Koizumi, the government was reluctant to do this. As we shall see, expanding the money supply with a 2 percent inflation target has been a cornerstone of Abenomics marking a departure from most policy during the slow growth era.

The preferred policy mechanism from 1990 to 2012 was the use of fiscal policy to stimulate the economy. Politics often interfered with the effectiveness of these packages. The recipients of stimulus funds often were LDP supporters, such as the construction industry. The monies were not necessarily sent to the areas of the economy, like the IT sector, which might have had a better chance of jump-starting the economy (Vogel 2006: 25).

The lack of decisive policies to deal with Japan's nonperforming loan problem also contributed to ongoing stagnation. Nonperforming loans became an increasing portion of bank portfolios throughout the 1990s. After the banking crisis of 1997–1998, the government continued to respond slowly. This slow response is seen as contributing to stagnation.

Government policies also slowed Japan's recovery. For example, the decision to raise the consumption tax in 1997 threw Japan's recovering economy back into recession.

In the end, some combination of policy and structural features influenced the prolonged stagnation.

The 2000s – a second lost decade?

To the surprise of many Japan's stagnation extended beyond the 1990s. Like in the 1990s, Japan's economy showed some signs of recovery during the 2000s, but setbacks emerged with the global economic recession in 2007–2008 and the triple disaster in 2011. Japan experienced GDP increases from 2003 to 2007. GDP is the market value of final goods and services in one year. In 2003 and 2004, GDP growth hovered around 2 percent. In 2005, this rate increased even further to 3.2 percent. A boom in exports promoted this growth. The exchange rate was weak which made Japanese exports cheaper. By 2005, there was some evidence that increased domestic demand was also promoting GDP growth. The first part of the 2000s also saw the growth of new businesses and increased investments in the information, communications, and non-manufacturing industries, due in large part to regulatory reforms detailed below. Overall, businesses were doing well in the early 2000s, especially in terms of increasing profits (Japan Echo 2006).

The U.S. housing and financial crisis of 2007–2008 spurred a global recession by 2008. The U.S. crisis occurred shortly after a domestic housing market bubble burst. The housing crisis exposed many risky investments by financial institutions. The U.S. crisis caused stock markets to plummet globally. Japan had been experiencing signs of recovery; however, the global crisis threw it back into recession. In fact, the Nikkei stock index fell from around 13,000 in August 2008 to a low of just under 7,000 in October (Arase 2009: 117). To the surprise of many, the global crisis also led to an appreciation of the yen – 24 percent against the U.S. dollar and 32 percent against the euro (Arase 2009: 119). While the higher yen increased Japanese purchasing power abroad, it made exports more expensive. The end result was that Japan ran a trade deficit for the first time in 28 years. Japan also dropped 1.3 percent of GDP in 2008 (Arase 2009: 118).

Statistics suggest that the individual was not fairing as well in the 2000s. Throughout the 2000s, deflation persisted. Deflation not only impacts consumer products, it also influences wages. Due to deflation, people's income levels have fallen. Moreover, the number of people in irregular employment has continued to increase. These circumstances have contributed to the rising number of people in working poverty.

Japan's unemployment rate has been low in comparison to other countries. The unemployment rate in August 2012 was 4.2 percent. This was higher than in the past. In 2016 the unemployment rate hovered around 3.2 percent (Japan Macro Advisors 2016). But a better measure is the aggregate number of hours workers work. This number has declined 8.6 percent since 2000 (Butkiewicz 2012: 5). The increasing number of irregular workers has influenced this trend.

Plenty of positive developments occurred in the 2000s, but these were overshadowed by persistent deflation. The prolonged stagnation has only increased calls for economic reform. The efforts to enact reform from Prime Minister Hashimoto (1996–1998) through Prime Minister Abe (2012–present) are considered below.

Economic reform

As we have seen in the 1990s, the LDP attempted to revive the economy through economic stimulus packages. The fiscal stimulus model tended to rely on some combination of tax cuts and spending increases. Fiscal stimulus packages were appealing because this approach nicely fit with the LDP machine model of pork barrel expenditures to reward supporters. Prime Minister Hashimoto was the only prime minister who veered from this path. He increased the consumption tax from 3 percent to 5 percent in 1997 to raise funds to support increased spending on health, welfare, and education. This increase came just prior to the banking crisis and is seen as throwing Japan back into recession. Following the banking crisis, Hashimoto implemented a stimulus plan, but it came too late to alleviate the economic problems (Noble 2011: 255). Prime Ministers Obuchi and Mori also implemented stimulus packages but to little avail. The LDP began to realize that its stimulus approach was not working. In addition, many began to worry about the growing deficit caused by the reliance on the stimulus approach.

When Prime Minister Koizumi was elected in 2001, he entered office with a desire to shift the focus from the fiscal stimulus approach to structural reform. Koizumi was classified as a neoliberal reformer. Neoliberalism is a market-oriented approach that calls for limited government intervention. This approach countered policies such as market controls, the protection of inefficient sectors, and efforts to redistribute wealth and profits, which were policies implemented during most of the postwar period.

Koizumi's reform agenda was large. Koizumi's reform desires included regulatory reform, fiscal reform, social security reform, pension reform, and tax reform. He also wanted to privatize public corporations and revise competition policy.

Koizumi used reforms initiated by Hashimoto to strengthen his position as prime minister and push for reform. One key feature of the reforms passed by Hashimoto was the creation of the Council on Economic and Fiscal Policy (CEFP) within the Cabinet Office in 2001. This agency assists the prime minister in developing economic and fiscal policies and includes experts from outside the government. Its functions are similar to the Office of Management and Budget in the United States. Prime Minister Koizumi appointed Takenaka Heizō to head the CEFP. Takenaka spearheaded the privatization of the postal system. Prior to privatization, Japan's postal system included postal delivery, postal banking, and postal life insurances. Its financial assets made it the largest bank in the world.

Prime Minister Koizumi's successes and failures are contested. Most scholars would classify the passage of postal privatization, regulatory reform, the mergers and privatization of public corporations, and the decrease in public works spending as successes (George Mulgan 2011: 262). Koizumi also significantly reduced the number of amakudari appointments and the amount of money funneled into the Fiscal Investment and Loan Program (FILP) (Noble 2006). Koizumi was not able to generate more revenue by realizing a consumption tax increase. He did not accomplish pension and medical reform. He only saw limited decentralization of the central government's tax and fiscal powers. Koizumi did stabilize Japan's debt, but he was unable to reduce the deficit (George Mulgan 2011: 262).

Koizumi made progress addressing the nonperforming loan problem. In 2003, the economy was showing signs of recovery. At this time, Koizumi had the Financial Services Agency (FSA) pressure banks to get rid of bad loans. Takenaka was in charge of tackling the nonperforming loan problem. Due to the efforts of the FSA, the ratio of bad debts held by major banks was cut by about 50 percent from October 2002 to the end of fiscal 2004 (Uchiyama 2010: 20). Government funds also went to the Resona banking group to help reinvigorate the financial sector. In 2002, nonperforming loans totaled 42 trillion yen. This figure had dropped to about 15 trillion yen by March 2006 (Japan Echo 2006). Several policies facilitated the disposal of nonperforming loans, including the restructuring of the banking system, the infusion of public funds, increases to the money supply and zero interest rates. Stock prices also increased during this time frame (Japan Echo 2006: 3).

Koizumi implemented several regulatory reforms that increased access to new markets. He created special deregulation zones where private corporations could compete in the realm of healthcare, agriculture, welfare, and education (Uchiyama 2010: 21).

Public works spending declined during Koizumi's time in office. Specifically, public works spending dropped from around 9.4 trillion yen in the fiscal 2001 budget to 7.2 trillion yen in the fiscal 2006 budget (Uchiyama 2010).

Koizumi oversaw the so-called "Trinity Reform" of the local tax and finance system. The three prongs of this reform included (1) the abolition of national subsidies to localities, (2) transfers of sources of tax from the national level to the local level, and (3) changes to the local tax allocation methods (Uchiyama 2010: 21). Some progress was made in this area. For example, subsidies declined by 4.7 trillion yen from 2004 to 2006 (Uchiyama 2010: 21).

The passage of postal privatization at the end of Koizumi's administration had serious potential ramifications for the Japanese economy. The postal system in Japan is significant because it entails much more than mail delivery. The postal system historically contained both an insurance component and a savings component. Before reform, 85 percent of all households had a postal savings account and 60 percent of households purchased insurance from the post office (Fiaola 2005). In fact, the postal savings system in Japan with its $3 trillion in deposits and 25,000 branches stood as the largest banking institution in the world at the time it was targeted for reform (Fiaola 2005). Significantly, postal savings funds were transferred to the FILP, which politicians used to fund particularistic projects, a second budget of sorts. Koizumi's postal reform sought to break up the various functions of the post office. With the passage of reform, Koizumi claimed that funds would be used more efficiently in commercial capital markets. That is, capital would be diverted from FILP; instead, private financial firms would compete for the capital/saving accounts.

Despite Koizumi's successes and his overall popularity, a backlash against Koizumi's neoliberalism occurred after he left office. Critics pointed out that neoliberal policies had increased income inequality and even threatened public safety. The revelation that the government had lost tens of millions of pension records fueled the distrust in the government and the backlash against neoliberalism (Noble 2011: 257).

Abe Shinzō (2006–2007), Fukuda Yasuo (2007–2008), and Asō Tarō (2008–2009) followed Koizumi in succession as LDP prime ministers. Each served a short term and none was able to make significant progress on economic reform. All three kept budget spending in check, although Asō initiated a significant fiscal stimulus package that marked a return to machine politics of old. These three prime ministers also continued to shrink the size of the FILP (Noble 2011: 257).

Prime Minister Fukuda pushed through a 1.8 trillion yen budget stimulus package to bolster the economy. These funds targeted small business loans, oil price offsets (to help farmers and fisheries dealing with higher oil prices), and elderly relief to counter the effects of a new medical insurance program (Arase 2009: 111). The stimulus package did not inspire much confidence, though. In fact, the Tokyo stock exchange fell 6.8 percent immediately after its passage in mid-October. Further stimulus was injected at the end of October as the LDP tried to mollify constituents prior to an election that had to be called no later than September 2009. The package included tax breaks for home loans, capital gains, and small businesses (Arase 2009: 112).

In the wake of the global financial crisis, Japanese banks were strong, illustrating the positive effects of reform following Japan's banking crisis. Evidence of this strength is the fact that several Japanese banks invested in the failing U.S. banks (Arase 2009: 117).

The DPJ took power in 2009. The DPJ administration also worked to reduce public works and other particularistic government expenditures. The DPJ's goal was not to reduce the deficit; it chose to use the savings from these cuts to fund increased government services, such as its child allowance program, which involved small monthly government payments to citizens with children to offset some of the costs of child rearing.

In general, the DPJ has had difficulties distinguishing itself from the LDP on economic policy issues (Schoppa 2011). Its tendency to shift its economic policy priorities is apparent when examining its manifestos. Its 2005 manifesto was more neoliberal. By 2009, the DPJ had eliminated many of its earlier commitments to neoliberal reform. In 2009, it supported child allowances, no tuition fees for public high school, pension reform, and labor reform, including a desire to strengthen unemployment support for irregular workers and establish allowances for non-permanent employees receiving training (George Mulgan 2011). It remained committed to spending reform, but many of its priorities were connected to strengthening the social safety net (George Mulgan 2011: 271).

While in office, the DPJ's newly inaugurated Administrative Reform Council was able to cut the LDP's stimulus budget by 3 trillion yen. The DPJ's new spending initiatives, however, cost 95 trillion yen, which exceeded the 2009 budget by 7 trillion yen (Arase 2010: 48). For 2010, the DPJ was able to eliminate 700 billion yen in cuts, but this was less than half what was needed to fund its expensive child allowance program (Rosenbluth 2012: 47).

The DPJ originally promised not to raise the consumption tax for four years upon taking office. Prime Minister Hatoyama stood by this promise, but just prior to the July 2010 upper house election Prime Minister Kan, his successor, announced his intention to push for a 5 percent increase in the consumption tax. This announcement certainly hurt the DPJ's performance in the 2010 upper house election where it suffered a devastating defeat to the LDP.

Following the triple disaster in 2011, the DPJ was forced to backtrack on many of its social safety net reforms. In particular, it realized that given the demands of reconstruction it could no longer fund its child allowance initiative. The cost of reconstruction made increasing the consumption tax more pressing. The main motivation for the tax increase, however, preceded the triple disaster. The goal of the tax was to bring Japan's rising debt, which was twice as much as its GDP in 2010, under control. Prime Minister Noda, Kan's successor, pushed through a bill that called for an increase from 5 percent to 8 percent in 2014 and a final increase to 10 percent in 2015.

Abenomics

The LDP regained control of the government following the 2012 lower house election, and Prime Minister Abe was elected to his second term as prime minister. Upon taking office, Abe announced an economic reform plan dubbed Abenomics (following similar labels such as Reganomics and Clintonomics). Abenomics is composed of three "arrows." These arrows include monetary policy, fiscal policy, and a growth strategy. The first two arrows were initiated shortly after Abe took office. Abe directed the Bank of Japan to begin the monetary policy of quantitative easing to induce a positive inflation rate. Quantitative easing is when a central bank purchases financial assets from commercial banks and other private institutions in order to increase the value of the assets and decrease their yield and simultaneously increase the monetary supply. In 2013, the Bank of Japan purchased a large amount of government bonds to push up prices and wages. Quantitative easing stands in stark contrast to the predominant approach, which has been an austerity policy, which keeps interest rates low in order to ensure price stability. Low interest rates reduce the effectiveness of monetary policy. In 2013, the Diet approved a 10.3 trillion yen fiscal stimulus package. The growth strategy has been slower to develop and includes structural changes in the labor market, healthcare, agriculture, and energy. Japan entered negotiations for the Trans-Pacific Partnership (TPP) as part of Abe's growth strategy. In June 2014, the cabinet approved several changes to labor regulations, pension fund investments, and corporate governance and tax policies. To encourage corporate investment and innovation, one proposal is to reduce the corporate tax from 35 percent to below 30 percent. For labor reforms, the Abe government is calling for greater gender equality and more foreign labor (Inman 2014).

The goals of Abenomics include moving away from the enduring deflation that has plagued Japan for more than a decade and instead reaching a 2 percent inflation target. The policies also hoped to spur public investment and reverse the trend of ongoing yen appreciation. At least initially, the bold monetary policy resulted in a depreciation of the yen and an increase in stock prices (Grimes 2013). Politically, however, inflation may be less popular since it will put an extra strain on people with fixed incomes, especially retirees, and decrease the purchasing power of current incomes. The stimulus package was meant to increase consumer demand. Its effectiveness will be weakened by the increases in the consumption tax. The structural reforms have been the slowest and most difficult policies to implement.

There are at least two major risks with Abenomics. Abe's drive to increase inflation might also lead to an increase in interest rates that could increase Japan's debt burden. Secondly, it is unclear whether LDP members or Kōmeitō politicians in coalition with the LDP will be willing to undertake the political risk of structural reform (Grimes 2013).

Conclusion: an economic prognosis

Despite all of Japan's economic challenges, it has the third largest GDP in the world. It remains a leader in automobiles and consumer electronics. It is also competitive in IT products and services. It has the highest life expectancy score and one of the highest rates of educational attainment among Organisation for Economic Co-operation and Development (OECD) countries (OECD 2014). However, Japan has had the second slowest per capita growth among G-7 countries since 1991. Japan's annual per capita growth rate has been 0.7 percent while the U.S.'s per capita growth rate has been 1.6 percent over the same time period (Butkiewicz 2012: 4). It sits in the middle of the 34 member countries of the OECD in terms of per capita income (OECD 2014: 5). It also performs comparatively poorly in terms of housing and work-life balance among OECD countries (OECD 2014: 5).

Several factors pose challenges for Japan's future economic growth. These factors include demographics, energy security, deficit financing, and lingering structural economic issues. Economic growth will be difficult to promote given the constraints of Japan's low birth rate and high life expectancy. With Japan's low birth rate, its population is projected to decline from 128 million in 2007 to 95 million in 2050 (Butkiewicz 2012: 2). Meanwhile, by 2055 life expectancy for women is expected to increase from 86 to 90 years and for men from 79 to 84 years. As a result of these trends, the government estimates that there will be less than two workers for every retiree. In the late 1990s, this ratio was closer to six workers for every retiree (Butkiewicz 2012: 3). Already from 1990 to 2010 the amount spent on social security has increased from 11 percent to 22 percent of GDP due to the aging population (OECD 2014: 8). Moreover, elderly people are more likely to save than spend. This trend impedes the government's attempt to spark domestic demand (Rosenbluth 2012: 20–21).

Energy security has always been a concern in Japan given its limited natural resources. This issue took on a new prominence following the Fukushima nuclear disaster. After the Fukushima incident, Japan's 50 nuclear power plants gradually were taken offline. Japan relied on nuclear power for about 30 percent of its energy supply. Since this time, Japan's demand for fossil fuels has increased significantly. The dramatic increase in natural gas and coal imports has been the primary cause behind recent trade deficits. The increased demand for electricity has resulted in higher prices as well as an increase in CO_2 emissions. This situation does not seem sustainable, but a consensus has not emerged on how best to secure Japan's energy security. The Nuclear Regulation Authority has approved five nuclear power plants for reopening and many more are under review (Patrick 2015). Even if these plants pass review, it is not clear if they will be brought back online. Prime Minister Abe's energy plan calls for a role for nuclear power, but public opposition remains high (Iwata 2014).

Deficit financing has been a growing problem since the bubble burst. The deficit has increased considerably during the last several decades given the dominance of the fiscal stimulus approach to economic recovery. The gross public debt has increased from 70 percent of GDP in 1992 to nearly 230 percent in 2014 (OECD 2014: 8). Both Prime Ministers Hashimoto and Koizumi attempted to reduce the deficit, but their approach was to decrease expenditures, not increase taxes. In the end, both of their attempts were stymied by recessions (Park 2011: 274). Currently, Japan is financing about 20 percent of its budget through borrowing; debt repayments account for 40 percent of the total budget (Park 2011: 273). This situation is even more dire given the demographic challenges Japan faces. The aging population means an increase in social security payments while the low birth rate will result in an ever-decreasing tax base.

Finally, several structural problems remain and impede growth. Inadequate daycare hampers the ability of women to work full time, an issue more fully considered in Chapter 9. The labor market's reliance on irregular workers is putting downward pressure on income and increasing the number of working poor. Little progress has been made on healthcare and pension reform. On the positive side, productivity is more connected to the bond and stock markets than to banks. This change makes it easier for investors to respond to new information. Companies are also more accountable to shareholders, something that puts positive pressure on efficiency (Lincoln 2011). Abenomics has given lip service to many of these problems, but decisive policies have not been implemented. The economic challenges Japan faces remain large. These issues are likely to dominate the policy agenda for several decades to come.

Notes

1 See Katz (1998, 2003) for a structural explanations for the bubble economy.

2 See Krugman (1999) for a policy explanation for the bubble economy.
3 Vogel cites Kikkawa (1998) as part of this school.

References

Arase, D. (2009) "Japan in 2008: A Prelude to Change?" *Asian Survey*, 49: 107–119.

Arase, D. (2010) "Japan in 2009: A Historical Election Year," *Asian Survey*, 50: 40–55.

Butkiewicz, L. (2012) "Implications of Japan's Changing Demographics," National Bureau of Asian Research. Available online at www.nbr.org/downloads/pdfs/ETA/ES_Japan_demograp hics_report.pdf (accessed 22 July 2014).

Cook, E. E. (2013) "Expectations of Failure: Maturity and Masculinity for Freeters in Contemporary Japan," *Political Science Japan Journal*, 16: 29–43.

Fiaola, A. (2005) "Japan Approves Postal Privatization," *The Washington Post.com*. Available online at www.washingtonpost.com/wp-dyn/content/article/2005/ 10/14/ AR2005101402163. html (accessed 22 July 2014).

Fujii, M. and Kawai, M. (2010) "Lessons from Japan's Banking Crisis, 1991–2005," *Asian Development Bank Institute Working Paper Series*, 222. Available online at www.adb.org/sites/ default/files/publication/156077/adbi-wp222.pdf (accessed 25 July 2016).

George Mulgan, A. (2011) "The Politics of Economic Reform," in A. Gaunder (ed.) *The Routledge Handbook of Japanese Politics*, London: Routledge.

Grimes, W. W. (2013) "Will Abenomics Restore Japanese Growth?" *NBR Analysis Brief*. June 25. Available online at www.nbr.org/publications/issue.aspx?id=286 (accessed 18 July 2014).

Inman, P. (2014) "Shinzo Abe Launches 'Third Arrow' of Japanese Economic Reform," *The Guardian.com*. June 24. Available online at www.theguardian.com/world/2014/jun/24/shinzo-a be-japan-economic-reform-corporation-tax (accessed 18 July 2014).

Iwata, M. (2014) "Safety Clearance for Japan Reactors Won't Guarantee Restarts," *The Wall Street Journal*, July 14. Available online at http://online.wsj.com/articles/safety-clearance- for-japan-reactors-wont-guarantee-restarts-1405340244 (accessed 21 July 2014).

Japan Echo (2006) "A Five-Year Economic Report Card," *Japan Echo*, 33: 1–4. Available online at www.japanecho.com/sum/2006/330512.html (accessed 22 July 2014).

Japan Macro Advisors (2016) "Japan Unemployment Rate." Available online at www.japanma croadvisors.com/page/category/economic-indicators/labor-markets/unemployment-rate/ (accessed 20 July 2016).

Katz, R. (1998) *Japan, the System that Soured: The Rise and Fall of the Japanese Economic Miracle*, Armonk, NY: M. E. Sharpe.

Katz, R. (2003) *Japan Phoenix: The Long Road to Economic Revival*, Armonk, NY: M. E. Sharpe.

Kikkawa, M. (1998) *Manee haisen* [The Money War Defeat], Tokyo: Bungei Shujū.

Krugman, P. (1999) "It's Baaack: Japan's Slump and the Return of the Liquidity Trap," *Brookings Papers on Economic Activity*, 2: 137–205.

Leheny, D. (2006) *Think Global, Fear Local: Sex, Violence and Anxiety in Contemporary Japan*, Ithaca, NY: Cornell University Press.

Lincoln, E. J. (2011) "The Heisei Economy: Puzzles, Problems, Prospects," *Journal of Japanese Studies*, 37: 351–375.

Miura, M. (2012) *Welfare Through Work: Conservative Idea, Partisan Dynamics and Social Protection in Japan*, Ithaca, NY: Cornell University Press.

Noble, G. W. (2006) "Koizumi and Neo-liberal Economic Reform," *Social Science Japan*, 34: 6–9.

Noble, G. W. (2011) "The Evolution of the Japanese Policymaking System," in A. Gaunder (ed.) *The Routledge Handbook of Japanese Politics*, London: Routledge.

OECD (2014) "Japan: Advancing the Third Arrow for a Resilient Economy and Inclusive Growth," *Better Policies Series: Japan 2014*, April. Available online at www.oecd.org/japan/ 2014.04_ JAPAN_EN.pdf (accessed 22 July 2014).

Ohno, K. (n.d.) "The Bubble Burst and Recession, 1990-." Available online at www.grips.ac.jp/teacher/oono/hp/lecture_J/lec13.htm (accessed 20 July 2016).

Park, G. (2011) "The Politics of Scarcity: Fixing Japan's Public Finances," in A. Gaunder (ed.) *The Routledge Handbook of Japanese Politics*, London: Routledge.

Patrick, H. (2015) "Japan's Post-Fukushima Energy Challenge," *East Asia Forum*. Available online at www.eastasiaforum.org/2015/11/23/japans-post-fukushima-energy-challenge/ (accessed 21 July 2016).

Posen, A. (1998) *Restoring Japan's Economic Growth*, Washington, DC: Institute for International Economics.

Rosenbluth, F. M. (2012) "Japan in 2011: Cataclysmic Crisis and Chronic Deflation," *Asian Survey*, 52: 15–27.

Schoppa, L. J. (2011) "Path Dependency in the Evolution of Japan's Party System since 1993," in L. J. Schoppa (ed.) *The Evolution of Japan's Party System: Politics and Policy in an Era of Institutional Change*, Toronto: University of Toronto Press.

Uchiyama, Y. (2010) *Koizumi and Japanese Politics: Reform Strategies and Leadership Style*, London: Routledge.

Vogel, S. K. (2006) *Japan Remodeled: How Government and Industry are Reforming Japanese Capitalism*, Ithaca, NY: Cornell University Press.

Vogel, S. K. and Zysman, J. (2002) "Technology," in S. K. Vogel (ed.) *U.S.-Japan Relations in a Changing World*, Washington, DC: Brookings Institution Press.

9 Policymaking

The policymaking process was fairly consistent in the 1955 system of LDP dominance. It has experienced some change since the 1990s due to electoral reform, administrative reform, and structural reform. This chapter focuses on the role and interactions of the key actors in the policymaking process. These actors include the bureaucracy, politicians, and interest groups. The courts have played a more limited role. The role of civil society organizations is considered in Chapter 10.

Building on the overview of the policymaking process, this chapter considers policy issues concerning women and immigration. These policy issue areas illustrate how structures provide opportunities and constraints for policy innovation. The discussion also addresses how and why the salience of these issues has changed over time.

Overview of the policymaking process

While policy initiatives have varied considerably during the postwar period, the policymaking process itself was quite stable, especially from the early 1960s to the early 2000s (Noble 2011). The main actors in the policymaking process included the bureaucracy, political parties, and interest groups. In addition, the prime minister and the cabinet as well as advisory councils often influenced the process.

The relative weight of each actor's influence in the policymaking process is contested and varied to a certain degree by issue area. Indeed, several different explanations for policymaking described Japan variously as Japan, Inc., the Capitalist Developmental State, New Japan, Inc., and Patterned Pluralism (Johnson 1982, 1987; Pempel 1987; Muramatsu and Krauss 1987). Despite the various contested views of policymaking, some general trends in the policymaking process can be observed.

Under the 1955 system, the LDP was the dominant political party. Limited support staff, however, circumvented politicians from taking the primary role in drafting policy. Instead, the LDP played an important role in delegating drafting legislation to the bureaucracy. The LDP was more directly engaged in proposals that involved pork or patronage such as public works. Private interests often influenced both politicians and bureaucrats. The relationship between bureaucrats, politicians, and private interests in some respects resembles an "iron triangle" as seen in American politics. In Japan, however, numerous iron triangles existed around any issue, making the process more similar to issue networks than a simple triangle (Campbell 1989; Curtis 1999).

The bureaucracy played a central role in drafting legislation. The bureaucracy's power in the policymaking process comes from its command of information and expertise (Curtis 1999: 60). The bureaucracy tended to draft policy using vague language, and then it added content during the implementation phase (Noble 2011). As detailed in Chapter 4, the bureaucracy is an elite institution in Japan, similar in strength and prestige to the French bureaucracy. Bureaucratic ministries attract the best and the brightest from Japanese universities. Like other professions in Japan, entrance into the bureaucracy requires passing a very demanding exam. The success rate on ministry exams is quite small.

Civil servants tend to spend their entire careers in one ministry. This practice increases the tendencies toward sectionalism between bureaucratic ministries. Politicians and interest groups have been known to exploit this sectionalism playing one ministry off another to get a desired policy result. Still, protection of turf, the area of authority of a bureaucratic ministry, has played a prominent role in Japanese politics.

Ministries and agencies often employ advisory councils (shingikai) to aid in drafting legislation. Advisory councils usually include professionals and academics with expertise in the policy area. Advisory councils might also include representatives from those touched by the policy coming from industry, civil society, social movements, or interest groups. Chapter 11 details how prime ministers have convened advisory councils to provide additional input into policy areas of particular interest. Prime Minister Nakasone in particular used advisory councils to achieve policy success.

The majority of legislation submitted under LDP dominance was cabinet bills. Policy was drafted by bureaucrats in consultation with politicians and considered by both the LDP's Policy Affairs Research Council (PARC) and Executive Council before being submitted to the cabinet for approval to move on to the Diet (Gaunder 2007: 124). The PARC was the main forum for policy debate and policy formulation under the 1955 system. It was particularly strong from the 1960s to the late 1980s. The PARC is divided into sections (bukai), which roughly correspond to certain bureaucratic ministries and the committee structure in the Diet. In the 1980s, there were as many as 17 different divisions.

Under the 1955 system, LDP Diet members were assigned to certain PARC committees (Curtis 1999: 201). LDP members were automatically assigned to the PARC committees that corresponded to their two Diet committees. Each LDP politician could be assigned to two additional PARC committees. Appointments were based on seniority and factional affiliation. Many politicians chose to participate on PARC committees that allowed them to influence areas of interest to their constituents (Curtis 1999: 201; Krauss and Pekkanen 2011: 156–157). Politicians who became specialists in certain areas were known as zoku giin. Zoku literally translates as "tribe." These politicians worked with bureaucrats and private interests to secure the passage of bills that favored their constituents. The most powerful zoku included the policy areas of agriculture and forestry, construction, and commerce and industry (Krauss and Pekkanen 2011: 184).

Bills are discussed in relevant PARC committees. The chairs and vice chairs of the PARC divisions serve as policy gatekeepers. The PARC also afforded backbenchers considerable influence, something that contributed to the fragmented policymaking in the LDP (Krauss and Pekkanen 2011). Opponents to party initiatives can use this structure to slow down, if not completely halt, progress on legislation. Participation on the PARC committees provides opportunities for credit claiming and fundraising as politicians can pursue the interests of their district and key interest groups.

While there are some similarities between the PARC divisions and the U.S. Congressional committee structure, these similarities are more related to structure than power. U.S. committees have a much stronger infrastructure to support crafting policy by members of Congress. Japanese politicians rely almost exclusively on bureaucrats (Curtis 1988: 113).

After the Policy Affairs Research Council approves policies, senior LDP politicians who serve on the Policy Advisory Council (Seisaku Shingikai) review them. This group then sends the proposals to the Executive Council, which is made up of LDP party leaders. The Executive Council sends approved policies to the cabinet that then introduces the proposals to the Diet (Krauss and Pekkanen 2011: 157–158). Because Japan is a parliamentary system the legislative and executive branches are fused. This means that most bills submitted to the Diet are cabinet bills, not bills of individual politicians.

During the period of LDP dominance, Diet deliberations were more performative. The real debate and discussion occurred in the PARC divisions and subcommittees. Once the cabinet submitted a bill, its passage was secure since the LDP had a clear majority in both houses until 1989 when it lost its majority in the upper house. Since parties vote down party lines in parliamentary systems, a majority guaranteed the passage of legislation.

The LDP, however, did not want to have the appearance of tyranny of the majority. As a result, it often took opposition interests into consideration, at least to some extent, especially after the contentious 1960s. These discussions, however, did not occur in Diet committees. Instead, the negotiations between the opposition and the LDP went on behind closed doors. The negotiations focused less on actual policy and more on the process of moving the legislation through the Diet. As Gerald Curtis explains, "the role of Diet committees in this system was to serve as formal agencies confirming informal understandings reached elsewhere" (Curtis 1999: 118).

When the LDP split and lost power in 1994, a policymaking vacuum emerged. This vacuum reflected the fact that most of the institutional structure for policymaking rested with the PARC that was an LDP institution. The rest of policy negotiations were based on personal relationships among bureaucrats, politicians, and private interests. As the opposition had been locked out of government for 38 years, it did not have access to the bureaucracy and its expertise. It struggled to pursue policy during its short tenure in 1993–4.

The DPJ experienced similar policymaking difficulties in 2009. The DPJ actually attacked the bureaucracy and tried to elevate the role of politicians in the process. As detailed later in this chapter, this move backfired.

Japanese prime ministers have had varying levels of success influencing the policymaking process. Chapter 11 details the constraints of resources of prime ministers. Briefly, the constraints on executive leadership are more pronounced in parliamentary systems where the prime minister is the first among equals on the cabinet. Most major legislation requires unanimous cabinet approval. This practice gives cabinet ministers significant influence. A cabinet minister can effectively veto legislation through this process (Noble 2011). The fact that the prime minister is selected from the majority party or majority coalition reduces the external barriers to policy passage. Prime ministers still have to get the government's backing before moving forward with legislation. Prime ministers, like other politicians, do not have significant resources for the formulation of policy and also tend to rely on the bureaucracy. Successful prime ministers have used informal resources such public popularity, media support, and personal ties to push their policy agendas (Shinoda 2000).

The courts have had limited influence on the policymaking process. According to the Constitution, the Supreme Court has the power of the judicial review. The Supreme

Court, however, has rarely used this power to rule on the constitutionality of laws. Instead, the courts have focused on preserving civil liberties and civil rights. As we saw in Chapter 4, the Court did declare apportionment provisions in the Public Office Election Law unconstitutional. It did not invalidate election results based on this decision. Litigation has played a role in raising the profile of several important issues including women's employment rights, social discrimination, and industrial pollution (Marshall 2011). As we shall see in Chapter 10, social movements related to the high-profile pollution cases in the 1970s effectively used the courts as a tool to influence policy. The courts, however, limited rulings to specific cases. These rulings did prompt the Diet to react and increase industrial regulations, something that negatively affected core LDP constituents. In this way, the courts have influenced the policy agenda of the Diet at times on important issues.

Reforms that influenced the policymaking process

The policymaking process was relatively stable under the 1955 system of LDP dominance. A series of reforms beginning in the 1980s, however, altered the dynamics of the policymaking process. These reforms included administrative reforms in the 1980s and 1990s, electoral reform in 1994, and structural reforms in the 2000s.

Administrative reforms refer to policy changes that affect the bureaucracy. The goals of administrative reform can be to influence the power, influence, efficiency, or capacity of the bureaucracy. Administrative reform can also be pursued for financial reasons.

Two successful attempts at administrative reform increased the power of politicians and the prime minister vis-à-vis the bureaucracy. The first successful administrative reform came in the early 1980s under the leadership of Prime Minister Nakasone. In 1981, Prime Minister Nakasone authorized the Ad Hoc Commission on Administrative Reform (known in Japanese as Rincho) to explore reforms. The calls for administrative reform came in the context of increased government debt following the oil shocks of the 1970s as well as the money and politics scandals under Prime Minister Tanaka. The main result of this round of administrative reform was the privatization of Japan National Railways (JNR), Nippon Telephone and Telegraph (NTT), and Japan Tobacco (JT). The Management and Coordination Agency (MCA) was also created through the merger of the Administrative Management Agency and the Office of the Prime Minister. The creation of the MCA was meant to increase the resources at the disposal of the prime minister to influence policy and monitor the bureaucracy (Bevaqua 1997). The privatization of JNR weakened the opposition, especially the Socialists, that had strong ties to public sector labor unions (Samuels 2003).

Prime Minister Hashimoto successfully led the second major efforts at administrative reform that also included changes to Cabinet Law. These reforms influenced the relative power of certain actors in the policymaking process. In particular, these reforms were meant to increase the power of politicians vis-à-vis the bureaucrats. The reforms also directly influenced the power of the prime minister. One of the most ambitious parts of this administrative reform effort aimed to decrease the size of the bureaucracy. In fact, the final legislation nearly cut the number of bureaucratic ministries in half. These reforms also clarified the power of the prime minister to lead the cabinet. The size of the cabinet was decreased while the size of the staff to support the prime minister was increased. The hope was that a smaller cabinet would promote more unified decision making. Four advisory councils were established in the cabinet, including the Council on Economic and Fiscal Policy (CEFP), which would end up playing a critical role in the postal reform process under Prime Minister Koizumi (Noble 2011). These reforms also limited the ability of bureaucrats to act as witnesses on technical matters during Diet deliberations. Instead, politicians are responsible for responding to questions from fellow members of parliament (Shinoda 2003: 24–25).

Prime Minister Koizumi was the first prime minister to utilize these administrative reforms. The reforms appeared to dramatically increase the power of the prime minister. The administrative reforms certainly increased the resources available to prime ministers to influence the policymaking process, but the lack of success of the three prime ministers who followed prime minister Koizumi (Abe, Fukuda, and Asō) illustrated that some of Prime Minister Koizumi's success was related to his own personal attributes as a leader (Gaunder 2007). Koizumi still faced obstacles, such as the ability of backbenchers and zoku to influence the policy agenda. He used the CEFP as well as his own powers as prime minister to pursue his agenda.

Electoral reform passed in 1994 prior to Hashimoto's administrative reforms. While not directly related to the policymaking process, electoral reform did influence the landscape of policymaking in Japan. In particular, as we have seen in other chapters, electoral reform changed the dynamics of party competition as well as the relative strengths of politicians and parties. Intra-party competition lessened and the power of party leaders increased. Coalition governments became the norm. The LDP was no longer the sole party involved in the policymaking process. It still has been in government for most of the post-electoral reform period, but it has been somewhat constrained by junior coalition partners.

When the DPJ came to office in 2009 it took action to significantly change the policymaking process. The goal of reform was to make the Japanese policymaking system more similar to the British Westminster system. The prime minister and the cabinet are at the center of the Westminster system of policymaking. The main motivations of the DPJ's reforms were to challenge the power of the bureaucracy and place politicians at the center of the policymaking process. The goal was to eliminate the constraints prime ministers faced in pursuing their policymaking agendas. According to George Mulgan, the DPJ's attempt at structural reform involved several steps, including "eliminating the intervention of the majority party in policymaking, destroying the party-bureaucracy nexus, and reversing the bureaucracy-led cabinet system" (George Mulgan 2011: 267).

Some of the reforms focused on the party, some focused on the cabinet, and some focused on the bureaucracy. Party-level reforms included the elimination of the party's policy research council and tax commission. More generally, the DPJ limited the submission of private member bills by DPJ Diet members. The goal was to limit the influence of party backbenchers. As we have seen during the period of LDP dominance, backbenchers could use the PARC to bog down or even circumvent legislation. Thus, in comparison to the UK model, the party held much more influence over policy.

In the Cabinet Office, the DPJ created and replaced the Council for Economic and Fiscal Policy with the National Strategy Bureau (NSB) and a Government Revitalization Unit (GRU). The National Strategy Bureau was charged with prioritizing policies and increasing the flexibility in the budgeting process. The GRU focused on promoting transparency and accountability in budgeting. Both bodies were meant to bolster the influence of politicians and decrease the reliance on the bureaucracy (George Mulgan 2011: 270).

The DPJ increased restrictions on the participation of bureaucrats in Diet proceedings. Bureaucrats could no longer testify on regular policy issues; instead, politicians would testify. Politicians were to become the policy experts. Under the LDP, policy-making had been a bottom up process with the bureaucrats playing the primary role in policy formulation. In the new system, the idea was that policy formation would be top down, more like the UK system. Bureaucrats are still involved, providing information for cabinet ministers. To this end, in each bureaucratic ministry, the DPJ made the minister, senior vice minister, and parliamentary secretary in charge of policy forma-tion. In addition, the cabinet's agenda was no longer decided by administrative vice ministers but by a cabinet-level committee (George Mulgan 2011: 269).

Finally, the DPJ limited the interactions between bureaucrats and Diet members. Bureaucrats could only meet with ministers and vice ministers (Noble 2011: 257). This final reform attacked the subgovernment relations between zoku politicians and bureaucrats. DPJ zoku were not allowed to emerge – only ministers or vice ministers could meet with bureaucrats (George Mulgan 2011: 268–269).

In the end, the DPJ's attempt to reform the policymaking process failed. The reforms alienated the bureaucracy and impeded the ability of politicians and bureau-crats to work together. The bureaucrats disengaged and in some instances were actively hostile toward the DPJ. This situation came to a dramatic head with the triple disaster (earthquake, tsunami, and nuclear incident in 2011). The new policymaking apparatus was not equipped to respond to the disaster. The DPJ looked inept and eventually the fallout from its policymaking and leadership failure would lead to the party's dramatic defeat in the 2012 lower house election (Hrebenar and Haraguchi 2015: 180).

Policy issues

This section explores the policymaking process in action. Numerous policies could be selected and discussed, and each would have its own unique aspects. This section dis-cusses a set of different policies related to the workplace as well as Japan's aging, low fertility society. Specifically, it will consider the goal of increasing women in the workplace and how to achieve this goal as well as an alternative to the labor issue – immigration. These policy issues illustrate the various strategies, constraints, and opportunities that might emerge when navigating the policymaking landscape. These examples are meant to give a sense of how the various actors interact to supplement the bird's eye view of the policymaking process given above.

Women

Policies that affect women are wide and varied. The next chapter explores the women's movement and discusses the role it played in the passage of the Equal Employment Oppor-tunity Law in 1986. This law encouraged companies to promote anti-discrimination against women in hiring, job assignments, and promotions and prohibited such dis-crimination in dismissals and training. It also sought to protect women from over-time or extra shifts. Revisions in 1997 made anti-discrimination provisions mandatory and added some sanctions if companies did not comply. The 1997 revisions framed anti-discrimination in terms of affirmative action. Revisions in 2006 extended the antidiscrimination provisions to both women and men (Schoppa 2006: 174–179).

More recent policy debates have focused on "Womenomics" (umano-mikusu) and 30 percent women in the civil sector, private sector, and politics by 2020. The Abe administration began highlighting these issues in 2012. Scholars and financial analysts have been touting the untapped potential of female labor in Japan for decades. Many contend that Japan could increase its GDP considerably by more effectively and comprehensively engaging women in the workplace. This notion is particularly appealing to Abe in the context of structural reform.

Womenomics and the 30 percent by 2020 goal are connected. The Third Basic Plan for Gender Equality released by the Gender Equality Bureau and approved by the cabinet in December 2010 featured the 30 percent by 2020 goal. This goal called for increasing female involvement in leadership roles in the civil service sector, private sector, and politics by 2020. The goal is related to the UN's emphasis on critical mass. Critical mass asserts that once women reach a certain percentage of a body, somewhere between 20 and 35 percent, the culture of the organization changes and results in more significant representation for women (Kanter 1977).

The 30 percent by 2020 goal is an ambitious one for Japan. In 2009, just prior to the release of the Third Basic Plan, women only comprised 16.7 percent of the lower house of parliament and held 6.5 percent of managerial positions (Gender Equality Bureau 2010). As Table 9.1 illustrates, the goal is particularly ambitious given the modest increasing trend of female representation in the Diet over the last two decades. The Third Basic Plan came out under the DPJ. Prime Minister Abe, however, latched on to the 30 percent by 2020 goal in this plan upon taking office.

Ironically, a key policy proposal regarding increasing female participation in the workplace died due to the dissolution of the lower house for the snap election. To further its goal of 30 percent by 2020, the LDP had proposed a bill to require companies with more than 300 employees to develop plans to promote women in the workplace. The bill included the promotion of numerical targets (*Yomiuri*, 1 December 2014, web). This policy proposal addressed Abe's goal of increasing female work participation from 68 percent to 73 percent by 2020. This increase would help improve Japan's performance on gender equality indexes. Japan is ranked 104th in gender equality by the World Economic Forum (*CSMonitor.com*, 11 November 2014).

Table 9.1 Number of female members of the lower house (% of women in party caucus)

	1996	2000	2003	2005	2009	2012	2014
LDP	4 (1.7%)	8 (3.4%)	9 (3.8%)	26 (8.8%)	8 (6.7%)	23 (7.9%)	25 (8.6%)
DPJ	3 (5.8%)	6 (4.7%)	15 (8.5%)	7 (6.2%)	40 (13%)	3 (5.2%)	9 (12.3%)
Komeito	n/a	3 (9.7%)	4 (11.8%)	4 (12.9%)	3 (14.3%)	3 (9.6%)	3 (8.6%)
JCP	4 (15%)	4 (20%)	2 (22%)	2 (22%)	1 (11%)	1 (12.5%)	6 (28.6%)
SDP	3 (20%)	10 (53%)	3 (50%)	4 (57%)	2 (29%)	0 (0%)	0 (0%)
Total*	23 (4.6%)	35 (7.3%)	34 (7.1%)	43 (9%)	54 (11.3%)	38 (7.9%)	45 (9.5%)

Source: Ministry of Internal Affairs and Communications (MIC), available online at www.soumu.go.jp/senkyo/senkyo_s/data/ (accessed February 1, 2015); Interparliamentary Union, available online at www.ipu.org/ (accessed March 16, 2015).

Note: * Total includes women elected from all political parties, including smaller parties and independents not listed on the table. The percentage that follows represents the total percentage of women in the Diet.

According to the 2013 White Paper on Gender Equality, women only hold 11 percent managerial positions (Cabinet Office 2013). To address the reality of the low percentage of women in management requires more serious structural reform. This reform to increase female participation would need to consider daycare and elderly care provisions, working conditions, and compensation.

Daycare

Daycare provision has been an important issue that has entered the Japanese policymaking process on numerous occasions in the last several decades. Daycare provision is related to issues that affect women and work as well as Japan's aging population and low fertility problem. In 2014, the fertility rate stood at 1.42 percent (MHLW 2015: 11). At the same time, the portion of the population over 65 continues to grow. It reached an all-time high of 33.8 million, which constitutes 26.7 percent of the population. These trends have been apparent for decades, but few policies have emerged to effectively address the problem.

The problem is multifaceted. One issue is the declining proportion of the Japanese in the workforce. Two potential solutions include increasing female participation in the workforce or increasing the number of immigrant workers. Womenomics discussed above partially addresses the woman and work issue. Adding in the declining fertility rate, however, complicates the pictures. The government has tried to incentivize childbirth with limited success.

Another way to increase female workforce participation is to increase the support for female professionals to have children through daycare provision. The Japanese government has pursued policies in this vein since the early 1990s when the potential impact of declining fertility rates became more salient. The first and second Angel policies in 1994 and 1999 along with the Plus One initiative in 2002 all focused on expanding daycare services. The first and second Angel plans set benchmarks for increasing the number of spaces in daycare centers, expanding the hours of daycare centers and providing services for sick children. There were also provisions for expanding community centers that provide child-rearing services as well as after-school programs. These initiatives had little impact on convincing women who had exited the workforce to stay in the workforce. The policies more directly applied to the 15 to 20 percent of mothers who had already chosen to stay in full-time jobs. Bureaucrats created these policies based on feedback from mothers and childcare providers, not women who might be making a choice between work and motherhood; the women they talked to had already made a choice. As a result, these policies had limited effect (Schoppa 2006).

Both the LDP and DPJ have attempted to increase daycare capacity by merging daycare centers and kindergartens. The LDP and DPJ governments both faced similar constraints. In 2011, the DPJ proposed to eliminate waiting lists for daycare centers by merging daycare centers and kindergartens over a ten-year period beginning in 2013. This proposal was meant to leverage the fact that kindergartens are under capacity while daycare centers have excess demand. In May 2009, kindergartens were at 69 percent occupancy while the number of children on waiting lists sat over 25,000. The waiting lists do not reflect the fact that a large number of people exit before putting their name on a list (Takahara 2010). The DPJ promoted this policy as a way to support working mothers with children. The LDP made a similar proposal in 2006.

Neither party was able to see the legislation through to passage. The major obstacle both parties faced was the bureaucracy. The Ministry of Education, Culture, Sports, Science, and Technology (MEXT) oversees kindergartens while the Ministry of Health, Labor, and Welfare (MHLW) administers daycare centers. Neither ministry was interested in reducing their influence; each ministry was invested in protecting its turf. Politicians who had strong ties to either ministry lobbied against the merger. Kindergarten administrators also did not wholeheartedly support the proposal. Many expressed concerns that a merger would lead to longer hours of operation and different educational content (Takahara 2010). In the end, the DPJ backed away from its merger proposal. Instead, it moved to supporting subsidies for daycare centers and kindergartens that chose to merge independently (Takahara 2011). This policy outcome illustrates the importance of policy networks and the significance of veto points in the Japanese political arena (Gaunder 2012).[1]

Immigration

Immigration policies have economic, cultural, and political ramifications. From an economic standpoint, there are both costs and benefits to promoting immigration. On the positive side, more open immigration might be a way to increase skilled labor. It can also provide labor for jobs that native citizens do not want to do. This influx of labor can have a strong impact in countries with an aging population. Critics of more open immigration policies worry that immigrants might place a larger burden on the state, especially if they are eligible for welfare benefits such as unemployment, healthcare, and education. The influx of immigrants also is coupled with fears that immigrants might take all the "good" jobs or drive down wages for all workers. The cultural ramifications are related to issues of national identity. Opponents to immigration fight to preserve ethnic homogeneity. Japan's initial response to labor shortages was to mechanize production and improve efficiency. Many companies also moved production overseas to take advantage of lower wages (Haig 2011). Moreover, the government has also promoted the notion that foreigners are dangerous, further cultivating resistance to foreign immigrants (Shipper 2005).

Politically several groups have a stake in immigration policy including bureaucratic ministries, political parties, local governments, citizens, and activist groups. Under the 1955 system of LDP dominance, the LDP and the Ministry of Justice (MOJ) had almost exclusive control over immigration policy. Since the 1990s, the landscape has become more pluralistic with several actors working as key veto points in the policymaking process. From a foreign relations perspective many countries in Asia, including the Philippines, China, and Thailand, would like to see more openness to immigrant labor.

In the postwar period Japan's immigration policies have been on the stricter side from a comparative perspective. Japanese citizenship is determined by blood not by birth in the country. It is very difficult to gain Japanese citizenship if you are not a Japanese national. For example, children of guestworkers cannot become citizens.

Immigration policy also involves policy debates between bureaucratic ministries. Policy priorities often vary with ministries with closer ties to business such as MITI (later METI) favoring more flexibility and the MOJ and Ministry of Labor (MOL) being more conservative. The MOJ, in particular, resisted policies to support foreign labor during Japan's rapid economic growth, often citing a connection to crime (Shipper 2005). The foundation for immigration policy after rapid growth was the 1990

Immigration Control and Refugee Recognition Act (ICRRA). ICRRA was written by the MOJ in consultation with the LDP and 17 other ministries (Haig 2011: 229). This policy maintained high barriers for immigration to Japan. It did allow for several "side door" opportunities for entrance into the country. These side doors included the Industrial Training and Technical Internship Programs. The initial motivation for these programs was to provide a mechanism to train foreign workers from developing countries among Japan's neighbors. These workers could eventually return to their home countries and promote development. In reality, these programs became a legal way to import manual labor to Japan through the side door (Haig 2011).

The ICRRA focused on migration. Another key component of immigration policy is integration. Integration policy outlines how immigrants are brought into society. Several bureaucratic ministries have an interest in an integration policy including the Ministry of Health, Labor, and Welfare, the Ministry of Economy, Trade, and Industry, the Ministry of Education, Culture, Sports, and Science, the Ministry of Justice, and the Ministry of Land, Infrastructure, and Transportation. Local governments with large proportions of resident aliens have promoted integration policies. These policies have included the provision of social services and local voting rights for non-Japanese residents.

Early on, the local and national government disagreed over the government's role in the provision of social services to non-Japanese residents. These tensions were resolved in the early 1980s when the national government conceded that the provision of social services to all legal foreign residents was necessary after Japan became a signatory of the UN Convention Relating to the Status of Refugees (Haig 2011). From this time on, legal foreign residents had access to public services. Nongovernmental organizations have played a significant role in additional service provision to the immigrant community. These services include information about marriage, divorce, and lodgings. Some unions offer consultations regarding labor disputes. Lawyers' associations are also a source of advice for a nominal fee (Shipper 2005).

Debate over voting rights for non-Japanese residents has also been an area of tension between the national and local governments. In 1995, the Japanese Supreme Court stepped into the policymaking process and clarified that granting local voting rights for non-Japanese nationals did not violate the Constitution. Opposition parties have submitted several bills to this effect. To date, national bills have failed. While the DPJ supported voting rights for permanent residents, it was not in power long enough to see any legislation passed. At the local level, several municipalities have granted non-Japanese citizens the right to vote on referendums (Kondo 2002). Maibaracho was the first municipality to pass a referendum in 2002. Over 200 municipalities followed suit. This movement to expand voting to non-Japanese citizens coincided with measures to merge local government (Mie 2014). Many politicians at the national level, especially in the LDP, worry about extending voting rights to non-citizens, even on local matters. LDP literature has encouraged local LDP chapters to oppose referendums for local voting rights for non-Japanese. Many in the LDP argue that extending the franchise can dilute the sovereignty of Japanese citizens. Foreigners who pay Japanese taxes counter that they should have a larger say in community issues (Mie 2014).

Overall, immigration policy illustrates the complexities of policymaking that involves a variety of actors and interests. The multitude of actors and interests often slow policy development and passage.

Conclusion

The policymaking process in Japan was fairly stable under the period of LDP dominance. With the split of the LDP, the change in the electoral system, and the changes in the political party composition, several administrative reforms have been implemented which have increased the role of some political actors, particularly party leaders and the prime minister. The courts have continued to play a relatively limited role. The passage of the Information Disclosure Act has increased the resources available to nonprofit organizations (NPOs) and nongovernmental organizations (NGOs) to be involved in the policymaking process, something that will be discussed in further detail in Chapter 10.

The discussion of policies related to an aging, low fertility society and immigration integration illustrate the various resources and constraints political actors have to influence policy outcomes. With daycare provision, interests of key ministries have impeded both the LDP and the DPJ efforts to increase access to childcare. With immigration integration policies, in particular, strains between the national and local level are exposed. Turf wars among bureaucratic ministries are also apparent.

Note

1 The discussion of daycare policy draws on Gaunder (2012).

References

Bevaqua, R. (1997) "Administrative Reform: Searching for the 'Hashimoto Vision'," *Japan Policy Research Institute Working Paper*, 36. Available online at www.jpri.org/publications/workingpapers/wp36.html (accessed 15 March 2016).

Cabinet Office (2013) "White Paper on Gender Equality 2013." Available online at www.gender.go.jp/english_contents/about_danjo/whitepaper/pdf/2013–2001.pdf (accessed 18 February 2015).

Campbell, J. C. (1989) "Bureaucratic Primacy: Japanese Policy Communities in an American Perspective," *Governance*, 2: 86–94.

Curtis, G. L. (1988) *The Japanese Way of Politics*, New York: Columbia University Press.

Curtis, G. L. (1999) *The Logic of Japanese Politics*, New York: Columbia University Press.

Gaunder, A. (2007) *Political Reform in Japan: Leadership Looming Large*, London: Routledge.

Gaunder, A. (2012) "The DPJ and Women: The Limited Impact of the 2009 Alternation of Power on Policy and Governance," *Journal of East Asian Studies*, 12: 441–466.

Gender Equality Bureau (2010) "The Third Basic Plan for Gender Equality." Available online at www.gender.go.jp/english_contents/pr_act/pub/pamphlet/women-and-men13/pdf/2–3.pdf (accessed 18 February 2015).

George Mulgan, A. (2011) "The Politics of Economic Reform," in A. Gaunder (ed.) *The Routledge Handbook of Japanese Politics*, London: Routledge.

Haig, K. (2011) "Japanese Immigration Policy," in A. Gaunder (ed.) *The Routledge Handbook of Japanese Politics*, London: Routledge.

Hrebenar, R. J. and Haraguchi, K. (2015) "The Fall of the DPJ and Return of the LDP Power: The December 2012 House Elections," in R. J. Hrebenar and A. Nakamura (eds) *Party Politics in Japan: Political Chaos and Stalemate in the Twenty-first Century*, London: Routledge.

Johnson, C. (1982) *MITI and the Japanese Miracle*, Stanford, CA: Stanford University Press.

Johnson, C. (1987) "Political Institutions and Economic Performance: The Government-Business Relationship in Japan, South Korea and Taiwan," in F. C. Deyo (ed.) *The Political Economy of the New Asian Industrialism*, Ithaca, NY: Cornell University Press.

Kanter, R. M. (1977) "Some Effects of Proportions on Group Life: Skewed Sex Ratios and Responses to Token Women," *American Journal of Sociology*, 82: 965–990.

Kondo, A. (2002) "The Development of Immigration Policy in Japan," *Asian and Pacific Migration Journal*, 11: 415–436.

Krauss, E. S. and Pekkanen, R. J. (2011) *The Rise and Fall of Japan's LDP: Political Party Organization as Historical Institutions*, Ithaca, NY: Cornell University Press.

Marshall, J. D. (2011) "Democratizing the Law in Japan," in A. Gaunder (ed.) *The Routledge Handbook of Japanese Politics*, London: Routledge.

MHLW (2015) "Vital Statistics in Japan – The Latest Trends." Available online at www.mhlw.go.jp/english/database/db-hw/dl/81-1a2en.pdf (accessed 7 July 2016).

Mie, A. (2014) "Debate on Foreigner Voting Rights Reignites Ahead of 2020 Olympics," *Japan Times*. Available online at www.japantimes.co.jp/news/2014/08/20/national/politics-diplomacy/debate-foreigner-voting-rights-reignites-ahead-2020-olympics/#.VthrFPkrK8p (accessed 3 March 2016).

Muramatsu, M. and Krauss, E. (1987) "The Conservative Policy Line and the Development of Patterned Pluralism," in K. Yamamura and Y. Yasuba (eds) *The Political Economy of Japan*, Stanford, CA: Stanford University Press.

Noble, G. W. (2011) "The Evolution of the Japanese Policymaking System," in A. Gaunder (ed.) *The Routledge Handbook of Japanese Politics*, London: Routledge.

Pempel, T. J. (1987) "The Unbundling of 'Japan, Inc.': The Changing Dynamics of Japanese Policy Formation," in K. Pyle (ed.) *The Trade Crisis: How Will Japan Respond?* Seattle: Society for Japanese Studies, University of Washington.

Samuels, R. J. (2003) "Leadership and Political Change in Japan: The Case of the Second Rincho," *Journal of Japanese Studies*, 29: 1–31.

Schoppa, L. J. (2006) *Race for the Exits: The Unraveling of Japan's System of Social Protections*, Ithaca, NY: Cornell University Press.

Shinoda, T. (2000) *Leading Japan: The Role of the Prime Minister*, Westport, CT: Praeger.

Shinoda, T. (2003) "Koizumi's Top-Down Leadership in the Anti-Terrorist Legislation: the Impact of Political Institutional Changes," *SAIS Review*, 23: 19–34.

Shipper, A. (2005) "Criminals or Victims: The Politics of Illegal Foreigners in Japan," *The Journal of Japanese Studies*, 31: 299–327.

Takahara, K. (2010) "Kindergartens, Day Care Centers May Merge," *Japan Times*, November 17. Available online at http://search.japantimes.co.jp/cgi-bin/nn20101117i1.html (accessed 29 December 2010).

Takahara, K. (2011) "Preschool, Day Care Integration Plan Eases," *Japan Times*, January 25. Available online at http://search.japantimes.co.jp/cgi-bin/nn20110125a5.html (accessed 15 June 2011).

10 State–society relations

This chapter explores state–society relations in Japan. In political science, the state is traditionally defined as "a set of ongoing institutions that develops and administers laws and generates and implements public policies in a specific territory" (Drogus and Orvis 2012: 39). While state and government are often used interchangeably, they are distinguished by the continuous existence of the institutions of the state. Governments come and go, but the state is more constant. Here, society is shorthand for civil society. Like many concepts in political science, civil society has a myriad of definitions. It can be defined more broadly or more narrowly, but in general it refers to the realm between the public and the private where people come together for a common purpose. According to Frank Schwartz, civil society is "that sphere intermediate between the family and state in which social actors pursue neither profit within the market nor power within the state" (Schwartz 2003: 93). Larry Diamond explains:

> Civil society is the realm of organized social life that is voluntary, self-generating, (largely) self-supporting, autonomous from the state, and bound by a legal order or set of shared rules. It is distinct from "society" in general in that it involves citizens acting collectively in a public sphere to express their interests, passions, preferences, and ideas to exchange information, to achieve collective goals, to make demands on the state, to improve the structure and functioning of the state, and to hold state officials accountable.
>
> (Diamond 1999: 221)

Civil society is distinct from the state and the market economy. Civil society is made up of independent, private associations, including nonprofit organizations (NPOs), non-governmental organizations (NGOs), and other voluntary associations. Civil society groups are voluntary in nature, and state–society relations are characterized by public debate. Still, civil society can only be understood in relation to the state. It cannot be investigated in isolation.

As the examples from Japan explored in this chapter will illustrate, state–society relations are characterized by both cooperation and conflict. Both entities have tools and resources to influence the other. These tools are often used to influence policy outcomes. This chapter investigates the tools at the state's disposal to influence civil society and the resources civil society organizations have to influence the state. It then provides an overview of civil society organizations, such as neighborhood associations, consumer groups, and agricultural cooperatives. It concludes by looking at social movements that often position themselves in opposition to the state.

Civil society

Different types of civil society organizations exist. Organizations fall into several categories, including economic associations, cultural groups, informational and educational groups, interest groups, developmental organizations, issue-oriented groups, civic groups, and institutions that promote independent cultural or intellectual activities (Diamond 1994). Examples of issue-oriented movements include environmental groups and women's rights organizations. Neighborhood associations are civic groups. Interest groups represent members such as workers in the policymaking process. Institutions that promote independent cultural or intellectual activities include think tanks and mass media (Diamond 1994).

In Japan, civil society organizations vary in part based on the level of institutionalization. The most formal organizations are institutionally recognized by the state. This category includes public interest corporations and nonprofits. A second category contains social establishments that are not recognized by the state but which have a formal office with employees, such as business, labor, and political associations. The final types of civil society organizations are active groups without state recognition or even a formal office and employees.

While small in comparison to the United States, the largest category of civil society organizations in Japan are those institutionally recognized by the state. In the late 1990s, there were twice as many of these groups compared to active groups without connections to the state (Tsujinaka 2003: 96). Social establishments make up the smallest category. When comparing Japan, the United States, and Korea on a per capita basis, Japan had about half as many state-recognized nonprofits as the U.S. but about four times as many as Korea (Tsujinaka 2003: 114). Japan has more business associations than both the U.S. and Korea on a per capita basis. It also has a relatively high number of active groups in the producer category (business, labor, and agricultural associations) (Tsujinaka 2003: 114).

The relative strength of civil society organizations vis-à-vis the state in Japan is contested. A focus on state-recognized institutions can lead to an emphasis on state regulations and restrictions. A focus on active organizations outside the state, however, can lead one to conclude that Japan is more pluralistic. All three categories need to be taken into consideration when assessing the overall strength of civil society organizations.

State–society relations focus on the interactions between the state and society. There is a level of interdependence between the state and society. A vibrant civil society is seen as an important factor influencing the effectiveness of democracy. In turn, the state influences the ability of society to organize and institutionalize. Some societal groups mostly cooperate with the state while others position themselves in opposition to the state. Social movements, in particular, often try to influence the policymaking process from the outside. Below we will explore the tools at the state's disposal to influence society and the resources and strategies of society to influence the state as well as the challenges faced by both the state and society.

State–society relations in Japan

The state shapes civil society organizations. This is especially true with the more institutionalized civil society organizations. The state controls the "rules of the game." The rules of the game include incentives and constraints posed by state rules and regulations. These incentives can promote some types of civil society organizations and make the environment more difficult to navigate for other groups. Neighborhood associations receive the most favorable incentives from the state, at least from a legal perspective. Large professionalized groups like Greenpeace have a much more difficult time navigating the legal landscape in Japan. These incentives can have consequences for the policymaking process and the relative involvement of certain voices. Small groups, like neighborhood associations, have strong ties to local governments and can influence outcomes on this level. Smaller groups are less able to carry out broader institutionalized movements (Pekkanen 2003: 117).

The state has direct and indirect influence on civil society organizations (Pekkanen 2003: 118–120). The direct influences of the state on civil society organizations come in the form of regulations and funding. The state controls the regulations guiding the formation and operations of organizations. Historically, the regulations on organization formation have been quite strict. The Civil Code favored the formation of organizations that promoted the "public interest." According to the Civil Code, public interest corporations include incorporated associations or foundations whose nonprofit activities focus on charity, worship, religion, education, art, or other public interest matters (Ogawa 2011: 187). Parent-Teacher Associations are an example of a common public interest association in Japan. Such associations are active on the local level but under the control of a national organization. Achieving the status of an incorporated foundation requires significant financial resources. The Civil Code requires an endowment of 300 million yen and an annual budget of 30 million yen. Several associations and foundations end up relying on the subsidies and commissions from the government to meet this requirement. In addition to financial requirements, official incorporation requires permission, approval, and recognition that involve bureaucratic discretion. Amakudari appointments of retired bureaucrats to public interest corporations is not uncommon as connections to the bureaucracy can be key in securing necessary funding and approval (Ogawa 2011).

In 1998, the Law to Promote Specified Nonprofit Activities (known as the NPO Law) eased the restrictions on small voluntary organizations to become incorporated nonprofit entities. The law seeks to recognize organizations that promote the interests of a variety of citizens in particular areas including health, medical care and welfare, social education, community development, culture, the arts, the environment, disaster relief, community safety, human rights, international cooperation, women's rights, and the nurturing of youth. In 2003 this list of activities was expanded to include consumer protection, scientific technology development, information technology development, the promotion of economic activities, and the promotion of employment opportunities (Ogawa 2011: 190). Political and religious activities are allowed as long as these activities are not the main activities of the organization. The NPO law eased the financial restrictions on becoming incorporated and decreased the barriers in the approval process. NPOs only require "recognition" which eliminates the bureaucratic discretion connected to permission and approval (Ogawa 2011: 191). After the passage of the NPO law, the number of nonprofits increased dramatically over the next decade. As of May 31, 2015 there were over 50,000 incorporated NPOs (The Cabinet Office 2015). The number has increased by 20 percent since 2009 when there were just over 40,000 (Ogawa 2011: 190). Some argue that the state has promoted the increase in NPOs as a way to promote structural reform and deregulation. Specifically, the state sees NPOs as a substitute for providing services that had been previously expected from the state (Ogawa 2011: 192).

The state can also direct government funding priorities. The state can make funds more readily available to organizations it wishes to promote. Funding to certain civil society organizations comes in the form of state subsidies or fees for projects. It also remains difficult for civil society organizations to gain certification from the state to receive donations that are tax deductible. The government also does not provide such organizations with discounts on bulk mailing, something that poses a barrier to communicating with members (Kawato, Pekkanen and Yamamoto 2011: 120). Funding barriers have reduced the ability of organizations to grow; small organizations have more difficulties influencing policy.

A reliance on the state for subsidies or fees for projects has limited the independence of some organizations. The state often finds a more collaborative relationship supported through this funding model an effective way to provide services it otherwise could not provide. This relationship is especially common between the state and social welfare organizations.

The relative strength of various state actors has an indirect influence on the shape of civil society. In general, as we saw in Chapter 9, the bureaucracy has played a larger role in policy formation and implementation in Japan. That is, ministries usually write legislation and always are in charge of implementing it. As a result, most civil society organizations direct attention at ministries as opposed to politicians. The state is interested in avoiding protests. As a result, it either provides concessions or works to "privatize" the issue (Pharr 1990; Upham 1987).

The relationship between civil society organizations and the relevant bureaucratic ministry varies. Agriculture cooperatives and business associations have close ties to bureaucratic ministries as well as members of the dominant LDP. Women, labor, and environmental groups have more oppositional relationships with the bureaucracy.

The media and the Internet are two potential tools that can be used by civil society organizations and social movements to influence public opinion and policy. The media and the Internet are significant aspects of the public sphere where debate and discussion occur. In Japan, civil society organizations have had less success utilizing the media due to the close connections among journalists, politicians, and bureaucrats. This relationship is institutionalized in press clubs (kisha kurabu). Press clubs have been described as information cartels (Freeman 2000). Membership of press clubs is limited to select journalists. Membership of the press club provides journalists access to sources and information. Journalists, in turn, agree to a set of informal rules about reporting information. This close relationship between the state, especially bureaucrats and politicians, and journalists has influenced the type of news coverage in Japan. Journalists tend to report stories in line with state interests. Civil society organizations are not part of the information cartel and thus have less influence on the dissemination of information to the public through traditional forms of media.

The growth of the Internet has provided an alternative mechanism for influencing public debate and discussion. The Internet has the potential of reaching a large number of people. It also does not require significant resources. Most civil society organizations in Japan have developed websites and email distribution lists. The formats used, however, are not very interactive (Ducke 2011). Email has been a particularly important tool to enhance networking.

Types of civil society organizations

Civil society organizations in Japan are characterized by a small number of members and staff, small budgets, and a small area of operation (Kawato, Pekkanen and Yamamoto 2011). Given these circumstances, organizations tend to be more active at the local level and work more closely with local government. The section below provides an overview of the kinds of civil society organizations in Japan.

Neighborhood associations

Neighborhood associations are the most prevalent civic organizations in Japan. Most Japanese are members of a neighborhood association. Membership is determined by residence. Neighborhood associations are community oriented and often serve as intermediaries between the local government and the neighborhood residents. The neighborhood associations are involved in a broad range of activities including maintaining roads, promoting recycling, supporting education, and organizing festivals. Membership in neighborhood associations was required during World War II. At this time, the organizations played a critical role in promoting the war effort through the distribution of rations, tax collection, and fire fighting. In the post-World War II era, these associations have become more democratic. The leadership of the organizations has expanded from farmers and the self-employed to include urban dwellers and women. In the postwar period, neighborhood associations have played an important role in promoting local government initiatives. The organizations are not instruments of the state as during World War II. They are more democratic and represent opportunities for service to the community (Haddad 2011).

Social welfare organizations

Social welfare organizations provide a variety of social services in the health, medical, and welfare fields. Social welfare organizations make up the largest percentage of NPOs in Japan. The majority of funding for these types of organizations comes from contract projects substantially supported by the state. Many argue that the LDP's main motivation for supporting the NPO law was to promote the establishment of social welfare organizations to supplement the state's provision of social welfare (Kawato, Pekkanen and Yamamoto 2011: 122–123).

Labor organizations

Labor organizations differ from typical civil society organizations in that labor organizations have relatively large memberships, staff, and budgets. Rengō is the largest trade union confederation in Japan. It was created in 1989 through a merger of the Japan Confederation of Labor (Dōmei), the Federation of Independent Labor Unions, and in 1990 the General Council of Trade Unions (Sōhyō). It raises funds through membership dues. It can mobilize these members to put pressure on policymakers. It currently has 6.75 million members and aspires to reaching 10 million members (JTUC-Rengo n.d.).

Since its creation Rengō has struggled to develop a strong relationship with a political party. Strong relationships with political parties had been a strong resource for labor unions in the 1955 system. Sōhyō was made up of public sector labor unions and backed the JSP; Dōmei was made up of private sector labor unions and backed the DSP and then the JCP. Rengō emerged just prior to the major party realignment due to the split of the LDP in 1993. When the Hosokawa anti-LDP coalition left office and the JSP joined the LDP in a coalition government, Rengō was greatly weakened. Some of its members supported the coalition due to previous connections with the JSP while other members had connections to former members of the DSP. The new electoral system also impeded Rengō's ability to influence the political process. The SMD portion of the electoral system does not support small niche parties.

Agricultural cooperatives

Not all scholars agree on whether agricultural cooperatives should be classified as civil society organizations. The main question has to do with whether these groups are primarily market actors. Those who object point to the strong ties between the LDP and farmers, and the economic interests and connections between these groups. Other scholars point out that agricultural cooperatives play a critical social and political role at the local level. Nōkyō is the major agricultural cooperative in Japan and boasts a membership that includes almost all farmers across Japan (Bullock 2003; George Mulgan 2000). It has more resources and more access than other types of civil society organizations due to its large membership and its close connections to the LDP.

Business associations

Business associations also fall into the category of economic interest groups. Business associations constitute the largest category of associational groups in Japan. The strongest voice for business associations comes from its peak association, Keidanren, the Federation of Economic Organizations. Keidanren has been a powerful actor vis-à-vis the state, asserting a strong voice on business and trade policies. The fact that Keidanren represents both efficient and inefficient sectors of the economy, however, has restricted its ability to advocate for economic reform that would promote increased competitiveness (Vogel 2001).

Social movements and civil society

Social movements are one way that citizens attempt to influence the government. Social movements often are concerned with civil rights, political equality, and freedom of speech and association. Social movements are made up of individuals who together are using noninstitutionalized tools to influence the state. This often involves protests and demonstrations. According to Patricia Maclachlan, "social movements can be viewed as political representatives of otherwise apolitical individuals within civil society that are designed to wrest favors from state and/or market institutions of which they are not a part" (Maclachlan 2003: 215).

The success of a social movement is related to the movement's organization and leadership as well as the movement's ability to create a group consciousness. The environment in which a social movement occurs also provides constraints and opportunities. That is, an environmental movement has more of an opportunity of influencing change in the aftermath of a nuclear accident. Such incidents can open a window of opportunity for policy change. This is known as the political opportunity structure (Tarrow 1998).

Group consciousness and organization can help overcome the collective action dilemma. The collective action dilemma emerges because individuals have very little incentive to participate in group activities when the cost of participation is high, and the likelihood that their actions will make a difference is low. Moreover, there is little incentive to participate if the same result can occur without their participation – that is, there is a strong incentive to "free ride" on the efforts of others.

Group consciousness often begins with ascribed characteristics such as race, ethnicity, and gender, but these characteristics are not sufficient to create a common mission. Group consciousness is a learned phenomenon; it does not automatically appear due to these ascribed characteristics. Instead, the movement needs to create a sense of membership in the group by emphasizing a common experience, such as discrimination. The group then needs to reject the status quo or tradition and create a new sense of pride and identity.

Even if you successfully create a group consciousness, the demand for change that emerges from the recognition that the problems lie in social institutions will only be realized if you also create a strong organization. A solid organizational structure can persuade members of a group to act in a certain way. Leaders can be critical in convincing others to put the group's interests above their individual interests.

In Japan, citizen movements (shimin undō) were quite active in the 1950s and 1960s. These movements involved labor union protests in the 1950s and the demonstrations against the U.S.–Japan Security Treaty in the 1960s, including the students' movement. Other citizen movements in Japan include the women's movement and the consumers' movement. The 1970s and 1980s were characterized by more local social movements (jūmin undō – local resident movements) related to Japan's high growth economy and the effects of industrialization on local regions. These movements focused on certain development projects, such as the building of nuclear plants as well as the environmental impact of industrialization. The prolonged economic recession coupled with neoliberal policies that have exacerbated the differences between the haves and have-nots have reinvigorated citizen movements that focus on issues of equality. For example, there is a union for friitaa and temporary workers. The Tōhoku Earthquake and Fukushima nuclear disaster also sparked national anti-nuclear protests.

This section provides an overview of the labor movement, women's movement, environmental movement, and anti-nuclear movement.

The labor movement

As explained above, the main participants in the labor movement have been labor unions. These labor unions often worked in cooperation with opposition parties. The labor unions did not have connections to the dominant conservative LDP. This outsider status often meant that these groups resorted to protests to influence policy.

Labor union protests and demonstrations were more prevalent during the 1950s and 1960s. In the 1950–1960s, several groups, including labor unions, worked with progressive parties to oppose the U.S.–Japan Security Treaty in the 1960s.

Traditionally the labor movement's main influence on the policymaking process came during the Spring Struggle. The Spring Struggle (shuntō) involves coordinated collective bargaining efforts primarily by enterprise unions just prior to the beginning of the fiscal year in Japan on April 1. In enterprise unions, membership comes at the firm or company group level. The Spring Struggle was devised as a way to centralize wage determination. The timing of wage negotiations was coordinated and as a result enterprise unions were able to overcome the information cost of carrying out negotiations in isolation (Carlile 2011: 167). Originally, the Spring Struggle had an explicitly political element to it as Sōhyō in particular emphasized the development of a class consciousness. In the 1970s, however, the Spring Struggle became a way for moderate wage increases to maintain Japan's economic competitiveness (Carlile 2011: 168). Since the inception of Rengō, the Spring Struggle has continued to evolve. Rengō has renamed the Spring Struggle the Spring Struggle for a Better Life. It includes larger social issues in its campaign; it is no longer just about wages and working conditions.

Rengō stills carries out protests, often in concert with other groups, but this mechanism has been less effective since the 1960s. The most common way to influence policy has been the creation and presentation of Institutional and Policy-related Demands. These demands are issued as a way to influence government policy and budget allocations (Carlile 2011: 168–169). Connections with parties are the final way that unions have attempted to influence the policymaking process.

The women's movement

The women's movement in Japan has been comparatively weak from a cross-national perspective. It also has mostly operated outside of the political realm. A historical investigation of the women's movement in Japan reveals two general categories of movements – one focused on women as wives and mothers and one concentrated on women's liberation. The National Housewives' Association and the Seikatsu (New Life) Club are examples of groups that attract women as wives and mothers. These groups target issues such as education and the environment, especially at the local level (Shin 2011). In contrast, women's liberation groups advocate liberation in marriage, sexuality, labor, and politics (Mackie 2003). The women who participated in these activities supported equality and had interests that conflicted with middle-class housewives. As a result, the women's movement in Japan has remained fragmented and weak.

Nevertheless, women's groups have had some success in influencing policy in two areas – gender equality and domestic violence. Feminist scholars, women's movement activists, and bureaucrats primarily associated with the Ministry of Labor worked together to implement the Equal Employment Opportunity Law (EEOL) in 1986 and its subsequent revisions in 1997 and 2006. Women activists gained strength and legitimacy from the UN's Convention on the Elimination of All Forms of Discrimination Against Women (CEDAW) passed in 1979 as well as their involvement in the UN's International Year of the Woman. The EEOL encouraged companies to promote anti-discrimination against women in hiring, job assignments, and promotions and prohibited such discrimination in dismissals and training. It also sought to protect women from overtime or extra shifts. Many feminists saw the initial law as inadequate. Revisions in 1997 strengthened the anti-discrimination provisions from voluntary to mandatory and added limited sanctions for noncompliance. It also framed anti-discrimination in terms of affirmative action. Revisions in 2006 extended the anti-discrimination provisions to both women and men. Overall, the EEOL and subsequent revisions have struggled to balance anti-discrimination provisions with protection (see Schoppa 2006: 174–179). Still, however, the EEOL does not effectively deal with wage differences based on sex or type of work (regular versus irregular workers) (Mikanagi 2011). No single women's group was decisive in pushing the EEOL, illustrating the fragmented nature of the movement.

Other groups such as the Women's Shelter Movement played an active role in hearings regarding domestic violence legislation by invoking the global norm of women's rights as human rights (Shin 2011: 182). The National Women's Shelter Network became an NPO in 2003. Key domestic violence legislation passed in 2001 prior to its official status as an NPO, but the organization of this network started following a National Symposium on Domestic Violence in 1998. The coordination among smaller, local groups across the country aided mobilization and added to the Shelter Movement's ability to influence the policymaking process (Shin 2011: 183). One effective strategy was to have survivors of domestic violence testify in front of Diet members. Such testimony brought to light the issue and influenced the passage of the initial law as well as subsequent revisions. Another distinct feature of this movement is that it worked in cooperation with state actors by formally participating in the policymaking process. The Shelter Movement had success without requiring formal membership in its organization. Instead, it achieved success by establishing a loose network with purely voluntary participation. The Shelter Movement can be seen as an example of a successful grassroots movement influencing policy (Shin 2011: 184).

The environmental movement

The Japanese environmental movement has experienced two stages. The first stage occurred in the 1950s–1970s and focused on local pollution issues that emerged due to industrialization and rapid economic growth. Most citizen protest groups were small and local in character. The focus of the more than 3,000 protests that occurred by the early 1970s was on compensation for victims of pollution or opposition to harmful public works projects (Lam 2011: 239).

National media attention aided several pollution cases and citizen protest movements. As discussed in Chapter 7, the most well-known cases of pollution-related diseases utilized citizen protest movements and the courts to pressure industries for compensation for victims. Minamata disease was caused by methyl mercury poisoning in Kumamoto and Nigata prefectures. Yokkaichi asthma was caused by sulfur dioxide and nitrogen dioxide emissions in Mie prefecture. Cadmium poisoning caused Itai Itai disease in Toyama prefecture. All these health hazards came to light in the 1960s and 1970s.

The traditionally pro-business, pro-industrialization LDP felt pressure to respond to the public outcry over industrial pollution. A large amount of this pressure came from the successful election of opposition party politicians to mayoral and gubernatorial positions due to the support of environmental activists. In 1967, the Diet passed the Basic Law for Environmental Pollution Control. This legislation was followed by the 1970 Pollution Diet, which saw the proposal and passage of 14 environment-related laws. Following the Pollution Diet, the Environmental Agency, currently known as the Ministry of the Environment, was established. These actions effectively redirected efforts to address environmental issues from the courts to the Diet and the bureaucracy (Upham 1987).

The Environmental Agency has had limited financial resources and little regulatory power. Its initiatives often were in conflict with MITI, LDP, and industry interests. As environmental protests declined, this Agency has had fewer tools to push for policy (see Broadbent 1998).

Environmental activism eventually shifted to focus on issues such as recycling and food safety. One example of a successful local environmental group was the Seikatsu (New Life) Club. The Seikatsu club is a consumer group that was formed as a cooperative to purchase environmentally sound household products. Its concern with safe household products has attracted housewives to its membership (Gelb and Estévez-Abe 1998: 268). Over time, the group's activities have become more political as members began to realize that securing safe products is greatly facilitated by government regulations that protect the environment. To directly influence politics at the local level, the consumer group established a separate branch of the organization – the Networks – that focuses on getting members elected to local office. Candidates supported by the Seikatsu Networks benefit from the aid of volunteers from the Seikatsu Club. Seikatsu Club members provide an initial support base from which candidates can build an even greater backing. These candidates can also draw on the Seikatsu Club's other resources to help them overcome the obstacle of financial backing. The Seikatsu Networks represent the success of a social movement translating its organizational power into political representation for women in the local areas where it is organizationally strong (Gelb and Estévez-Abe 1998; LeBlanc 1999; Gaunder 2009).

In the late 1980s, the focus of environmental movements began to shift to global environmental issues, such as ozone depletion and global warming. The Kiko network is an example of an NGO that emerged to combine local efforts to fight climate change. It sees its major activities as providing information, lobbying domestic policymakers, and participating in the international conversation on these issues. Interestingly enough, while the United States has many more environmental NGOs than Japan, Japan has done more to address issues such as climate change (Schreurs 2003).

Scholars have observed that environmental policymaking has become increasingly pluralistic in Japan. According to Schreurs (2003), the state has started to recognize that NGOs can be important sources of information. These groups have knowledge concerning public opinion, policy initiatives and options, and international movements. Policy initiatives are mostly to be successful when the Environmental Agency and the METI's interests align.

The anti-nuclear movement

The anti-nuclear movement also has experienced several stages. In the 1950s through the early 1960s, most opposition was local. From the late 1960s through the 1980s, however, opposition to nuclear power became more organized and extended beyond the local realm. Anti-nuclear associations appeared at the regional and national levels. Two significant national organizations emerged in the 1970s – the Citizens' Nuclear Information Center and the National Liaison Conference of the Anti-nuclear Movement. Both these groups functioned to provide information about nuclear power and coordinate actions of smaller anti-nuclear groups in localities potentially affected by nuclear power. From the 1980s to the present, civil society organizations have had greater success at stalling and preventing the siting of nuclear power plants in localities. One of the main tools used by anti-nuclear groups has been citizen referenda. Groups have also filed lawsuits against both private utility companies and even the central government.

The anti-nuclear movement faces a formidable opponent. The so-called nuclear village in Japan is comprised of pro-nuclear utility companies, METI, business federations, the LDP, media, and some academics. The state, in particular, has developed several strategies to sway key constituents, including local officials, fishermen, and farmers, in local areas potentially affected by nuclear power. While opposition groups focused on safety concerns, the national government emphasized the economic benefits of siting a nuclear power plant, including increased tax revenue, job creation, and national subsidies for infrastructure. The government often would fly local officials to Tokyo to offer strategies for how to quell local opposition. MITI would send officials to localities as well to explain how nuclear energy was key to Japan's energy security. The state has disseminated pro-nuclear information in paid newspaper ads and through the science curriculum in public schools. It also collects information to allay health and safety concerns among fishermen and farmers in localities near potential nuclear power plants. The state strategically has focused on localities for nuclear power plants based on the relative weakness of civil society organizations in those areas (Aldrich 2012: 131). While this strategy was particularly effective early on, it has become less effective as local opposition has gained more support from umbrella anti-nuclear civil society organizations. Only about half of the government's nuclear siting attempts have succeeded in the postwar period, a much lower success rate than for the siting of dams and airports (Aldrich 2008: 151).

The Fukushima nuclear accident opened a window of opportunity for changes in nuclear power policy; however, the anti-nuclear movement has not gained significant momentum. The areas that house nuclear power plants are economically dependent on the plants. Local governments in these areas receive incentives from the national government and are dependent on the relationship. Social networks were more important in disaster relief following the tsunami, earthquake, and nuclear incident than in mobilizing protests against nuclear power. Prime Minister Kan was able to get a feed-in tariff passed before leaving office as a condition of his resignation. Feed-in tariffs support renewable energy by promoting long-term contracts for developers of renewable energy as well as stable pricing. The anti-nuclear movement had little involvement in this process. It came about due to individual agency (Kingston 2012: 189).

Conclusion

Civil society organizations are seen as an important component of democracy. Vibrant civil societies indicate debate and discussion is occurring in the realm between the public and the private. Civil society organizations can function with varying levels of institutionalization. The creation of NGOs and NPOs in Japan requires state approval. This process has become less prohibitive than in the past, but it still provides the state opportunities to exert influence on the types of civil society organizations recognized by the state. The state uses regulations or monetary incentives to promote actions by certain groups in society. In general, neighborhood associations and social welfare organizations receive positive incentives from the state in Japan.

Civil society organizations have tools and resources to influence the state. The greatest resource of civil society organizations is their ability to mobilize citizen support. Such mobilization is not easy due to the collective action dilemma. Organizations have more success overcoming this dilemma with strong organization and leadership. Strong organization and the creation of a group consciousness are particularly important for social movements. In general, civil society organizations have been more effective at creating social capital and influencing local government initiatives

(Pekkanen 2006: 8–9). The ability of civil society organizations to influence national policy has been more limited and has varied based on the type of organization (Pekkanen 2006).

Many outside observers have classified Japan as a consensus-based society. The exploration of civil society organizations and social movements illustrates that organizations do challenge the state. Examples of both cooperation and conflict abound. Responses to the pollution protests and anti-nuclear referenda illustrate how social movements can use the courts or other tools of democracy to influence outcomes. The state remains strong but not above influence from citizen movements.

References

Aldrich, D. P. (2008) *Site Fights: Divisive Facilities and Civil Society in Japan and the West*, Ithaca, NY: Cornell University Press.

Aldrich, D. P. (2012) "Networks of Power: Institutions and Local Residents in Post-Tōhoku Japan," in J. Kingston (ed.) *Natural Disaster and Nuclear Crisis in Japan*, London: Routledge.

Broadbent, J. (1998) *Environmental Politics in Japan: Networks of Power and Protest*, New York: Cambridge University Press.

Bullock, R. (2003) "Redefining the Conservative Coalition: Agriculture and Small Business in 1990s Japan," in F. J. Schwartz and S. J. Pharr (eds) *The State of Civil Society in Japan*, New York: Cambridge University Press.

Carlile, L. E. (2011) "The Labor Movement," in A. Gaunder (ed.) *The Routledge Handbook of Japanese Politics*, London: Routledge.

Diamond, L. (1994) "Rethinking Civil Society: Toward Democratic Consolidation," *Journal of Democracy*, 5: 4–18.

Diamond, L. (1999) *Development Democracy: Toward Consolidation*, Baltimore, MD: The John Hopkins University Press.

Drogus, C. A. and Orvis, S. (2012) *Introducing Comparative Politics: Concepts and Cases in Context*, Los Angeles, CA: CQ Press.

Ducke, I. (2011) "Civil Society and the Internet," in A. Gaunder (ed.) *The Routledge Handbook of Japanese Politics*, London: Routledge.

Freeman, L. A. (2000) *Closing the Shop: Information Cartels and Japan's Mass Media*, Princeton, NJ: Princeton University Press.

Gaunder, A. (2009) "Women Running for National Office in Japan: Are Koizumi's Female 'Children' a Short-term Anomaly or a Lasting Phenomenon?" in S. Reed, K. M. McElwain, and K. Shimizu (eds) *Political Change in Japan: Electoral Behavior, Party Realignment, and the Koizumi Reforms*, Washington, DC: Brookings Institution.

Gelb, J. and Estevez-Abe, M. (1998) "Political Women in Japan: A Case Study of the Seikatsusha Network Movement," *Social Science Japan Journal*, 1: 263–279.

George Mulgan, A. (2000) *The Politics of Agriculture in Japan*, London: Routledge.

Haddad, M. A. (2011) "Volunteer Organizations (Re)making Democracy in Japan," in A. Gaunder (ed.) *The Routledge Handbook of Japanese Politics*, London: Routledge.

JTCU-Rengo (n.d.) "About Rengo." Available online at www.jtuc-rengo.org/about/ (accessed 13 July 2016).

Kawato, Y., Pekkanen, R. J., and Yamamoto, H. (2011) "State and Civil Society in Japan," in A. Gaunder (ed.) *The Routledge Handbook of Japanese Politics*, London: Routledge.

Kingston, J. (2012) "The Politics of Natural Disaster, Nuclear Crisis and Recovery," in J. Kingston (ed.) *Natural Disaster and Nuclear Crisis in Japan*, London: Routledge.

Lam, Peng Er (2011) "Japan's Environmental Politics and Change: Local, National and Global," in A. Gaunder (ed.) *The Routledge Handbook of Japanese Politics*, London: Routledge.

LeBlanc, R. (1999) *Bicycle Citizens: The Political World of the Japanese Housewife*, Berkeley: University of California Press.

Mackie, V. (2003) *Feminism in Modern Japan*, Cambridge: Cambridge University Press.

Maclachlan, P. L. (2003) "The Struggle for an Independent Consumer Society: Consumer Activism and the State's Response in Postwar Japan," in F. J. Schwartz and S. J. Pharr (eds) *The State of Civil Society in Japan*, New York: Cambridge University Press.

Mikanagi, Y. (2011) "The Japanese Conception of Citizenship," in A. Gaunder (ed.) *The Routledge Handbook of Japanese Politics*, London: Routledge.

Ogawa, A. (2011) "The New Prominence of the Civil Sector in Japan," in V. L. Bestor and T. C. Bestor (eds) *Routledge Handbook of Japanese Culture and Society*, London: Routledge.

Pekkanen, R. (2003) "Molding Japanese Civil Society: State Structured Incentives and the Patterning of Civil Society," in F. J. Schwartz and S. J. Pharr (eds) *The State of Civil Society in Japan*, New York: Cambridge University Press.

Pekkanen, R. (2006) *Japan's Dual Civil Society: Members Without Advocates*, Stanford, CA: Stanford University Press.

Pharr, S. J. (1990) *Losing Face: Status Politics in Japan*, Berkeley: University of California Press.

Schoppa, L. J. (2006) *Race for the Exits: The Unraveling of Japan's System of Social Protection*, Ithaca, NY: Cornell University Press.

Schreurs, M. A. (2003) *Environmental Politics in Japan, Germany and the United States*, Cambridge: Cambridge University Press.

Schwartz, F. J. (2003) "What is Civil Society?" in F. J. Schwartz and S. J. Pharr (eds) *The State of Civil Society in Japan*, New York: Cambridge University Press.

Shin, Ki-young (2011) "The Women's Movements," in A. Gaunder (ed.) *The Routledge Handbook of Japanese Politics*, London: Routledge.

Tarrow, S. (1998) *Power in Movement: Social Movements and Contentious Politics*, New York: Cambridge University Press.

The Cabinet Office (2015) *Naikakufu NPO homepage*. Available online at www.npo-homepage.go.jp/ (accessed 12 July 2016).

Tsujinaka, Y. (2003) "From Developmentalism to Maturity: Japan's Civil Society Organizations in Comparative Perspective," in F. J. Schwartz and S. J. Pharr (eds) *The State of Civil Society in Japan*, New York: Cambridge University Press.

Upham, F. K. (1987) *Law and Social Change in Postwar Japan*, Cambridge, MA: Harvard University Press.

Vogel, S. K. (2001) "The Crisis of German and Japanese Capitalism," *Comparative Politics* 34: 1103–1133.

11 Prime ministerial leadership

Political leadership is difficult to exercise. Nevertheless, citizens in democracies demand effective leadership. What constitutes effective leadership varies. Some equate political leadership with the ability to get elected to office. Others focus on the ability of the leader to pass policies related to their initial policy agenda. Those who hold an even higher bar maintain an effective leader is transformational and leaves institutional legacies. The ways leaders accomplish goals are also plentiful. Executive leaders in democracies are granted a certain set of formal powers in the constitution. But, perhaps even more important are the informal powers leaders exercise to pursue their goals. These powers include the ability to persuade the public through effective speaking or the use of media, personal ties, and popularity.

Political leadership is important because in certain instances leaders, whether it be prime ministers, presidents, or politicians, can influence change. While several factors, such as history, culture, structures, rules, or even rationality, might constrain a leader's ability to realize change, effective leaders can take these constraints into account and use formal and informal powers to creatively navigate a path to achieve their policy or political goals.

This chapter explores executive leadership in Japan. When addressing the question of where power rests in Japan, few would argue that the prime minister is a decisive player. The conventional wisdom suggests that Japanese prime ministers are given limited formal powers and therefore are inherently weak. Prime ministers are not seen as ideologically driven but instead as reactive, only paying attention to issues that cannot be ignored or that are ongoing (Hayao 1993: 27). The most successful prime ministers are characterized as good managers who can effectively secure consensus among key political actors. Indeed, under the 1955 system of LDP dominance when money politics and backroom deals ran rampant, the focus tended to be on the political bosses, the so-called "shadow shoguns" influencing politics behind the scenes (Schlesinger 1997). A consideration of both the formal and informal powers at the disposal of Japanese prime ministers, however, reveals a more complicated picture. Case studies of several postwar prime ministers illustrate common constraints faced by all prime ministers and expose some of the variations in political leadership due to personal attributes and informal resources.

A comparison of parliamentary and presidential executives

When comparing the ideal types of parliamentary and presidential executives, several key differences emerge. In parliamentary systems, the executive and legislative branches are fused. This connection is directly related to how the prime minister is selected. In a classic parliamentary executive, a prime minister is selected from the majority party or coalition following a national election. This process puts political parties at the center. It also means that prime ministers ultimately rely on the legislative branch for their ultimate legitimacy. In most systems, the prime minister's term in office is not fixed. After being selected, the prime minister then appoints members of the national assembly to be cabinet members. Cabinet ministers remain members of parliament. The prime minister and the cabinet are referred to as the government, illustrating the fused nature of these bodies. The prime minister is seen as first among equals and collective decision making and collegiality are the norms. The fact that the prime minister is selected by the legislature guards against divided government. The legislative body can terminate the prime minister and the cabinet. If this happens, then the prime minister and the cabinet members return to serve as members of parliament. A dissolution of the body by the prime minister and/or a vote of no confidence can also lead to new elections of the entire parliamentary body.

In contrast, in presidential systems, individuals are elected by the public and receive legitimacy by virtue of being elected by the people. A president's term in office is fixed, and the term is not related to the term of the legislative body. Separation of powers is the guiding principle behind this institutional design. A president appoints members to the cabinet; these members must not be sitting politicians. The president and the cabinet are referred to as the executive branch, not the government as in parliamentary systems. One of the greatest strengths of this system is that one individual can be held accountable. It is more difficult to hold an entire collegial body accountable for a decision. The checks and balances inherent in this system of separation of powers is often seen as a positive; however, this institutional design does allow for divided government which can impede the passage of legislation.

The prime minister

Formal powers

Japan is a parliamentary system with a prime minister. Japan's parliamentary executive functions much like the classic system described above. The prime minister is the head of the cabinet, and the cabinet is the center of executive authority. The prime minister has limited formal powers and an array of informal powers, which vary by the person holding the office.

According to the Japanese Constitution, the prime minister is the head of the cabinet and appoints and dismisses cabinet ministers (Article 68). The cabinet can dissolve the lower house by calling new elections. The prime minister must attend a Diet session when requested to address questions (Article 63).

At least on paper, many features would suggest that a Japanese prime minister could exercise real influence. Japan is a unitary system, and thus the central government is not constrained by powers delegated to local governments. The cabinet functions based on collective responsibility and has not faced strong challenges from the lower house, particularly during the 1955 system of LDP dominance. The more regular occurrence of a twisted Diet where an opposition party has control of the upper house has added a potential constraint on cabinet activity as has the trend toward coalition government since electoral reform.

Reforms in 1999 and 2001 increased the resources that support the prime minister. Cabinet reforms decreased the size of the cabinet to fourteen in hopes of facilitating the ease of unified decision making. This reform enhanced the centralization of the cabinet. These reforms also reduced the role of bureaucrats by limiting their role to act as witnesses on technical matters during Diet deliberations. Instead, politicians are responsible for responding to Diet member concerns (Shinoda 2003: 24–25). This change provided prime ministers with an incentive to select cabinet ministers with more knowledge and expertise. The reforms also established the Council on Economic and Fiscal Policy (CEFP). The CEFP is under the cabinet and the goal is for it to advise the prime minister on economic policy.

Administrative reforms supported by Prime Minister Hashimoto and implemented in 2001 gave the prime minister and the Cabinet Secretariat clear authority to initiate policy. The law clearly established the prime minister's ability to propose policies at cabinet meetings. It is also called for a reorganization of the Cabinet Secretariat, and its staffing increased over threefold. The three policy offices that were part of the Secretariat were merged into one unit. This reform increased policy coordination (Shinoda 2003; Nyblade 2011).

Constraints on prime ministerial power

The constraints on prime ministerial power have changed over time. In the 1955 system of LDP dominance, the greatest constraint on prime ministerial power was the LDP and its factional structure. Under the 1955 system, being LDP president was synonymous with becoming prime minister. The LDP had the majority in the lower house and its leader automatically became prime minister. The selection of the LDP president could be a complicated, political affair. In general, the largest faction either chose one of its members to serve as prime minister or its leaders served as kingmakers naming a leader from a smaller faction. Factional balancing became the norm for cabinet selection. Cabinet ministers were not known for their policy expertise. Prime ministers often reshuffled the cabinet frequently to maximize the number of senior LDP politicians who could be rewarded. Thus, while the LDP's position was secure during this period, the prime minister was often beholden to faction leaders. Action independent from the party was difficult. Prime ministers often found themselves serving a party manger role (Ansell and Fish 1999; Wiliarty 2008).

Opposition control of the upper house has become a more relevant constraint on prime ministerial power since electoral system reform. In 1989, the Japan Socialist Party (JSP) received a majority in the upper house. With this majority, the JSP could block policies considered by both houses. Twisted Diets became even more common following electoral reform in 1994. The DPJ effectively used its control of the upper house to slow some key initiatives of the Koizumi government as we will see in the case study below.

Since electoral reform, coalition governments have become the norm. Coalitions can serve as an effective response to a twisted Diet. That is, even if a party has a majority in the lower house it might find it advantageous to join forces with a smaller opposition party to secure a majority in the upper house by forming a coalition. Coalitions can constrain the prime minister and the cabinet's legislative agenda. Policy compromises are often necessary to maintain a coalition. Coalitions certainly favor more consensual decision making (George Mulgan 2003).

The policymaking dynamic in Japan has also been seen as a constraint on prime ministerial power. As discussed in Chapter 9, in the 1950s and 1960s policy in some areas was seen as being controlled by iron triangles consisting of politicians, bureaucrats, and special interest groups. In this Japan Incorporated view of policymaking, politicians only gave legitimacy to the system (Johnson 1982). These actors did not play a decisive role in policymaking. In the 1970s, the view of policymaking shifted to a New Japan Incorporated paradigm. The New Japan Inc. asserted that interest groups and business led the policy agenda with politicians and bureaucrats responding based on their own goals and priorities (Pempel 1987). Subgovernments organized around policy areas constrain the action of individual politicians (Campbell 1989).

The combined SMD/PR electoral system has created new constraints and opportunities for prime ministerial leadership. As elections have become more nationalized, the importance of party label has increased. Party leaders have assumed greater responsibility for creating long coattails for party rank and file to ride on during elections. As the media has increasingly focused on party leaders, these leaders have become more susceptible to shifts in public opinion. More media coverage allows voters to reassess their attitudes towards leaders more frequently. Some argue that this new "hyperaccountability" explains an increased volatility (i.e., shorter average terms) for prime ministers (Nyblade 2011).

Informal powers[1]

Informal powers of prime ministers include certain resources that emerge from experience as well as personal attributes. Informal powers are more idiosyncratic; however, these resources and personal attributes often allow leaders to overcome the institutional constraints they face.

The importance of a resource depends on the goal. In the case of policy passage, the main goals are persuasion and mobilization. To reach these goals several resources can be significant. Many of these resources are related to personal ties. Connections with the bureaucracy, opposition parties, and within your own party can facilitate policy passage. Intra- and inter-party ties can be particularly important for building coalitions. Connections to businesses can also be key. In addition, popularity and public relations through media coverage can be important in securing support for a policy (Shinoda 2000). "Going public," the strategy of taking the policy directly to the people to garner public support for a policy, is especially effective in presidential systems (Kernell 1986). It is more difficult for prime ministers given their first among equals status. However, some argue that media savvy has become increasingly important for prime ministers (Krauss and Nyblade 2005; Rose 2001). Finally, previous experience can provide policy expertise that might be relevant in building support (Gaunder 2007; Shinoda 2000).

In Japan, a political leader's resources are often related to their level of seniority. Politicians with greater seniority are more likely to have served in party and Diet positions and therefore had time to develop connections with ministries, industries, and opposition leaders. Access to backroom dealings also comes with seniority and is quite significant in the Japanese case (Gaunder 2007: 11–12).

As with resources, the import of certain personal characteristics varies with the goal in mind (Gaunder 2007). The relationship between a leader's personal attributes and a leader's ultimate success has been considered for centuries. For example, in *The Prince*, Machiavelli (1985) asserts that feared leaders, rather than beloved ones, are more likely to retain power. Max Weber (1947) connects charismatic leadership to social change. Here, charisma is more than effective speaking. Charisma refers to the superhuman power to convince individuals to give up their identity and take on the leader's identity as their own. Richard Samuels emphasizes "bricolage" or the ability to connect the desire for change to the "useable" past (Samuels 2003a: 8). The charismatic and the bricoleur are both transformational leaders seeking change that is larger in scope than the passage of policy. Indeed, transformational leaders are often revolutionary.

In his classic study of leadership, James MacGregor Burns looks at more practical "transactional leadership" which is characteristic of policymaking in democratic countries. He asserts transactional leadership "requires a shrewd eye for opportunity, a good hand at bargaining, persuading, reciprocating" (Burns 1978: 169). Risk-taking, vision, and commitment have been connected to the effective support and passage of political reform (Gaunder 2007). Some of these personal attributes can be honed; others emerge from innate ability, making many political scientists uncomfortable as they cannot be predicted or replicated. Nevertheless, these attributes cannot be ignored as a leader's willingness to have "reached out for the impossible" often allows a leader to overcome structural, cultural, or rational constraints that might stand in the way (Weber 1946: 128).

Case studies: prime ministerial leadership in postwar Japan

While many look at Prime Ministers Koizumi and Abe and contend that prime ministerial leadership is a new phenomenon in Japan, a historical look at a handful of postwar prime ministers reveals a variety of leadership styles and strategies. Successful and failed cases are explored to illustrate how prime ministers use their formal and informal powers to promote certain policy outcomes. Table 11.1 lists all postwar prime ministers, their party affiliation, and the dates of their terms in office.

Yoshida Shigeru

Yoshida Shigeru served two terms as prime minister in 1946–1947 and 1948–1954. As we saw in Chapter 3, he played a critical role in establishing the postwar political system. He drew largely on informal resources and personal attributes to achieve his policy goals. He reframed history to support the postwar reality. He asserted that the emperor had always been a symbol, making this shift less jolting. He painted the military as villains who had circumvented the Meiji Constitution. This claim established a historical context for democracy. The roles of the emperor and the military were seen as the aberration, and democracy was conceived as the true basis for modern governments (Samuels 2003a: 203).

Yoshida used the window of opportunity created by the outbreak of the Cold War to gain support for U.S. troops stationed in Japan. Yoshida also argued Japan needed assistance since it was constrained by Article 9. He forged strong ties with General MacArthur to further pursue his goals. Yoshida also supported the creation of the National Police Reserve (NPR). He did not frame the NPR as a military, though. He framed it as a defense force (Samuels 2003a).

Alcide De Gasperi had similar success using the outbreak of the Cold War to overcome some of the negative legacies of being an aggressor in World War II. He created the narrative that neutrality would not work in the context of the Cold War. This

Table 11.1 Postwar prime ministers

Prime minister	Party affiliation	Dates in office
Higashikuni Naruhiko	Imperial family	17 August 1945–9 October 1945
Shidehara Kijūrō	The Japan Progressive Party	9 October 1945–22 May 1946
Yoshida Shigeru	The Japan Liberal Party	22 May 1946–24 May 1947
Katayama Tetsu	Japan Socialist Party	24 May 1947–10 March 1948
Ashida Hitoshi	Democratic Party	10 March 1948–19 October 1948
Yoshida Shigeru	Democratic Liberal Party/ Liberal Party	19 October–10 December 1954
Hatoyama Ichirō	Liberal Party/ Liberal Democratic Party	10 December 1954–23 December 1956
Ishibashi Tanzan	Liberal Democratic Party	23 December 1956–25 February 1957
Kishi Nobusuke	Liberal Democratic Party	25 February 1957–19 July 1960
Ikeda Hayato	Liberal Democratic Party	19 July 1960–9 November 1964
Satō Eisaku	Liberal Democratic Party	9 November 1964–7 July 1972
Tanaka Kakuei	Liberal Democratic Party	7 July 1972–9 December 1974
Miki Takeo	Liberal Democratic Party	9 December 1974–24 December 1976
Fukuda Takeo	Liberal Democratic Party	24 December 1976–7 December 1978
Ōhira Masayoshi	Liberal Democratic Party	7 December 1978–12 June 1980
Suzuki Zenkō	Liberal Democratic Party	17 July 1980–27 November 1982
Nakasone Yasuhiro	Liberal Democratic Party	27 November 1982–6 November 1987
Takeshita Noboru	Liberal Democratic Party	6 November 1987–2 June 1989
Uno Sōsuke	Liberal Democratic Party	2 June 1989–8 August 1989
Kaifu Toshiki	Liberal Democratic Party	8 August 1989–5 November 1991
Miyazawa Kiichi	Liberal Democratic Party	5 November 1991–6 August 1993
Hosokawa Morihiro	Japan New Party	6 August 1993–28 April 1994
Hata Tsutomu	Shinseitō	28 April 1994–29 June 1994
Murayama Tomiichi	Japan Socialist Party	29 June 1994–11 January 1996
Hashimoto Ryūtarō	Liberal Democratic Party	11 January 1996–30 July 1998
Obuchi Keizō	Liberal Democratic Party	30 July 1998–5 April 2000
Mori Yoshirō	Liberal Democratic Party	5 April 2000–26 April 2001
Koizumi Junichirō	Liberal Democratic Party	26 April 2001–26 September 2006
Abe Shinzō	Liberal Democratic Party	26 September 2006–26 September 2007
Fukuda Yasuo	Liberal Democratic Party	26 September 2007–24 September 2008
Asō Tarō	Liberal Democratic Party	24 September 2008–16 September 2009
Hatoyama Yukio	Democratic Party of Japan	16 September 2009–8 June 2010
Kan Naoto	Democratic Party of Japan	8 June 2010–2 September 2011
Noda Yoshihiko	Liberal Democratic Party	2 September 2011–26 December 2012
Abe Shinzō	Liberal Democratic Party	26 December 2012–

narrative helped him re-establish Italy as part of the Western Alliance and Pax Americana. He, like Yoshida, used his personal attributes to mold his country's national identity following World War II (Samuels 2003a).

Tanaka Kakuei

Prime Minister Tanaka became LDP president and prime minister in 1972 and served for two years. He is credited with creating machine politics in Japan. If effective leadership is defined as winning elections, building party loyalty, and securing backroom deals, then Tanaka is most certainly a success. In many ways, Tanaka was the quintessential shadow shogun (Schlesinger 1997). His policy record was more mixed.

Tanaka followed Prime Minister Satō Eisaku as prime minister. Informally, Satō had backed Fukuda Takeo to be his successor. Tanaka, however, beat Fukuda in the race for party president. Tanaka's popularity with the public was quite high. His approval ratings hovered above 60 percent after taking office (Curtis 1988). Tanaka was known for supporting populist policies. For example, he addressed the pollution issues associated with rapid economic growth. He also introduced reforms to the pension and healthcare system. In fiscal year 1973, public works spending increased 32 percent, and social welfare spending was not far behind at 29 percent (Curtis 1988: 64). The government's commitment to social welfare policies, such as national health coverage and pensions, continued long after Tanaka left office.

Prior to his bid for prime minister, Tanaka released a book titled *Building a New Japan: A Plan for Remodeling the Archipelago*. The plan outlined in this book became the signature policy initiative of his administrative. The book highlighted many of the problems associated with industrialization and rapid growth including pollution, long commutes, and the difficulty of buying homes in urban areas. Tanaka's solution was to redirect growth to other areas of Japan. Specifically, his plan involved promoting industrialization in medium-sized Japanese cities and increasing government spending on infrastructure projects. This plan responded to the reality of Japan's rapid economic growth, which had resulted in a massive increase in the urban populations of large Japanese cities, most notably Tokyo and Osaka. The goal was to promote the development of industry outside large metropolitan areas and in essence build the population to create medium-sized cities. These cities would need to be developed and connected to the larger cities with infrastructure, mainly railway and highway development.

This policy initiative attracted great interest from politicians and ministries. One of the main appeals was the amount of potential pork associated with the plan. Public works spending was at the heart of the remodeling plan. The most significant problem was that very few areas were targeted for depopulation, and over 86 percent of the surface area of the country was marked for expansion (Masumi 1995: 142).

Tanaka was also unable to secure support from small- and medium-sized enterprises as well as many large firms associated with Keidanren. The idea of taxing large firms in overpopulated areas met strong resistance from large firms, especially ones that did not produce significant amounts of pollution. Other industries were frustrated by the possibility of relocating workers and coordinating with localities (Masumi 1995: 142).

The economic environment also did not favor policy success. The oil shocks in 1973 occurred in the middle of Tanaka's term. Japan experienced rampant inflation and high economic uncertainty. This situation made Tanaka's early large deficit spending unsustainable. In the wake of these developments, the largest issue that Japan faced was dramatic increases in land prices. Land prices in Tokyo were increasing at an annual rate of over 30 percent. This trend also made the remodeling plan unrealistic.

Leaders can inspire, bully, or buy to "stretch constraints" (Samuels 2003a: 17). Tanaka employed bullying and buying. These strategies secured backroom deals but did not result in the passage of his policy agenda. His informal powers of public support and ties with the business community did not provide him enough leverage to overcome the obstacles to his signature policy. The business community did not support the expulsion tax, and public support waned as the economic situation worsened. Raising government deficits and land prices also made an ambitious program based on increased public works spending unsustainable.

In the end, Tanaka's time in office was cut short by political scandal. Money politics became the focal point of the July 1974 upper house election due to questionable campaign contributions solicited by Prime Minister Tanaka. Tanaka essentially asked 2,000 large- to medium-sized corporations to support specific candidates in the elections. The focus was on vote getting, with executives encouraging employees in subsidiaries in localities to vote for LDP candidates (Masumi 1995). The public did not look favorably on such blatant coordination between big business and the LDP.

Three months after the campaign controversy, a Japanese magazine published an article that implicated Tanaka in illegal real estate and construction deals. This article exposed Tanaka's "money for power politics" and turned what had been speculation into direct accusation (Johnson 1986). The approval ratings for the Tanaka cabinet plummeted to 12 percent approval and 69 percent disapproval (Masumi 1995: 153). Tanaka's popularity, which had been a strong informal power, decreased dramatically. In the face of public anger over the scandal, LDP party leaders pushed for Tanaka's resignation.

In many ways, Tanaka became more powerful after leaving the prime ministership. After his fall from grace, he focused on building his faction. His motto was that "politics is power; power is numbers" (Schlesinger 1997: 108). He realized that a large faction could control the selection of the prime minister and the policy agenda from behind the scenes. Tanaka used several informal powers to influence politics after leaving office. He built ties with the opposition parties and the bureaucracy. He influenced committee assignments and provided money to opposition parties to attain favorable results in negotiations. He used amakudari (the revolving door) and money to influence the bureaucracy. He also recognized when bureaucratic ministries could be played off one another to secure favorable outcomes (Schlesinger 1997).

Tanaka's case illustrates how the external environment can constrain prime ministers with considerable informal resources. Tanaka's resources fostered his success as a faction leader after stepping down from the prime ministership.

Nakasone Yasuhiro

Prime Minister Nakasone became LDP president and prime minister in 1982 and served for five years. He was from a small faction and successfully elected with the backing of the Tanaka and Suzuki factions. He was a fiscal conservative and pursued classic liberal policies similar to his contemporaries Margaret Thatcher in Great Britain and Ronald Reagan in the United States. He also possessed a nationalistic vision for Japan's foreign policy. His leadership has often been described as presidential, partly because he took a more active role in the policymaking process (Hayao 1993: 47). He favored increasing defense spending, strengthening the U.S.–Japan Security alliance and revising the Constitution. His hawkish stance was quite controversial. He also pursued several classically liberal reforms, including education reform, tax reform, and railroad and telecommunication privatization.

Nakasone targeted education reform but was much less successful in achieving his goals in this area compared to other policy initiatives. His main goal was to diminish the control of the Ministry of Education over the education system. To this end, he sponsored a bill to establish the National Council of Educational Reform to develop reform proposals. His proposals for liberalization met opposition from this body, which was heavily influenced by the Ministry of Education and LDP zoku politicians. Nakasone also pushed to end the first stage of the college entrance exams for public and national universities. This plan differed from the Ministry of Education, which favored revising the process as opposed to abolishing it. In the end Prime Minister Nakasone was less able to challenge the education subgovernment because he was unable to find allies to back his position. As we shall see below, with privatization he had support from others in the LDP, business interests, and the public. Without these informal resources, he was not able to do more than highlight the importance of some education issues such as the overly demanding examination process (Hayao 1993: 46–67).

Nakasone's biggest success was administrative reform and the privatization of the Nippon Telegraph and Telephone Public Corporation (NTT) and Japan National Railway (JNR). Administrative reform was a popular issue because it was seen as a way to cut government spending and address the budget deficit. Prime Minister Nakasone had several informal powers at his disposal to pursue this agenda. In particular, he had strong public support. His main slogan for pushing reform was "Clearing the Postwar Political Legacy." This slogan indicated that administrative structures that had facilitated rapid economic growth were no longer necessary (Shinoda 2000: 135). The implication was that privatization was more appropriate given Japan's economic success. In the case of JNR, increasing fares and low quality service bolstered the case to privatize with the hope of increasing efficiency. He also had the support of significant business interests. One way he secured this support was by appointing a prominent, well-respected business leader to head the commission that would oversee the implementation of reform. These informal resources allowed Nakasone to challenge the ties between bureaucrats, zoku politicians, and big business.

The most significant resource for Prime Minister Nakasone came in the form of advisory councils. His advisory councils for railroad and telecommunication privatization provided him with a mechanism to consider policy free from the factional politics and power wielding within the LDP. These advisory councils reported directly to the prime minister. The prime minister then would act on the recommendations of the councils. Nakasone chose political allies to participate on the advisory councils and created links between the councils and the LDP. He also threatened to punish any bureaucrat who hindered the process (Samuels 2003b: 12–13). Building on public and business support and using the advisory councils and his connections within the LDP, Nakasone was able to push through both privatizations (Gaunder 2007: 126–127).

The privatization of JNR was the most difficult politically. JNR had over 400,000 employees with strong union connections to the JSP. JNR also had a debt of 13 trillion yen. Many LDP politicians were at least initially opposed to the privatization of JNR due to the pork connected to its operation (Samuels 2003b: 20). In the end, though, the privatization hurt the JSP much more as it weakened Shōyō.

Nakasone's leadership and policy agenda is often compared to other prominent contemporaries. Margaret Thatcher served as prime minister of the UK from 1979 to 1990. Deregulation and privatization were key features of her neo-conservative agenda. In fact, during her time in office over 30 public corporations underwent privatization including oil and electronics, public utilities, and water. Prime Minister Thatcher faced some similar obstacles to reform. She initially had to fight to receive the leadership role in the Conservative Party, and it took time to build the support of the cabinet and the bureaucracy. In the interim, she used outside think tanks, such as the Institute of Economic Affairs, and cabinet subcommittees to pursue her agenda. She also had a clear vision and a personal tenacity. Strong public support for the Conservatives also reduced the obstacles in her way. Prime Minister Thatcher navigated a different environment but had success using some of the same tools and resources as Prime Minister Nakasone.

Koizumi Junichirō[2]

Koizumi Junichirō served as prime minister from 2001 to 2006, a comparatively long term for a Japanese prime minister. Many political pundits and scholars characterized Koizumi as a maverick. This language probably emerged due to the fact that Koizumi was willing to challenge his own party, at least rhetorically. One of his most famous slogans was "change the LDP, change Japan."

Koizumi was an advocate for small government, free and open markets, and individual responsibility. His main goals centered on increasing Japanese economic competitiveness and implementing fiscal structural reform. Increasing economic competitiveness meant decreasing government support of protected and privileged sectors, such as public works. Deregulation and privatization were key pillars of fiscal structural reform.

The extent of Koizumi's success in pursuing this agenda is contested. Under Koizumi's leadership several reform measures passed including highway, construction, postal savings, public works, and health insurance reform. Quite significantly, however, Koizumi made very little progress on his overarching goal of comprehensive economic reform. Compromise characterized all his policy successes. These compromises often meant some special interests were protected and the overall change was narrower than initially desired. Many of the reforms that Koizumi pursued went against the interests of fellow LDP members or key LDP constituents. This circumstance made compromise more appealing, if not necessary. Despite the compromises, the reforms together did mark a gradual weakening of old-style pork barrel politics.

Postal saving system reform was the signature policy initiative of Koizumi's tenure in office. Post offices in Japan offer financial accounts in addition to mail services. At the time Koizumi was considering reform, the postal saving system was essentially the largest bank in the world based on deposits. Significantly, the government had access to these funds through the Fiscal Investment and Loan Program (FILP) and often used this money to support politically motivated public works projects.

During his time in office, Koizumi secured the passage of two postal reform bills. The first postal reform bill opened the postal system to competition in a very limited way. His second proposal was more comprehensive. His 2005 Postal Reform bill called for the privatization of the postal system and the division of Japan Post into four different operational units which focused on four distinct sectors – banking and savings, insurance, branch network management, and courier services. This proposal emerged from the cabinet-based Economic Financial Policy Council. This resource was independent from the bureaucracy. The initial bill passed the lower house, but it failed in the upper house. Some members of the LDP voted against the bill in both houses. After this failure, Koizumi dissolved the lower house and called for new elections. He immediately kicked any LDP lower house politician who voted against the bill out of the party. Koizumi then successfully made the lower house election a referendum on postal reform. The LDP won an outright majority in this election.

Entrenched interests remained intact following electoral reform and party realignment. The ties among bureaucratic agencies, LDP politicians, and special business interests were a major constraint on all of Koizumi's efforts. In the case of the postal system, the postal family of LDP zoku politicians and postmasters were a major constraint.

Koizumi had several informal powers that allowed him to challenge these constraints. Initially, strong public support was Koizumi's greatest resource. When Koizumi first came to office, his support ratings were at an unprecedented level, sitting around 80 percent. By his fifth year, public support had waned to around 30 percent. While 30 percent sounds small comparatively speaking, this level of support was still within the normal range. This public support meant that Koizumi could often put forward reform that went against the party's interest without fearing retribution. The party was not necessarily obligated to pass his policy initiatives, but the party was unwilling to consider sacking him despite his controversial policy agenda due to his public support. Koizumi used the media, the Internet, and grassroots town hall meetings to build support for his policy agenda.

Koizumi also effectively used the media to push his policy agenda. He developed several slogans, which translated into effective sound bites. Some slogans included "structural reform without sacred cows," "from the public sector to the private sector," "what the private sector can do, it should do." All these slogans highlighted his privatization and economic reform goals. The slogans consistently appeared in the media and remain strongly associated with the Koizumi era.

Several environmental factors also favored policy success. The fact that Japan had been in an economic recession for over a decade made the public more primed for economic reform. Moreover, the opposition parties remained fragmented and weak. The DPJ, in particular, was unable to challenge Koizumi as he co-opted their general position by taking on his own party.

Koizumi also used advisory councils and the new resources of the prime minister to push for policy. These resources rested outside the Diet, which gave Koizumi more independence from his party. For postal reform, Koizumi established an outside advisory council on the three postal services to develop his reform proposal. This advisory council did include some cabinet ministers. The inclusion of cabinet ministers instead of solely relying on outside experts eased the eventual cabinet approval (George Mulgan 2002).

Finally, Koizumi had several personal attributes that aided his ability to pursue his policy agenda. He was an effective speaker with a clear vision of reform. These attributes contributed to his success in garnering media coverage and public support. He was also willing to take risks to secure policy passage. The willingness to take risks was particularly relevant to the eventual passage of the more comprehensive postal reform bill (Gaunder 2007). When the upper house rejected the initial bill, Koizumi dissolved the lower house and kicked party rebels who voted against the bill out of the party. The ability to dissolve the lower house is a formal power of the prime minister. Using this power following a party dispute at a time when the party is divided, however, was risky. This risk paid off. The LDP won a landside victory, and the reform passed a little over a month after the lower house election. Koizumi's willingness to take this risk resulted in a weakening of the constraints he faced, most notably opposition within his own party. It was not a foregone conclusion that the public would overwhelmingly support Koizumi and the LDP in the snap election. The results of the election changed the political landscape and increased the possibilities for him to achieve his policy goals.

Koizumi certainly did not achieve all of his policy goals. Many also would not classify postal system reform as a victory, especially in the long term. In particular, several provisions have been watered down in the years since its initial passage. Prime Minister Abe allowed the postal rebels to re-enter the party in his first term in office following Koizumi's departure. When the DPJ came to power in 2009 it included the People's New Party (PNP) in its coalition to secure a majority in the upper house. Postal rebels formed the PNP after Koizumi dissolved the Diet in 2005. The PNP worked to dilute postal reform during its time in government with the DPJ. Whether Koizumi's leadership resulted in policies that left a legacy remains an open question.

Abe Shinzō

Abe Shinzō presents an interesting case of prime ministerial leadership because he has served two non-consecutive terms as prime minister. His second term has been more successful than his first term. Abe first came to office immediately following Koizumi. Abe was Koizumi's handpicked successor. He was relatively young and assumed office with a high level of public support. He was one of the few postwar prime ministers to assume office with support ratings just above 50 percent support (Nyblade 2011: 197). He also had a strong media presence.

In his first term, Abe championed revising the Constitution as well as taking a hard stance against North Korea following its nuclear testing. He also focused on pensions and healthcare. The fact that it was revealed that the government had been mishandling pension records for over a decade harmed these efforts. In the end, Abe served less than a year before resigning due to the LDP's poor performance in the upper house election and the outbreak of financial scandals.

Abe was re-elected LDP president and prime minister in September 2012 following the LDP landside victory over the DPJ. While Abe still supports revising the Constitution, his main focus since resuming the prime ministership has been on economic reform. His reform platform has been dubbed "Abenomics." As discussed in Chapter 8, Abenomics has three "arrows." These arrows include fiscal stimulus, monetary easing, and structural reform. The main short-term goal of Abenomics is to combat deflation by increasing domestic demand and stimulating GDP growth. In the long term, structural reform aims to increase Japan's competitiveness.

During his first two years in office, Abe's economic plan focused on fiscal stimulus and monetary easing, the first two arrows of Abenomics. The more difficult component of Abenomics is the third arrow – structural reform. Many elements of structural reform are unpopular with certain business sectors. Structural reform includes corporate tax cuts, the liberalization of agriculture as well as energy, environment, healthcare, and labor reforms. The Trans-Pacific Partnership (TPP) is a key component of reform aimed to stimulate trade. It is a free trade agreement negotiated with the U.S. and eleven other Pacific Rim countries.

The environment has become increasingly favorable for Prime Minister Abe to pursue his policy agenda. In 2014, he called a snap election to the lower house in an attempt to receive a mandate for his reforms. The LDP along with its coalition partner, the Kōmeitō, retained a majority in the lower house. Following the strong performance in the lower house election, Abe focused on passing a controversial security bill; little progress was made on his economic agenda. In the July 2016 upper house election, the LDP coalition won a two-thirds majority in the upper house. The coalition's strong majorities in both houses open the door to Constitutional revision.

Japan's continued economic woes have not provided Abe as much leverage as he would have liked to push structural reform. This circumstance is even more surprising given the LDP coalition's strong position in the Diet. Several vested interests are strongly opposed to deregulation and liberalization. This constraint seems to have prevented significant action on structural reform. Abe is an effective speaker; he has developed slogans, but the rhetoric has not been enough in isolation to get major movement on structural reform.

Conclusion

Prime ministers are one of several potential key actors in the Japanese policymaking process. The case studies of prime ministerial leadership in the postwar era discussed above illustrate many of the constraints prime ministers face as well as the informal and formal powers used to overcome these constraints. These case studies focused primarily on policy successes, although it should be clear from this discussion that prime ministers are often forced to compromise. The prime ministers highlighted above tended to have a large reserve of informal powers. Yoshida had a clear vision for postwar Japan and reshaped the narrative of Japan's history to support his vision. Tanaka had money, strong personal ties inside and outside his party, and initially at least strong popular appeal. Nakasone and Koizumi both used advisory councils to push their agendas and overcome internal party constraints. Koizumi was a risk taker willing to put his own party's electoral fortunes on the line by dissolving the Diet after postal reform was denied. Abe has had more success in his second term than in his first. Abe is telegenic and has created a synergy around Abenomics. Still, it is unclear if Abe will be able to weaken the special interests that have a stake in opposing structural reform. To date, Abe has not taken real risks to pursue his goals. Risk taking is not essential to all policy success, but it is often an effective strategy for overcoming constraints.

Notes

1 This section draws on Gaunder (2007), especially pp. 12–15.
2 This section draws on Gaunder (2007), pp. 121–134.

References

Ansell, C. K. and Fish, M. S. (1999) "The Art of Being Indispensable: Noncharismatic Personalism in Political Parties," *Comparative Political Studies*, 32: 283–312.
Burns, J. M. (1978) *Leadership*, New York: Harper and Row.

Campbell, J. C. (1989) "Bureaucratic Primacy: Japanese Policy Communities in an American Perspective," *Governance*, 2: 86–94.

Curtis, G. L. (1988) *The Japanese Way of Politics*, New York: Columbia University Press.

Gaunder, A. (2007) *Political Reform in Japan: Leadership Looming Large*, London: Routledge.

George Mulgan, A. (2002) *Japan's Failed Revolution: Koizumi and the Politics of Economic Reform*, Canberra: Asia Pacific Press.

George Mulgan, A. (2003) "The Dynamics of Coalition Politics in Japan," in J. Amyx and P. Drysdale (eds) *Japanese Governance: Beyond Japan Inc.*, London: RoutledgeCurzon.

Hayao, K. (1993) *The Japanese Prime Minister and Public Policy*, Pittsburgh, PA: University of Pittsburgh Press.

Johnson, C. (1982) *MITI and the Japanese Miracle*, Stanford, CA: Stanford University Press.

Johnson, C. (1986) "Tanaka Kakuei, Structural Corruption, and the Advent of Machine Politics in Japan," *Journal of Japanese Politics*, 12: 1–28.

Kernell, S. (1986) *Going Public: New Strategies of Presidential Leadership*, Washington, DC: Congressional Quarterly Press.

Krauss, E. S. and Nyblade, B. (2005) "Presidentialization in Japan? The Prime Minister, Media and Elections in Japan," *British Journal of Political Science*, 35: 357–368.

Machiavelli, N. (1985) *The Prince*, trans. H. C. Mansfield, Jr., Chicago, IL: The University of Chicago Press.

Masumi, J. (1995) *Contemporary Politics in Japan*, trans. L. E. Carlile, Berkeley, CA: University of California Press.

Nyblade, B. (2011) "The 21st Century Japanese Prime Minister: An Unusually Precarious Perch," *Journal of Social Science*, 61: 195–209.

Pempel, T. J. (1987) "The Unbundling of 'Japan, Inc.': The Changing Dynamics of Japanese Policy Formation," in K. Pyle (ed.) *The Trade Crisis: How Will Japan Respond?* Seattle: Society for Japanese Studies, University of Washington.

Rose, R. (2001) *The Prime Minister in a Shrinking World*, Cambridge: Polity Press.

Samuels, R. J. (2003a) *Machiavelli's Children: Leaders and Their Legacies in Italy and Japan*, Ithaca, NY: Cornell University Press.

Samuels, R. J. (2003b) "Leadership and Political Change in Japan: The Case of the Second Rincho," *Journal of Japanese Studies*, 29: 1–31.

Schlesinger, J. M. (1997) *Shadow Shoguns: The Rise and Fall of Japan's Postwar Political Machine*, New York: Simon and Schuster.

Shinoda, T. (2000) *Leading Japan: The Role of the Prime Minister*, Westport, CT: Praeger.

Shinoda, T. (2003) "Koizumi's Top Down Leadership in Anti-Terrorism Legislation: The Impact of Political Institutional Changes," *SAIS Review*, 23: 19–34.

Shinoda, T. (2011) "Prime Ministerial Leadership," in A. Gaunder (ed.) *The Routledge Handbook of Japanese Politics*, London: Routledge.

Weber, M. (1946) "Politics as Vocation," in H. H. Gerth and C. W. Mills (eds) *From Max Weber: Essays in Sociology*, trans. H. H. Gerth and C. W. Mills, New York: Oxford University Press.

Weber, M. (1947) *The Theory of Social and Economic Organization*, trans. A. M. Henderson and T. Parsons, New York: Free Press.

Wiliarty, S. E. (2008) "Angela Merkel's Path to Power: The Role of Internal Party Dynamics and Leadership," *German Politics*, 17: 81–96.

12 National security and foreign policy

While Japan clearly achieved economic superpower status by the 1980s, it has not experienced commensurate political superpower status in the international arena. This chapter explores the challenges Japan has faced at the international and regional levels. It investigates the legacies of its imperialistic past, the consequences of prioritizing growth over defense in the postwar period, and the constraints its domestic political institutions have posed at the international level. It also considers the dynamics of significant bilateral relationships, including Japan–U.S. relations, Japan–EU relations, and Japan–East Asia relations. It concludes with a discussion of Japan's soft power.

Legacies of World War II

Several legacies of World War II influence Japanese politics in general and its national security and foreign policy more specifically. The largest institutional legacies emerge from the postwar settlement and the Japanese Constitution. Article 9, the renunciation of war clause, in particular has constrained Japan's ability to play an active role in its own national security. The interpretation of the Constitution has expanded throughout the postwar period, and the possibility of revising the Constitution has increased in recent years under the tenure of Prime Minister Abe.

The way World War II is remembered has had a large impact on Japan's foreign relations with its neighbors. China and South Korea in particular remain wary of Japan. China opposed Japan's bid to gain a seat on the UN Security Council. Gaffes and denials of past violence and even attempts at apology have negatively impacted Japan's foreign relations. Controversies over comfort women, textbooks, and prime ministerial visits to Yasukuni shrine, a shrine for Japan's war dead including war criminals, have increased distrust by China and South Korea.

The way that Japan has remembered the war has changed over time. In the immediate postwar period, Japan mostly pushed the war into the background. Once the U.S. left, a tendency to glorify Japan's colonial expansion in economic terms and pose the Japanese people as victims of a military regime emerged. After it got back on its feet economically in the mid-1960s, Japan began to engage in the discourse of war responsibility. With the end of the Cold War, the split of the LDP, and the economic stagnation that emerged in the 1990s, the issues surrounding remembrance became much more contentious, influencing both domestic and international issues (Lind 2008).

During the Occupation, Japan's main focus was on building an alliance with the United States. Japan cast World War II as caused by militarism and saw the Occupation as an opportunity to move toward democracy. The Occupation put the focus on

Japan–U.S. relations. Neither Japan nor the U.S. apologized for aggressions or atrocities committed during the war, but each was able to move forward. This focus on the bilateral relationship allowed Japan to largely ignore its relations with its Asian neighbors (Conrad 2010). Moreover, the focus on the way the war ended with atomic bombs dropped on Hiroshima and Nagasaki allowed Japan to take on the role of victim. The atrocities committed by Japan in Asia were overshadowed.

Interestingly enough, Japan's remembrance of World War II contrasts with Germany's remembrance. Some people argue that differing attitudes and beliefs explain the different ways of remembering the war. Here, the argument is that Germany is a guilt culture. As such, it feels that it did something wrong and should be punished for it. Japan, in contrast, is a shame culture. In a shame culture getting caught is worse than the actual action. As a result, the incentive to admit wrongdoing is lower (Benedict 1946). The cultural argument is problematic given that West Germany, East Germany, and Austria would all fall under the category of guilt culture, yet each country dealt with war remembrance quite differently.

Others point to the geopolitical context to explain differences in remembrance (Conrad 2010). Japan's main point of reference was the United States, and its desire was to further its bilateral relations with the U.S. Germany, in contrast, had both the United States and East Germany as its main points of reference. It wished to integrate back into Western Europe. This desire provided incentives for self-critique and apology (Conrad 2010). Denials of war atrocities had the potential of interfering with conservative party goals such as reunification, rearmament, and integration with the West (Lind 2008). As a result, there was very little conservative backlash in Germany.

Japan began to more directly engage in calls for contrition from its neighbors from the mid-1960s through the 1980s. Its apologies often were deemed inadequate. Since the 1990s, the Japanese government has attempted more far-reaching apologies. Prime Ministers Hosokawa, Murayama, Obuchi, and Koizumi all issued a variety of different apologies. In 1995, the Diet passed a resolution to "renew the determination for peace on the basis of lessons learned from history," but contrition tended to produce a domestic conservative backlash that undermined the initial apology (Lind 2008: 62–63). Despite apologies, China and South Korea continue to distrust Japan. The way that World War II has been remembered has had a significant effect on its national security and foreign relations.

National security

After the postwar settlement was negotiated, Japan's national security policy was relatively stable. From the end of World War II until the U.S.–Japan Security Treaty controversy in 1960, Japan was refining its interpretation of Article 9 and what self-defense entailed. With the end of the Cold War, however, the foreign policy landscape opened up, and the possibility of revising the Constitution or further reinterpreting it increased.

In general, as we saw in Chapter 3, the so-called Yoshida Doctrine initially molded Japan's foreign policy. Prime Minister Yoshida negotiated a postwar settlement that called for the most limited defense policy and instead relied on the U.S. for national security. The U.S. was allowed to establish bases on Japanese territory. The U.S.–Japan Security Treaty put Japan under U.S. protection during the Cold War. The Yoshida Doctrine changed over the course of the Cold War. As Japan developed into an economic superpower, it began to share more of the burden of its defense.

Japan's Constitution has influenced Japan's national security policy. Article 9, the renunciation of war clause, states that Japan will not develop the capabilities to pursue acts of aggression. As written, Japan was not supposed to maintain land, sea, or air forces for the purposes of war or aggression (Reischauer 1990: 192). Over time the clause was reinterpreted to allow Japan to create and support a national self-defense force.

Partisan dynamics, as well as public opinion, influenced national security policy under the 1955 system. The JSP was a party defined by its commitment to protecting Article 9 and preventing the revision of the Constitution. Even though the JSP was never close to attaining control of government from 1955 to 1993, the presence of pacifist Diet members helped constrain the debate. Conservatives who supported Japan regaining its military independence stood at the other end of the spectrum. Most of the public had positions between these two extremes. As a result of these dynamics, developments in defense policy were limited. Arms exports were restricted, defense spending was kept under 1 percent of GDP, and the SDF was not allowed overseas. Nuclear weapons were developed, though (Oros 2011: 322). Over time, the issues surrounding Article 9 became somewhat less charged or at least overshadowed by the focus on economic growth.

Public opinion polls from the 1970s to the late 1980s show an increasing flexibility on defense issues (Hyde 2009: 86–89). The JSP, however, retained its strong pacifist stance throughout this period. The JSP's last significant battle related to Article 9 came in 1990, following the outbreak of the first Gulf War. At this juncture, the U.S. criticized Japan for its checkbook diplomacy. In response, the LDP submitted a Peace-keeping Operation (PKO) Bill to the Diet, which would support the deployment of Self-Defense Forces (SDF) troops in UN peacekeeping operations. The JSP was staunchly opposed to this bill. Its opposition was seen by the public as outdated. Indeed, the JSP's public support dropped dramatically after its protests against the PKO bill, and its seats were cut in half in the 1993 lower house election. Hyde suggests that the JSP lost its less committed supporters following the first Gulf War and then lost its hard core supporters following the formation of the LDP-JSP government in 1994 when the JSP was seen as abandoning all of its postwar principles to be in government (Hyde 2009: 96–97).

The reinterpretations of the Constitution have meant that policy and practice now veer considerably from the original intent of Article 9. The Supreme Court has been unwilling to step into the fray, claiming that the establishment of the SDF, for example, is a political policy issue. The Cabinet Legislative Bureau interpreted the Constitution as not preventing Japan from using force to defend its territory (Oros 2011: 323). Many constraints remained under the 1955 system, though. The SDF was small, offensive weapons were banned, and Japan could not aid allies that had been attacked, a practice known as collective self-defense.

Many politicians have argued that Article 9 and Japan's pacifist Constitution have prevented Japan from becoming a "normal country." Here, normal country refers to a country that is able to employ the military as part of its foreign policy. LDP politician and kingmaker Ozawa Ichirō sparked the debate on Japan's "normalcy" in his book *Blueprint for a New Japan*. In this book, Ozawa argued that Japan should change its electoral system in order to have greater party alternation and more political debate on the issues. He hoped that this switch would allow Japan to become a "normal country" and participate in UN operations beyond financial support, as was the case in the first Gulf War (Ozawa 1994).

Several factors have opened up the foreign policy space, especially issues surrounding national security, since the 1990s. With the end of the Cold War, the U.S.'s commitment to maintaining Japan's national security became less certain. In addition, since the 1990s several regional developments have increased Japan's national security concerns and made it more interested in expanding its international presence (Mochizuki 2007: 5). These developments include the push to develop nuclear weapons in North Korea, North Korea's increased acts of aggression via missile testing over Japan, and increased military exercises in China (Mochizuki 2007: 5).

In addition to this system-level change, several changes in Japan's domestic environment have influenced the politics of national security, including electoral reform, party realignment, more policy-focused elections, the alternation of power, and the increased power of the prime minister. Party realignment, policy-focused elections, and the alternation of power all stem from electoral reform (Oros 2011; Rosenbluth and Thies 2010). With party realignment, the JSP has been diminished to all but a few members. No new parties adopted the JSP's inflexible position on Article 9. Moreover, no political party sees the SDF as unconstitutional (Oros 2011). These developments have lessened the constraints on expanding the interpretation of the Constitution.

Japan and the United States have reaffirmed their relationship in the post-Cold War era. Prime Minister Hashimoto and President Bill Clinton issued a joint security declaration in 1996. Among other things, Japan and the U.S. agreed to develop a more advanced ballistic missile defense system (Mochizuki 2007: 13).

Following the September 11, 2001 terrorist attacks in the United States, the Diet passed the Anti-Terrorism Special Measure Law. This law expanded the activities permitted by the SDF. The SDF could participate in noncombat areas, provide fuel and supplies to other countries, transport weapons by sea, provide medical assistance to wounded soldiers, and help refugees (Tsuchiyama 2007: 47). In 2003, the Diet passed the military emergency law to set up guidelines for a response to acts of aggression against Japan. It also passed a Law Concerning Measures on Humanitarian and Reconstruction Assistance that authorized the dispatch of Japanese troops to Iraq (Tsuchiyama 2007: 47–48).

Clearly, constitutional interpretation has expanded since the end of the Cold War. The government deployed the SDF to Afghanistan in 2001 and Iraq in 2003. The peacekeeping role of the SDF has expanded to include refueling activities. Surveillance satellites and ballistic missile defense have also been adopted (Oros 2011).

On July 1, 2014 Prime Minister Abe successfully received unanimous cabinet approval to dramatically reinterpret the Constitution to include collective self-defense. Collective self-defense states that a country can come to the aid of an ally in the case of an act of aggression against that ally if that country's national security is threatened. Throughout the postwar period, collective self-defense has long been deemed in conflict with Article 9 and its renunciation of war. Abe reversed this interpretation. Significantly, however, Abe did not attempt to revise the Constitution. Constitutional revision would require the approval by two-thirds of both houses of parliament and 50 percent approval from the public. Prime Minister Abe got the formal process for revising the Constitution approved during his previous stint as prime minister. He was not in office long enough during his first term, however, to pursue his security agenda. The reinterpretation approved on July 1, 2014 will also allow Japanese SDF to carry weapons in certain instances in peacekeeping operations.

Prime Minister Abe pursued this reinterpretation despite the fact that public opinion polls indicated significant public opposition to the move. For example, three months prior to the cabinet approval an Asahi Shimbun poll indicated that 63 percent of those polled opposed collective self-defense (only 29 percent approved of it). Of those who approved of collective self-defense, a majority (56 percent) still believed that such a shift required an amendment of the Constitution; only 40 percent (of the 29 percent in favor of collective self-defense) supported the reinterpretation through government approval as it eventually happened (Asahi Shimbun 2014).

The cabinet resolution was followed by the introduction of eleven provisions related to Japan's peace and security to the Diet. These provisions outlined the circumstances Japan could be involved in foreign combat and solidified the government's commitment to collective self-defense. The legislation passed both houses in September 2015 despite public protests outside the Diet and declining approval of the Abe government. Whether collective self-defense is unconstitutional and in conflict with Article 9 of the Constitution remains an open question.

Japan–U.S. relations

The Japanese–United States bilateral relationship has been the central and most significant relationship for Japan in the postwar period. Both countries have positive attitudes about the bilateral relationship. According to Gallup's country ratings, 69 percent of Japanese polled said they had a favorable opinion of the U.S. (Global Asia 2013). Similarly, 81 percent of Americans had a favorable opinion of Japan. In fact, Japan joined Canada, Great Britain, and Germany at the top (in the fourth place) of countries attracting the most favorable attitudes from U.S. citizens. All these countries are democracies and strong U.S. allies (Newport and Himelfarb 2013).

In general, Japan–U.S. relations have centered on security, military bases, and economic issues, especially trade. As we have seen above, the Yoshida Doctrine and the U.S.–Japan Security Treaty have significantly influenced Japan's national security. As discussed in Chapter 3, the Yoshida doctrine established Japan as a Western ally. Japan and the U.S. would cooperate to ensure Japan's defense, with the U.S. carrying much of the burden, and Japan would focus on reviving its economy. Japan was able to use Article 9 to avoid getting pulled into wars in Asia. The U.S.–Japan Security Treaty was originally signed in 1951 and renewed in 1960 with a hope on Japan's part of making it more "mutual." No longer a defeated power, Japan hoped to increase its influence over the defense of its soil. In 1967, the U.S. and Japan refined their agreement to include that nuclear weapons would not be housed on Japanese soil. Prime Minister Sato established no production, possession, or introduction of nuclear weapons on Japanese soil. These non-nuclear principles began Japan's participation in the U.S. nuclear weapons umbrella. In 1978, Japan and the United States further refined their relationship in the Guidelines for Defense Cooperation. These guidelines established sea-lane defense and joint exercises.

Japan signaled its commitment to the U.S.-led world order even more clearly under Prime Minister Nakasone (1982–1988). Prime Minister Nakasone and President Reagan had a strong personal relationship. During Nakasone's tenure, Japan agreed to cooperate with the U.S. more explicitly in its Cold War efforts against the Soviet Union. These efforts included an expansion of U.S. troops in Japan as well as an increase in the number of SDF troops.

The Japan–U.S. relationship underwent some strain after the outbreak of the first Gulf War in 1989. The United States criticized Japan for its "checkbook" diplomacy and pressured Japan to increase its involvement. In response, LDP lawmakers introduced the Peacekeeping Operations (PKO) Bill. This bill got bogged down in the Diet, mainly due to staunch opposition from the Japan Socialist Party. The Gulf War was complete before the PKO bill passed the Diet making it a moot point for that incident. Japan, however, did begin to deploy its SDF troops on UN-sponsored missions, and it had a much more efficient response to the 9/11 terrorist attacks when it passed the Anti-Terrorism Special Measure Law. It has dispatched troops to both Iraq in 2001 and Afghanistan in 2003 mainly as backup support in refueling operations.

The United States and Japan revised the joint defense guidelines after the end of the Cold War. For example, the U.S.–Japan Defense Guidelines in September 1997 permitted Japan to conduct military operations from Japan to situations in the area surrounding Japan – another expansion of Japan's responsibility for its own defense (Green and Szechenyi 2011: 334). In 2013, Japan and the United States reopened dialogue of revisions to address issues such as the ballistic missile and nuclear threat from North Korea, cyber attacks, and terrorism. The United States continues to see Japan as an important stronghold in Asia, especially with more aggressive actions from North Korea and China in territorial disputes. With Abe's recent reinterpretations of the Constitution to include collective self-defense, Japan–U.S. security relations are likely to continue to evolve.

Military bases

U.S. bases in Japan have been a central point of dispute between the United States and Japan since their initial establishment. The United States took control of Okinawa as part of the postwar settlement and only returned it to Japanese control in 1972. While Okinawa makes up less than 1 percent of Japan's total land mass, it contains the majority of U.S. bases. The strategic significance of U.S. troops in Okinawa has changed over time. In the beginning, troops in Okinawa were seen as an important piece of regional security during the Cold War. Now territorial disputes as well as the North Korean nuclear threat are often cited as reasons for a continued U.S. presence.

These bases have been the center of many controversies. The local residents have filed complaints and initiated heavily attended grassroots protests about noise, environmental damage, and misconduct by U.S. troops. The most high-profile case of sexual misconduct involved an alleged gang rape of a 12-year-old Okinawan by three members of the U.S. military personnel in 1995. This case was resolved in the U.S. military justice system to the dissatisfaction of the Okinawans. In 1996, Prime Minister Hashimoto asked then U.S. President Bill Clinton to return the Futenma base to Japanese control. This began ongoing conversations about lessening the U.S. presence on the island. In addition to sovereignty concerns, the Okinawans also are interested in recovering base lands to develop tourism and other potential industries. The details of this agreement have changed over time. In 2006, Japan and the U.S. agreed to move Futenma and transfer 8,000 troops to Guam. In 2009, Prime Minister Hatoyama opposed the relocation of Futenma. Prime Minister Hatoyama's stance on Futenma was related to his larger position on Japan–U.S. relations. Specifically, Prime Minister Hatoyama pushed for a more "equal" relationship with the U.S. He also rejected market fundamentalism and called for yuai (fraternity) to define Japan's relations with its neighbors (Chanlett-Avery et al. 2010). President Obama refused to entertain

Japanese requests, and Hatoyama eventually resigned largely due to his mishandling of this issue. Prime Minister Abe has further revised the agreement. Currently, the plan no longer connects the transfer of troops to Guam with the construction of a new base on Okinawa. As of 2013, the U.S. had agreed to return Futenma and five other bases in Japan to the Japanese by the 2020s.

Economic relations

Economic issues have been an important component of Japan–U.S. relations throughout the postwar period. In the immediate postwar, reviving the Japanese economy in the wake of the Cold War became an important priority of Occupation officials during the reverse course. As Japan experienced rapid economic growth, trade frictions increased and dominated the Japan–U.S. economic relationship in the 1970s, 1980s, and early 1990s. Trade frictions subsided with the stagnation of the Japanese economy that occurred about the same time as the U.S. technology boom in the 1990s. Trade frictions have never returned to the heightened levels of the 1980s partially due to the establishment of the World Trade Organization (WTO) as a forum for filing and resolving trade disputes. WTO procedures have lessened the need for Japanese bilateral trade negotiations. Japan and the United States have shifted most recently to pursuing regional free trade agreements.

When trade friction reached its height in the mid-1980s, the governments experimented with various bilateral trade frameworks to resolve disputes. In March 1985, the United States initiated the Market Oriented Sector-Specific (MOSS) talks with Japan. These negotiations focused on disputes in telecommunications, medical equipment, pharmaceuticals, forestry products, electronics, and later auto parts. The focus was on removing export barriers to U.S. products in these sectors. Market access was improved through these negotiations, but U.S. exports to Japan did not increase substantially. In 1989, Japan and the United States entered into Structural Impediments Initiative (SII) talks that targeted nontariff trade barriers. Nontariff barriers included the Japanese retail distribution system, its keiretsu business conglomerates, and exclusionary business practices. The SII did influence Japan's decision to revise its Large Retail Store Law, which had protected small mom and pop shops and prevented the entry of large retail discount stores such as Walmart and Toys R Us. In the early 1990s, the United States focused more on deregulation and competition policy (Cooper 2014).

Following 9–11, national security returned as the dominant issue in the bilateral relationship. Discussions on banking reform, regulatory reform, and competition policy continued, but trade disputes moved to the WTO from 1995 on.

Japan joined twelve other countries including the United States, in Trans-Pacific Partnership talks in 2013. These discussions had been going on since 2005. The TPP negotiations got bogged down on several issues including agriculture, intellectual property rights, services, and investments. The TPP seeks to significantly reduce if not completely eliminate tariffs for hundreds of products. Twelve countries, including Australia, Brunei, Canada, Chile, Japan, Malaysia, Mexico, New Zealand, Peru, Singapore, the United States, and Vietnam, signed the agreement in February 2016. The next step involves ratification by the TPP countries. Strong opposition to several of the provisions could threaten ratification in several countries. If passed, the agreement will establish common standards in several areas for 40 percent of the world's economy (Glenza 2015). Significantly, while China was asked to participate in the trade agreement, it chose not to participate due to the number of restrictions.

Japan–EU relations

The bilateral relationship between Japan and the European Union has not been central to either country. Japan has focused on the United States and the Asian region. The European Union has focused more on its 27 member states (Gilson 2011). In general, Japan welcomed the formation of the EU. From an economic perspective, the EU offers Japan a larger market with standardized rules. The EU market, however, is a potential competitor in some regards. Japan has also found itself facing competition from South Korea and other countries for opportunities in the EU market (Gilson 2011: 353).

Both Japan and Europe see the other as playing a positive role in international politics. Several European countries gave Japan high ratings in this regard including Spain (69 percent), Great Britain (57 percent), Germany (54 percent), Italy (48 percent), and France (47 percent) (BBC 2006).

Japan and the EU participate in several multilateral international organizations including the WTO, OECD, G20, G8, and UN. Several policy issues are relevant to the relationship including trade, the environment, and energy.

Japan is the EU's second largest trading partner in Asia, falling behind China. Japan's main exports to Europe include machinery and transport equipment as well as chemical products. Japan imports agricultural products from the EU as well as machinery and transport equipment and chemical products (European Commission 2016). Of the EU member countries, Germany is both the largest exporter to Japan and importer from Japan. Historically, Japan has run a large trade surplus with the EU, but the relationship has become more balanced in recent years due mainly to a decline in imports to the EU from Japan. Japan and the EU have frequently discussed the promotion of business and investment, and the two countries have several significant agreements surrounding anti-competitive practices and product conformity. Japan and the EU began discussions of a free trade agreement (FTA) in March 2013. A one-year review process of the five rounds of negotiation began in 2014 (European Commission 2014). Japan's interest in an FTA with the EU is based on a desire for greater market access. The EU has high tariffs on cars and electronics that Japan would like to see reduced (Solis 2011).

Japan and the EU have had intentional dialogue on energy policy since 2007. These discussions have focused on sustainable energy, energy security, and energy research and innovation (European Commission 2014). The environment and energy are two areas where Japan and the EU can move to increased multilateralism (Gilson 2011).

Japan–East Asia relations

Japan's relations with its neighbors in East Asia are influenced by the legacies of World War II. While Japan has established positive economic relations with Korea and China, its foreign relations with its neighbors are strained. On the positive side, Japan has been in active negotiations with South Korea and China for FTAs. On the negative side, it has ongoing territorial disputes with these nations as well.

Japan, South Korea, and China all have comparatively negative attitudes toward each other. Japanese attitudes toward South Korea are more favorable than South Koreans' attitudes towards Japan. In Japan, 39.2 percent of people polled said they had a favorable opinion towards South Korea. In comparison, only 21 percent of South

Koreans polled had a favorable attitude towards Japan. A similar picture emerges when investigating Japanese and Chinese attitudes toward each other's countries. In Japan, only 18 percent of those polled had a favorable opinion of China, much lower than those who had a favorable opinion of South Korea. Similarly, only 28.6 percent of Chinese polled had a favorable attitude towards Japan (Global Asia 2013). In 2012, the number of Japanese surveyed who saw South Korea and China as friendly was lower than ever. That is, negative feelings of Japanese towards both countries have been increasing (Fisher 2012). The cause of these increasing negative feelings is not completely straightforward. There are several potential causes, including China's economic and political rise in the region, territorial disputes between the countries, and some would even say rising Japanese nationalism. This trend is worthy of attention moving forward.

Territorial disputes

Japan has ongoing territorial disputes with both South Korea and China. These disputes have historical, economic, and nationalistic dimensions.

South Korea and Japan have competing claims to islands known as the Dokdo islands in Korea and Takeshima in Japan. South Korea has had jurisdiction of the islands since 1954, but Japan claims that these islets are its territory. The dispute is inextricably tied to Japan's colonization of Korea in 1905. Both countries claimed these islands prior to colonization. South Korea claims that it established Dokdo as Korea territory in 1696. Dokdo was placed under the jurisdiction of Uldo County in 1900. According to South Korea, Dokdo was annexed by Japan in 1905, but it was given back to Korea at the end of World War II. Japan claims that it gained official control of the islands by the mid seventeenth century and that it became part of Shimane prefecture in 1905. It claims that South Korea acted outside its rights in claiming jurisdiction in 1954 since the islands were not part of the San Francisco Peace Treaty (BBC 2012). The islands can be described as two small atolls with about 30 smaller surrounding rocks. They are found in between South Korean and Japanese territory in what South Korea calls the East Sea and Japan refers to as the Sea of Japan. The islands are in the middle of ripe fishing grounds and many have speculated that the area around the islands contains gas reserves, but this is unclear (BBC 2012).

The islands hold a symbolic significance for each nation connected to history and national identity. Japan has called for the dispute to be heard by the International Court of Justice. A hearing, however, requires South Korean consent. South Korea has refused to consent to a hearing. It has jurisdiction and fears that if the International Court of Justice ruled in Japan's favor it would be legitimizing Japan's colonization from the South Korean perspective (Park and Chubb 2011).

Both sides have used the islands to fuel domestic support and nationalism. In 2005, Shimane prefecture in Japan declared February 22 Takeshima Day, a move that touched off protests in South Korea. At several points, Japan has asserted sovereignty over the islands in its textbooks. South Korea in turn has beefed up security in the area to maintain control. Allies of both Japan and South Korea would like to see the dispute resolved, but a way out is not clear due to the charged history connected to the island dispute.

Japan and China also have an ongoing territorial dispute that has escalated in the last decade. The history of the dispute over islands in the East China Sea referred to as the Senkaku Islands by the Japanese and the Diaoyu Islands by the Chinese has its origins as far back as the Sino-Japanese War in 1894–1895. After Japan defeated China in the Sino-Japanese War, it claimed control of Taiwan as well as the Senkaku/Diaoyu islands. Japan asserts that its rights to the territories actually emerged from the fact that the islands were uninhabited and unoccupied when one of its citizens, Koga Tatsuhiro, a merchant from Fukuoka, first came upon the islands in 1884. The Japanese government made the islands part of Japan following the end of the Sino-Japanese War in 1895 (Lee 2011). Japan lost control of the islands to the United States after World War II, but the islands returned to Japan's control at the same time the U.S. released control of Okinawa. Since this time Japan, China, and Taiwan have all laid claim to the islands. The islands while uninhabited are believed to be surrounded by deposits of oil and natural gas, something uncovered in the 1960s.

The dispute over the islands in the East China Sea has escalated in the last decade. In 2010, a Chinese fishing boat ran into the Japanese coast guard in the area. Following the crash, the Japanese coast guard boarded the Chinese fishing boat and arrested the captain. Video footage suggested that the Chinese captain intentionally rammed the fishing boat into the coast guard. Regardless of motivation and guilt, the incident sparked protests in cities across China (Lee 2011). China felt further provoked when the right-wing mayor of Tokyo, Ishihara Shintarō, attempted to purchase three of the islands from private owners. In an attempt to diffuse the situation, the Japanese government stepped in to purchase the islands. This action did not succeed in calming the Chinese. Instead, the Chinese government focused on the fact that the territory did not have the right to change owners since ownership was in dispute (Schiavenza 2013). China responded in November 2013 by establishing an air-defense identification zone (ADIZ) over parts of the East China Sea. This law requires foreign aircraft to inform China when flying over areas in the East China Sea. Both Japan and the United States registered opposition to the ADIZ. At this point, a resolution to the territorial dispute appears elusive.

Economic relations

Despite the territorial disputes and other legacies of Japan's imperialism, Japan has fostered positive economic relations with South Korea and China.

Japan is South Korea's third largest export market and second largest import market. South Korea exports more to China and the United States and imports more from China.[1] Only the United States and China import more into Japan than South Korea does; it ranks third. South Korea is Japan's third largest export market (behind the U.S. and China).[2] Japan's major exports to South Korea include machines, electronic equipment, iron and steel, organic chemicals, and medical equipment. Japan's major imports from South Korea include oil, electronics, machines, iron and steel, and plastics.[3]

Economic interdependence between Japan and China is high. China is Japan's largest trading partner, and Japan is China's third largest trading partner. In 2014, China's share of Japan's total trade was 20.5 percent. In 2014, China ranked first in the value of Japanese total trade and imports, and ranked second after the U.S. in terms of exports (JETRO 2015). Japan's major exports to China are electronic equipment, machines, vehicles, medical equipment, and organic chemicals.[4] In recent years, Japan has become the largest exporter of automobiles for China (JETRO 2015). Japan's major imports from China include electronic equipment, machines, clothing, and plastics.[5] Since the early 2000s, however, Japan's total share of Chinese trade has declined. That is, China has become less reliant on the Japanese market. Over the same time period, Japan's reliance on the Chinese market has increased (Todo 2014). While economic interdependence persists, political tensions do pose some threats to smooth economic relations in the future.

Japan as a regional leader

Japan is a member of several regional organizations. Most of these organizations are built around economic cooperation. The historical legacy of Japan's imperial expansion has complicated its leadership role on all fronts, but especially politically. Finding economic common ground has been more possible.

Japan began building ties in the Asia-Pacific region in the 1950s and 1960s, finding a strong partner in Australia. Following the creation of several groupings, the efforts culminated in the creation of a multilateral grouping in 1989 referred to as the Asia-Pacific Economic Cooperation (APEC). APEC initially included twelve countries: Japan, Australia, New Zealand, Canada, the United States, South Korea, Thailand, Singapore, Indonesia, the Philippines, Malaysia, and Brunei. Membership later expanded to include twenty-one countries in Asia, adding China, Hong Kong, and Chinese Taipei in 1991, Mexico and Papua New Guinea in 1993, Chile in 1994 and Vietnam, Russia, and Peru in 1998.

The main goal of APEC has been to promote free and open trade and investment in the Asia-Pacific region. APEC members committed to achieving this goal for developed country members by 2010 and for developing country members by 2020. Over time, its focus has expanded from trade and investment liberalization to include energy security, climate change, human security, food security, data privacy, human security, and other issues.[6]

Japan's soft power

Many argue that the constraints of Article 9 have limited Japan from becoming a political superpower. As we have seen, domestically politicians have struggled because Japan has been unable to function as a "normal" country due to the renunciation of war clause.

With the constraints on the use of military force many politicians, policymakers, and scholars have argued that Japan would be best served to focus on developing its soft power. Soft power refers to the dissemination of values and beliefs to ellicit desired behavior from other countries. While most treatments of soft power only focus on popular culture, it also includes ideology and the legitimacy of foreign policy (Sun 2012: 5–7). According to Sun, through soft power "a country can get another country to do what it desires by launching charm offensives, convincing other countries to perceive the wooing country as an example and to voluntarily follow its preferences" (Sun 2012: 5). Soft power does not require the use of force. For soft power to be effective, a country needs to consider the target country carefully. In the absence of common values, soft power's effectiveness is limited. Just because a country like Japan has exported popular cultural items such as sushi, karaoke, manga, anime, etc. does not mean it will be able to elicit the desired behavior from another country. The context matters. That is, the target country needs to have shared values. Leaders also play important roles in mobilizing soft power.

In the context of Asia, especially in China, Japan's soft power has been limited. Japanese products are popular in China. Manga, anime, J-pop, and J-drama all have appeal. The problem rests with the context. History impedes any efforts to charm China. The positives of popular culture have been unable to diminish the resentment and hurt over World War II.

Japan has made some efforts to disseminate its values or at least increase its positive image and promote education about Japan. These efforts have come about through several government-sponsored agencies including the Japan Foundation, the Japan Exchange and Teaching Program, Japan Overseas Cooperation Volunteer Program, and Official Development Assistance (Lam 2007). These programs are not directly linked to specific policy goals, weakening the potential for them to turn into power. Soft power is most effectively wielded when a leader has connected values, popular culture, and ideology to specific foreign policy goals (Sun 2012).

Conclusion

This chapter has illustrated the significance of the legacies of Japan's imperialistic past on its national security policy and its foreign relations, especially in East Asia. The way Japan has remembered World War II has been highly criticized by its neighbors, and a lack of trust prevails in the security realm. Recent moves by the Abe government to reinterpret the Constitution have not helped to allay these fears. Moreover, territorial disputes continue to plague Japan–South Korea and Japan–China relations. Despite these concerns, though, Japan has successfully established economic relations in the region. As illustrated in this chapter, its economic interactions with South Korea and China are significant.

Japan has prioritized the bilateral relationship with the United States in the postwar period. During the Cold War, Japan was part of the U.S.-led world order. The U.S.–Japan Security Treaty was quite significant in setting the parameters of the relationship. Many observers assert that Japan was able to grow so rapidly because it did not have to focus as many resources on self-defense due to being under the U.S.'s security umbrella. On the economic front, relations with the United States have been more harried, especially in the 1980s, with the U.S. accusing Japan of unfair trade practices. The TPP could be a very significant free trade agreement involving the United States, Japan, and other countries in the Asia-Pacific.

Finally, Japan has not gained political superpower status despite being the third largest economy in the world. Its soft power has increased, but it is unclear that soft power is enough to influence the actions of other countries in any significant way.

Notes

1 See http://countries.bridgat.com/South_Korea_Trade_Partners.html.
2 See www.tradingeconomics.com/japan/exports.
3 See www.worldsrichestcountries.com.
4 See www.worldsrichestcountries.com.
5 See www.worldsrichestcountries.com.
6 See www.apec.org.

References

Asahi Shimbun (2014) "Special Public Opinion Poll," The Maureen and Mike Mansfield Foundation, April 7. Available online at http://mansfieldfdn.org/program/research-education-and-communication/asian-opinion-poll-database/listofpolls/2014-polls/asahi-shimbun-special-public-opinion-poll-040714/ (accessed 28 July 2014).

BBC (2006) "Global Poll: Iran Seen Playing Negative Role," *Global Scan*. Available online at www.globescan.com/news_archives/bbc06-3/ (accessed 6 August 2014).

BBC (2012) "Profile: Dokdo/Takeshima Islands," *BBC News*. Available online at www.bbc.com/news/world-asia-19207086 (accessed 13 August 2014).

Benedict, R. (1946) *The Chrysanthemum and the Sword: Patterns of Japanese Culture*, New York: Houghton Mifflin.

Chanlett-Avery, E., Cooper, W. H., and Manyin, M.E. (2010) "Japan-U.S. Relations: Issues for Congress," Congressional Research Service, February 24. Available online at https://books.google.com/books?id=xOkv75brxqcC&pg=PA1&lpg=PA1&dq=futenma+and+dpj&source=bl&ots=KzR7tcHG-y&sig=JSzi9P6bcoMfA6UQRT4cuTz793s&hl=en&sa=X&ved=0ahUKEwj16p2Z25nOAhVCRyYKHdb9D_0Q6AEIRzAG#v=onepage&q=futenma20and%20dpj&f=false (accessed 28 July 2016).

Conrad, S. (2010) *The Quest for the Lost Nation: Writing History in Germany and Japan in the American Century*, trans. A. Nothnagle, Berkeley: University of California Press.

Cooper, W. H. (2014) "U.S.-Japan Economic Relations: Significance, Prospects, and Policy Options," Congressional Research Service, February 18. Available online at Fas.org/sgp/crs/row/RL32649.pdf (accessed 6 August 2014).

European Commission (2014) "Japan." Available online at http://ec.europa.eu/trade/policy/countries-and-regions/countries/japan/ (accessed 7 August 2014).

European Commission (2016) "Japan." Available online at http://ec.europa.eu/trade/policy/countries-and-regions/countries/japan/ (accessed 18 July 2016).

Fisher, M. (2012) "12-Year Survey: Japanese View of China and Korea Hits Record Low," *The Washington Post*. Available online at www.washingtonpost.com/news/worldviews/wp/2012/11/29/12-year-survey-japanese-view-of-china-and-korea-hits-record-low/ (accessed 11 August 2014).

Gilson, J. (2011) "Drifting Apart? Japan-EU Relations," in A. Gaunder (ed.) *The Routledge Handbook of Japanese Politics*, London: Routledge.

Glenza, J. (2015) "TPP deal: US and 11 Other Countries Reach Landmark Pacific Trade Pact," *The Guardian*. Available online at www.theguardian.com/business/2015/oct/05/trans-pacific-partnership-deal-reached-pacific-countries-international-trade (accessed 18 July 2016).

Global Asia (2013) "The Politics of Trust: How East Asia Can Secure a Peaceful Future," *Global Asia*, 8, 3 (Fall): 24. Available online at Globalasia.org/Template/DownloadArticle/459 (accessed 5 August 2014).

Green, M. J. and Szecheneyi, N. (2011) "Janap–U.S. Relation," in A Gaunder (ed.) *The Routledge Handbook of Japanese Politics*, London: Routledge.

Hyde, S. (2009) *The Transformation of the Japanese Left: From Old Socialists to New Democrats*, New York: Routledge.

JETRO (2015) "JETRO survey: Analysis of Japan-China Trade in 2014 (Based on Imports of Both Countries)." Available online at www.jetro.go.jp/en/news/releases/2015/20150225183-news.html (accessed 18 July 2016).

Lam, Peng Er (2007) "Japan's Quest for 'Soft Power': Attraction and Limitation," *East Asia*, 24: 349–363.

Lee, J. (2011) "Senkaku/Diaoyu: Islands of Conflict," *History Today*, 61. 5. Available online at www.historytoday.com/joyman-lee/senkakudiaoyu-islands-conflict (accessed 12 August 2014).

Lind, J. M. (2008) *Sorry States: Apologies in International Politics*, Ithaca, NY: Cornell University Press.

Mochizuki, M. M. (2007) "Japan's Changing International Role," in T. U. Berger, M. M. Mochizuki, and J. Tsuchiyama (eds) *Japan in International Politics: The Foreign Policies of an Adaptive State*, Boulder, CO: Lynne Rienner.

Newport, F. and Himelfarb, I. (2013) "Americans Least Favorable Toward Iran," *Gallup.com*. Available online at www.gallup.com/poll/161159/americans-least-favorable-toward-iran.aspx (accesses 5 August 2014).

Oros, A. L. (2011) "The Politics of National Security," in A. Gaunder (ed.) *The Routledge Handbook of Japanese Politics*, London: Routledge.

Ozawa, I. (1994) *Blueprint for a New Japan: The Rethinking of a Nation*, trans. L. Rubinfien, Tokyo: Kodansha International.

Park, Dong-Joon and Chubb, D. (2011) "South Korea and Japan: Disputes over the Dokdo/ Takeshima Islands," *East Asia Forum*. Available online at www.eastasiaforum.org/2011/08/17/ south-korea-and-japan-disputes-over-the-dokdotakeshima-islands/ (accessed 13 August 2014).

Reischauer, E. O. (1990) *Japan: The Story of a Nation*, 4th edn, New York: McGraw Hill Publishing Company.

Rosenbluth, F. M. and Thies, M. F. (2010) *Japan Transformed: Political Change and Economic Restructuring*, Princeton, NJ: Princeton University Press.

Schiavenza, M. (2013) "How a Tiny Island Chain Explains the China–Japan Dispute," *The Atlantic*. Available online at www.theatlantic.com/china/archive/2013/12/how-a-tiny-island-cha in-explains-the-china-japan-dispute/281995/ (accessed 12 August 2014).

Solis, M. (2011) "Japan and East Asian Economic Regionalism," in A. Gaunder (ed.) *The Routledge Handbook of Japanese Politics*, London: Routledge.

Sun, J. (2012) *Japan and China as Charm Rivals: Soft Power in Regional Diplomacy*, Ann Arbor: University of Michigan Press.

Todo, Yasuyuki (2014) "For Coin and Country: Easing Japan-China Tensions Through Social, Economic, and Political Equilibrium," *Georgetown Journal of International Affairs*, December 12. Available online at http://journal.georgetown.edu/for-coin-and-country-easing-japan-china -tensions-through-social-economic-and-political-equilibrium/ (accessed 18 July 2016).

Tsuchiyama, J. (2007) "War Renunciation, Article 9, and Security Policy," in T. U. Berger, M. M. Mochizuki, and J. Tsuchiyama (eds) *Japan in International Politics: The Foreign Policies of an Adaptive State*, Boulder, CO: Lynne Rienner.

13 Conclusion

Now that we have explored Japanese history, political institutions, economic development, political economy, policymaking, state–society relations, foreign relations, and national security it is important to revisit the major themes of the text. Indeed, our examination of Japanese politics has shed light on many of the key questions in comparative politics including modernization, democratization, the role of institutions, and the relationship between culture and structure. The first part of this chapter revisits these themes. The final section of the conclusion looks at the major challenges and opportunities facing Japan moving forward. It highlights the significance of the alternation of power in the 2009 lower house election. It also addresses many ongoing issues in Japanese politics and economics.

Revisiting the themes of the text

Our examination of Japanese politics has shed light on many key questions in comparative politics. As we have seen, Japan presents an interesting case of modernization. Japan was a late modernizer. It avoided colonization by the West when forced to open its ports in the mid-1850s. Many of the legacies of feudalism would prove to favor an accelerated path to modernity for Japan. The fact that Japan was a relatively unified feudal country with high levels of agricultural development and internal trade helped Japan remain independent. Nevertheless, the West treated Japan as a second-class citizen with unequal treaties in force until the early 1900s. Japan began to build an empire close to home with the hope of gaining economic resources and security. It also adopted a Western constitution. The ambiguity of sovereignty, however, made it unclear whether the oligarchs, politicians, or militarists were in charge. In the end, the military interests prevailed and Japan turned to fascism.

An exploration of the causes of fascism is the reverse of exploring why countries democratize. Some posit that fascism emerged as a way to return to more traditional ways of the past (Turner 1972). Others maintain that fascism was more likely to emerge in countries that were trying to modernize (Chirot 1977). Japanese fascism differed some from the variants in Europe, particularly with its focus on the emperor. Still, many of the defining features of fascism are apparent – the focus was on the state and on war.

The Occupation played a key role in putting Japan on a path to becoming one of the leading modern industrialized countries. The Occupation focused on demilitarization and democratization. It built on institutions from prewar Japan such as a bicameral legislature and a multiple-member district electoral system. Institutional legacies from the Taishō period (1912–1926) provided a strong foundation for the solidification of Japanese democracy.

The causes of the Japanese economic miracle are a bit more difficult to untangle. Some argue that the bureaucracy played a key role in picking economic winners and losers through its use of industrial policy (Johnson 1982). Others posit that liberal countries inherently tend toward growth and point to key indicators such as savings and investment rates (see Noble 1989). Initially, cultural explanations saw group-oriented societies, such as Japan, as antithetical to growth (Weber 1930). The Japanese case called these assertions into question. Given this, some wondered if there was something particular in Japanese culture that promoted growth. In the end, the most suitable explanation for Japanese growth depends a great deal on the time period and industrial sectors under investigation. Certainly, the Japanese state through the bureaucracy played a larger role in the economy than in other countries. That said, by the 1970s pluralistic explanations with a focus on policy networks involving bureaucrats, politicians, and interest groups more accurately captured the policymaking dynamics (Pempel 1987).

When Japan is placed into comparison with the West in general and the United States in particular, cultural explanations are particularly enticing. This exploration of Japanese politics has acknowledged that cultural differences certainly exist between Japan and the West. These differences, however, have existed for long periods of time and are thus more difficult to establish as the decisive factor explaining change. Instead, culture is often an intervening factor that explains why certain practices or processes might look differently in Japan than in the U.S. For example, as more and more countries have developed a recognition that capitalism can look differently in different countries more attention has been put on institutional legacies of late development as well as varying values and beliefs informing the institutions of capitalism (Hall and Soskice 2001).

Many chapters in this text have focused on institutions. Institutions are important because they outline the rules of the game that provide incentives and constraints for political actors. In this way institutions often influence political outcomes. Under the multiple-member district electoral system, for example, factions emerged as a way to respond to the rules of the game. In large parties seeking a majority in the lower house of parliament, members had to compete against one another for seats in any given district. Politicians sought factional support mainly for financial reasons. Factions, in turn, asked politicians to support their candidate for the prime ministership and only supported one factional candidate per district. Changes to electoral system rules in 1994 changed the incentives and constraints political parties, politicians, and voters faced. To the surprise of some, factions have remained despite the switch to single-member district elections. Part of the explanation for their longevity rests with the fact that factions have non-electoral functions as well. Factional power has diminished and changed in the new system in response to new incentives. Nevertheless, factions are an institutional legacy of the old system (Krauss and Pekkanen 2011). This example of the role of institutions in framing politics is just one of many that can be extracted from this text.

Future challenges and opportunities

Japan faces several challenges and opportunities in the political and economic realm. Politically, there is the possibility of party realignment or at least redefinition. Since resuming power in 2012, the LDP has faced an apathetic public. Will unpopular governments and weak leadership continue to define Japanese politics in the twenty-first century as it has for most of the postwar period?

Economically the situation remains bleak. Economic stagnation has continued despite Prime Minister Abe's Abenomics. The quality of life for the individual has decreased in the last decades. Per capita income is less in real terms than during economic growth. Unemployment remains low comparatively, but part-time employment has increased at the expense of full-time employment. Poverty rates have also increased. Finally, life expectancy continues to increase. This increased life expectancy coupled with Japan's decreasing birth rate poses severe economic strains. Comparatively speaking, however, Japan weathered the Great Recession better than many other developed countries where the economic contraction was worse and the political fallout was more severe. Indeed, the LDP has maintained its hold on power after a brief period of DPJ rule from 2009 to 2012. This section considers some significant political and economic issues facing Japanese society moving forward.

Political issues

The Democratic Party of Japan won a landslide victory in the 2009 lower house election. With the exception of a ten month period in opposition in 1993–1994 following an internal party split, the LDP controlled the majority in the lower house or ruled in coalition from 1955–2009. Given this history, the ascendance of the DPJ was met with great anticipation. In the end, however, the party fumbled. The party's poor performance in office was only exacerbated by the triple disaster in March 2011. What does the 2009 alternation in power tell us about the future of Japanese politics?

The election of the DPJ in 2009 signaled that the party system had become more nationalized, and the LDP and DPJ were becoming the major parties competing in single-member districts (McElwain 2012). These trends have increased the need for parties and candidates to appeal to the broader public. Party leaders and party manifestos continue to play a larger role in elections, and the appeal to the median voter more heavily guides electoral politics (Scheiner 2012). The new electoral environment has also increased the potential for larger partisan swings as seen in the 2005, 2009, and 2012 lower house elections. Party popularity has been a strong predictor of candidate performance in recent elections (Reed, Scheiner, and Thies 2012).

Interestingly enough, the policy outcomes during the DPJ's time in office were not dramatically different from those of prior LDP coalition governments. The DPJ's limited success in realizing its policy agenda is directly related to the incentives and constraints posed by the institutions considered throughout the text. Fiscal constraints made it difficult for the DPJ to keep campaign promises related to child care allowances and transportation policies (Gaunder 2012; Lipscy 2012). Key veto points, including bureaucratic ministries, also played a role in inhibiting progress on the party's agenda (Gaunder 2012). Weak leadership and party disorganization plagued DPJ success. The result was that the DPJ did not accomplish much while in office.

The LDP has resumed a dominant position in the government as the "least bad option" (Pekkanen 2012). The dramatic victory of the LDP in the 2012 lower house election showed its strength in single-member districts. The LDP's performance in the PR portion barely increased. In addition, voter turnout was 10 percent lower than in 2009 (Pekkanen 2012).

Prime Minister Abe shored up support for the LDP when he called a snap election for the lower house in 2014. The Diet has to be dissolved for new elections every four

years. The 2014 lower house election was called only two years after the Abe government had taken control, much earlier than anticipated. Prime Minister Abe explained
that he wanted a mandate for his government so that he could continue his policy
agenda. He got this, partly due to a weak opposition. The LDP won 291 seats and its
coalition partner, the Kōmeitō won 35 seats, giving the coalition a two-thirds majority
in the lower house. A two-thirds majority allows the lower house to overturn any
potential veto from the upper house. The DPJ increased its seats from the previous
defeat but only won 73 seats in all. The DPJ was not even able to run candidates in all
the single-member districts, and its leader lost his seat. Voter turnout was significantly
lower in the 2014 election falling to 52.7 percent from 59.3 percent in the 2012 election
(Economist 2014).

Prime Minister Abe's performance has been stronger than in his first stint as prime
minister in 2006. In 2012, his cabinet approval ratings were around 60 percent. His
approval ratings dipped below 40 percent in 2015 following the passage of controversial
security bills in the lower house in July. These bills centered on increasing Japan's collective self-defense. The security legislation was not popular with the public and
prompted the opposition to walk out of the lower house in July 2015. Prime Minister
Abe was committed to the passage of this legislation regardless of the negative reaction from
the public. After the 2014 lower house election, the LDP's position was so strong that the
legislation passed both houses without a problem after securing the support of the
Kōmeitō. The DPJ and other opposition parties were unable to mobilize public discontent
with the security bill into support for their parties (Pekkanen and Pekkanen 2016).

In 2016, Abe's approval ratings had recovered to above 50 percent. The DPJ has
gained little ground since losing to the LDP in 2009. That is, when LDP approval ratings wane, this has not translated into increased support for the DPJ. Given Abe's
support for several controversial initiatives including reopening nuclear plants, the
security bill, and the Trans-Pacific Partnership (TPP), it is remarkable that the DPJ has
gained so little ground.

In March 2016, the Democratic Party of Japan merged with the Japan Innovation
Party (Ishin no Tō) to create the Democratic Party (Minshintō). Many members of the
Japan Innovation Party had been former members of the DPJ. The merger of the first
and third largest opposition parties brought the new party's strength to 153 members of
parliament. The hope is to consolidate opposition power. Given the number of new parties
and party mergers in recent years, this particular merger did not garner a large amount of
attention (Ueda 2016). The new Democratic Party will suffer from the same problems as
the DPJ – distinguishing itself from the LDP as well as illustrating its ability to rule by
establishing an effective party organization and appealing party leadership.

The 2016 upper house results suggest the merger has had a limited impact. The
Democratic Party did not perform strongly, winning 31 of the 121 contested seats.
The LDP/Kōmeitō coalition gained five seats with the LDP securing 55 seats and the
Kōmeitō winning 14 seats. Following this election, the coalition holds a two-thirds
majority in both the lower and upper houses (The Japan News 2016).

Economic issues

This text has highlighted several economic challenges that Japan faces in upcoming
decades. These challenges take on even greater significance in the context of the political environment. Without the potential challenge from an opposition party, the LDP

once again has less incentive to address some of the structural issues that could negatively impact its constituencies. Prime Minister Abe's mandate has resulted in the passage of security bills, but significant movement on economic reform has not occurred. Growth has remained at or below 1 percent, and structural change has been limited to this point. Major economic challenges include debt service, energy security, and employment issues related to an aging, low fertility society.

Debt service

Japan has the largest debt service of any OECD country. With decades of a weakened economy, Japan has run government deficits since 1993. As a result, gross government debt as a percentage of GDP has increased from 70 percent in 1992 to 230 percent in 2015 (OECD 2016: 7). The government deficits are a result of increased public social spending on such things as pensions and healthcare. Government revenues have not increased due to a weak economy. The government increased the consumption tax from 5 percent to 8 percent in 2014 in an attempt to raise revenue for debt service. This increase had a negative effect on consumer spending. Another increase is scheduled for 2017. The government is still debating whether to move forward with this increase given the mixed effects of the previous increase (Kennedy 2015).

Slow growth, low productivity and a rapidly aging population have had a negative effect on per capita GDP. Japan now ranks below the top half of OECD countries on this measure (OECD 2016: 2). Prime Minister Abe is encouraging companies to increase wages. The government lowered the corporate tax rate from 32 percent to just below 30 percent in April 2016 to incentivize companies to increase wages. The hope is that increased wages will increase consumption (Kennedy 2015: 3)

Finally, the value of the yen has declined about 30 percent since 2012. The declining value of the yen has both positive and negative consequences. On the positive side, it means greater profits for export-based companies. The weaker yen makes Japanese products cheaper abroad. On the negative side, the weaker yen makes imports more expensive for Japanese consumers. Higher prices for imported food and imported energy can have a negative effect on consumer demand (Kennedy 2015).

Energy security

Energy security was a pressing issue for Japan even prior to the triple disaster in 2011. The incident at the Fukushima nuclear power plant following the earthquake and tsunami, however, made nuclear power an unpopular option and has thrown Japan's energy policy into an uncertain future. All of Japan's nuclear power plants went off line following the disaster, and only two had reopened by 2015. Japan had hoped to increase its reliance on nuclear power prior to the disaster. Now, Japan is struggling to balance several, at times competing, priorities including self-sufficiency, economic efficiency, environment protection, and safety (Koyama 2015: 42).

With the closure of most nuclear power plants, Japan has had to import more fossil fuels. In fact, in 2014 Japan imported over 90 percent of its energy supply (Patrick 2015). The reliance on energy imports causes concern both in terms of energy security and in terms of economic impact. Japan has always worried about its limited natural resources. Nuclear power provided a domestic source of energy that could reduce reliance on imports. When all nuclear power plants went off line following Fukushima,

Japan became the second largest importer of fossil fuels, only following China (EIA 2013). Japan is the world's largest importer of natural gas, the second largest importer of coal, and the third largest importer of oil behind the U.S. and China (Patrick 2015). The increased fuel imports have produced trade deficits. These deficits have only exacerbated Japan's debt situation. In addition, the cost of electricity rose following the disaster, putting pressure on the individual consumer. The weakened yen has also increased costs of fuel imports. Prime Minister Abe is in favor of resuming nuclear energy production. The Nuclear Regulation Authority has implemented increased safety standards for nuclear power plants. Under this regime five plants have been approved for reopening and many more are under review. Given the age of many of the plants, it is estimated that only about seven existing plants will reopen (Patrick 2015). Nevertheless, a report released by METI concerning energy goals for 2030 places nuclear power in the mix, providing about 10 percent of Japan's electricity needs. The majority of the energy supply will be met through fossil fuels (75 percent) and renewables (13 percent) (Patrick 2015).

Japan has implemented a feed-in tariff to promote renewable energy. Technological innovations have made solar power more affordable. In addition, Abe has liberalized the electric industry as part of Abenomics. This liberalization will increase competition and should provide a downward pressure on the price of electricity that soared following the Fukushima disaster (Patrick 2015). Energy policy is sure to be one of the most important issues facing Japan during the next decade as Japan tries to grapple with its vulnerabilities in this area.

Aging, low fertility society

As we saw in Chapter 10, another policy challenge facing Japan in the decades to come is its aging, low fertility society. Japan leads the OECD countries when looking at the elderly population as a share of the working-age population. Currently this ratio is 42 percent. It is projected to increase to 75 percent by 2050 (OECD 2016, 3).

In September 2015, Prime Minister Abe set new economic goals for Japan in the spirit of the original three arrows of Abenomics (monetary policy, fiscal policy, and structural reform). The first goal is to increase Japan's nominal GDP from 500 trillion yen to 600 trillion yen by around 2020. The second goal is to increase the birth rate from 1.4 to 1.8 children per woman. The third goal is to provide elder care so that no workers would have to quit their jobs to care for an elderly relative (OECD 2016: 4). It is unclear whether the government will be able to develop policies that will forward these goals. As we have seen, the government has been trying to provide incentives to increase the birth rate for decades to little avail.

Women and immigrants are the two populations that can be tapped to respond to a decline in the number of people of working age. As we saw in Chapter 10, though, little progress has been made on liberalizing immigration. Increasing women's participation has received much attention in the media as Abe continues to tout a 30 percent by 2020 goal for women in several critical areas. Constraints on achieving these goals remain.

While Japan faces many economic challenges, it also has many strong economic features that will aid it as it faces these challenges. Japan's workforce is highly educated. Japanese companies invest heavily in research and development, and as a result Japan is a world leader in technology. While the aging population strains government resources, high life expectancy has a positive effect on wealth. Indeed, Japan ranks near the top of OECD countries in net household wealth. Japan's employment rate is also higher than average in comparison to other OECD countries (OECD 2016, 1).

Conclusion

Japan remains a very important country to study. It merits attention not only because it is the third largest economy, but also because it has much to tell us about theories of comparative politics. Politically, Japan is a particularly interesting case for electoral system and political party studies. From 1955–1993, Japan was a one-party predominant system. It was not the only country in this category. Sweden, Italy, and Israel have also had periods of one-party predominance (Pempel 1990). Electoral reform in 1994 provides a nice natural experiment to test the effects of changes to electoral system rules. By 2009, it appeared that Japan had settled into a party system of two large parties that mainly competed in the SMDs and several smaller parties kept alive by PR. The disintegration of the DPJ following its first stint in office (2009–2012) has reinitiated party realignment. The new Democratic Party may or may not strengthen its leadership and organization and truly challenge the LDP. We can continue to look to the Japanese case to consider the factors that influence party realignment.

With its firm control on power, the LDP is now grappling with many policy challenges including debt service, energy security, and an aging, low fertility society. Its progress in these areas remains an open question. This text has illustrated how institutions and historical legacies can constrain reform. These issues face many other industrialized democracies. Placing Japan's performance and policies in comparative perspective places Japan as a "case of" as opposed to a unique nation. This frame of analysis is critical when investigating any country from a comparative perspective.

References

Chirot, D. (1977) *Social Change in the 20th Century*, New York: Harcourt Brace Jovanovich, Inc.

Economist (2014) "Romping Home," *The Economist*, December 15. Available online at www.econom ist.com/news/21636467-shinzo-abe-wins-easily-weak-mandate-voters-romping-home (accessed 21 July 2016).

EIA (2013) "Today in Energy," U.S. Energy Information Administration, November 7. Available online at www.eia.gov/todayinenergy/detail.cfm?id=13711 (accessed 23 July 2016).

Gaunder, A. (2012) "The DPJ and Women: The Limited Impact of the 2009 Alternation of Power on Policy and Governance," *Journal of East Asian Studies*, 12: 441–466.

Hall, P. A. and Soskice, D. (2001) *Varieties of Capitalism: The Institutional Foundations of Comparative Advantage*, London: Oxford University Press.

Johnson, C. (1982) *MITI and the Japanese Miracle*, Stanford, CA: Stanford University Press.

Kennedy, J. (2015) "3 Economic Challenges Japan Faces in 2016," *Investopedia*, December 30. Available online at www.investopedia.com/articles/investing/123015/3-economic-challenges-japan-faces-2016.asp (accessed 22 July 2016).

Koyama, K. (2015) "Inside Japan's Long-term Energy Policy," *Japan SPOTLIGHT*, IEEJ, September/October. Available online at http://eneken.ieej.or.jp/data/6291.pdf (accessed 23 July 2016).

Krauss, E. S. and Pekkanen, R. (2011) *The Rise and Fall of Japan's LDP: Party Organizations as Institutions*, Ithaca, NY: Cornell University Press.

Lipscy, P. Y. (2012) "A Casualty of Political Transformation: The Politics of Energy Efficiency in the Japanese Transportation Sector," *Journal of East Asian Studies*, 12: 409–439.

McElwain, K. M. (2012) "The Nationalization of Japanese Elections," *Journal of East Asian Studies*, 12: 323–350.

Noble, G. W. (1989) "The Japanese Industrial Policy Debate," in S. Haggard and C. Moon (eds) *Pacific Dynamics: The International Politics of Industrial Change*, Boulder, CO: Westview Press.

OECD (2016) "Boosting Growth and Well-being in an Ageing Society," OECD. Available online at www.oecd.org/publications/japan-boosting-growth-and-well-being-in-an-ageing-society-9789 264256507-en.htm (accessed 22 July 2016).

Patrick, H. (2015) "Japan's Post-Fukushima Energy Challenge," *East Asia Forum*. Available online at www.eastasiaforum.org/2015/11/23/japans-post-fukushima-energy-challenge/ (accessed 21 July 2016).

Pekkanen, R. J. (2012) "The 2012 Election Paradox: How the LDP Lost Voters and Won the Election," The National Bureau of Asian Research. Available online at http://nbr.org/resea rch/activity.aspx?id=297 (accessed 22 July 2016).

Pekkanen, R. J. and Pekkanen, S. M. (2016) "Japan in 2015: More about Abe," *Asian Survey*, 56: 34–46.

Pempel, T. J. (1987) "The Unbundling of 'Japan, Inc.': The Changing Dynamics of Japanese Policy Formation," in K. Pyle (ed.) *The Trade Crisis: How Will Japan Respond?* Seattle: Society for Japanese Studies, University of Washington.

Pempel, T. J. (1990) *Uncommon Democracies: The One Party Dominant Regimes*, Ithaca, NY: Cornell University Press.

Reed, S. R., Scheiner, E., and Thies, M. F. (2012) "The End of LDP Dominance and the Rise of Party-Oriented Politics in Japan," *Journal of Japanese Studies*, 38: 353–376.

Scheiner, E. (2012) "The Electoral System and Japan's Partial Transformation: Party System Consolidation without Policy Realignment," *Journal of East Asian Studies*, 12: 351–379.

The Japan News (2016) "Upper House Election 2016," *The Japan News* (by the Yomiuri Shimbun). Available online at http://the-japan-news.com/news/article/0003069791 (accessed 22 July 2016).

Turner, A. T. (1972) "Fascism and Modernization," *World Politics*, 24: 547–564.

Ueda, M. (2016) "Split, Merge and Lose: The Future of Party Politics in Japan," *The Diplomat*, March 25. Available online at http://thediplomat.com/2016/03/split-merge-and-lose-the-future-of-party-politics-in-japan/ (accessed 22 July 2016).

Weber, M. (1930) *The Protestant Ethic and the Spirit of Capitalism*, London: Allen and Unwin.

Index

Note: tables are indicated by **bold** page numbers

Abenomics 101, 105–6, 107, 146, 147, 165, 168
Abe Shinzō 65, 102, 104, 105–6, 107, 114, 139, **140**, 146–7, 155, 165–6, 167; Constitution and 146, 147, 149, 152, 153, 154, 160; gender equality and 106, 115–16, 168
administrative reforms 7, 38–9, 52, 61, 110, 113–15, 120, 137, 143
advisory councils (shingikai) 110, 111, 113–14, 143, 145, 147
Afghanistan 78, 152, 154
aging population 6, 7, 42, 106, 107, 117, 120, 165, 167, 168–9
agriculture 11, 25, 33, 69, 86, 87, 98, 104, 106, 111, 146, 163; agricultural associations 122, 123, 125, 127; reform 25, 59; and trade 89, 155, 156
Akahata 37, 55
amakudari ("descent from heaven") 38, 98, 103, 124, 142
Anti-Terrorism Special Measure Law 152, 154
APEC (Asia-Pacific Economic Cooperation) 159
Article 9 (peace clause) *see* Constitution
Ashida Hitoshi 25, 28, **140**
Asia 21, 37, 90, 118, 150, 153, 156, 159–60; East Asia 6, 19, 20, 28, 92–3, 156–9
Asō Tarō 104, 114, **140**
Australia 19, 52, 155, 159
automobile industry 84, 85, 101, 106, 155, 156

banking 3, 14, 26, 84, 85, 97, 103, 104, 145, 155; crisis 38, 98–9, 101, 103, 105
Bank of Japan 26, 84, 97, 98, 99, 105, 106
birth rates 100, 106, 107, 117, 165, 168
Blair, Tony 44
Blueprint for a New Japan 60, 151
bubble economy 59, 76, 90, 94, 96–9
Buddhism 10, 35, 36, 56
budgets: bureaucracy and 37, 38, 64, 114; Diet and 31, 32, 68; Dodge Mission 25; DPJ and 64, 114; growth and 94; LDP and 52; pre-modern 15, 16; slowdown and 104, 105, 107

Building a New Japan 141
bureaucracy 11, 37–9, 44, 45, 83, 86–7, 111, 120, 164; amakudari 38, 98, 103, 124, 142; civil society and 124, 125, 129; DPJ and 39, 50, 64, 112, 114–15, 165; industrial policy 83, 85, 91, 164; Meiji period 14, 16, 37; Occupation 22–3, 26; policymaking 37, 38, 46, 83, 85, 86, 110–11, 112, 115, 117, 118, 119, 125; pre-modern 3, 11, 12; reform 113–14, 137
Burns, James MacGregor 139
business associations 123, 125, 127

cabinet: bureaucracy and 114, 115, 137; Diet and 32, 112, 136; legal system and 39; policymaking and 106, 110, 111, 112, 116, 137, 153; political parties and 23, 35, 51, 52, 57, 61; Meiji period 15, 16–17; prime minister and 32, 61, 112, 113, 136, 137; reforms 32, 113–14, 137
Cabinet Law 32, 113
Cabinet Secretariat 32, 137
campaigning 34, 57, 63, 68, 75, 76, 77–8, 80
Canada **1**, 52, 153, 155, 159
Canon 84
capitalism 3, 87, 90–1, 164; Japanese 26, 28, 29, 83, 86, 91–2, 101
CEFP (Council on Economic and Fiscal Policy) 103, 114, 137
CGP (Clean Government Party) (Kōmeitō) *see* Kōmeitō
China 1, **1**, 6, 27, 79, 115, 149, 150, 156–7; disputes with 154, 156, 157–8, 160; in East Asia 92, 118, 159, 160; World War II 19, 149, 150, 156, 160
Chisso Corporation 88
Christianity 10
citizen movements (shimin undō) 128, 133
Civil Code 124
civil rights and liberties 4, 15, 31, 45, 46, 113, 127

civil service 14, 16, 22, 38, 44, 111, 116; *see also* bureaucracy
civil society 4, 46, 68, 88, 110, 111, 122–33
clientelism 41, 51, 76, 78, 80
Clinton, Bill 152, 154
"closed country" policy (sakoku) 10, 11
coalitions 24, 32, 43, 54, 57, 58, 73, 80, 112, 138; anti-LDP 42, 49, 53, 60, 61, 62, 71, 99; DPJ 146; LDP/JSP 54, 60, 61–2, 99, 127; LDP/Kōmeitō 36, 46, 62, 65, 106, 147, 166
Cold War 21, 25, 27, 28, 30, 56, 57, 59, 139, 150, 153, 154, 160
collective action dilemma 128, 132
collective self defense 151, 152–3, 154, 166
colonization *see* imperialism
comfort women 149
Communists 22, 35, 55; *see also* JCP
Confucianism 4, 6, 86
conglomerates (keiretsu) 25–6, 91, 93, 155
conglomerates (zaibatsu) 14, 24, 25, 26, 91, 93
Constitution 21, 23, 24, 31, 33, 44, 46; Article 9 (peace clause) 23, 28, 40, 53, 54, 139, 149, 150, 151, 152, 153, 159; Article 41 (Diet) 31; Article 76 and 81 (courts) 39; Articles 92–95 (local government) 41; Meiji 9, 14–15, 16, 21, 23, 29, 30, 46; prime minister and cabinet (Articles 68 and 63) 136; revising 146, 147, 149, 150, 151, 152, 160
construction industry 33, 50, 51, 69, 86, 97, 99, 101, 111, 142, 144
consumer groups 76, 128, 131
consumption tax 54, 59, 62, 63, 64, 98, 103, 105, 106, 167
corporate tax 106, 146, 167
corruption 25, 33–4, 38–9, 46, 58, 68, 69, 71, 74–5, 78, 80, 99
courts 39–40, 88, 130, 133; and policymaking 110, 112–13, 119, 120
Crichton, Michael 90
cultural explanation for growth 2, 86–7, 164
Curtis, Gerald 51, 112

Daiichi 26
Datsun 84
daycare 107, 117–18, 120
debt 99, 103, 143; national 105, 106, 107, 113, 167, 168
decentralization 42, 44, 76, 103
deflation 14, 17, 96, 102, 106
De Gasperi, Alcide 139–40
demilitarization 22, 23, 26–7, 29, 163
democracy 2, 3–4, 5, 9, 28, 30, 40, 45, 46–7, 58, 68, 123, 139, 149; Buddhist 36, 56; and civil society 123, 132, 133; LDP dominance and 57, 59, 93; Taishō period 3, 15–19, 23, 46, 164
Democratic Party (Minshintō) 35, 64–5, **65**, 166

democratization 3–5, 22, 23, 26, 29, 163
Diamond, Larry 122
Diaoyu Islands 154–5
Diet 7, 31–2, 46, 88, 99, 130; financial 99; pollution 88, 130; Meiji period 14, 15, 16, 17; twisted 31–2, 43, 62, 136, 137; *see also* lower house; upper house
Dodge Mission 25, 26, 83
Doi Takako 53, 54, 77
Dokdo islands 157
Dōmei (Japan Confederation of Labor) 36, 53, 56, 126, 127
DPJ (Democratic Party of Japan) 61, 62–5, 74–5, 137, 145, 165; 2012 split 34, 37, 64, 72, 80, 169; bureaucracy and 39, 64, 112, 114–15; daycare 117–18, 120, 165; formation 37, 62–3; policies 63, 105, 119, 165; policymaking 112, 114, 115; prime ministers **140**; triple disaster 50, 64, 65, 105, 115; women 77, 116, **116**, 117
DPJ (Democratic Party of Japan), elections: 2005 63, **72**; 2009 37, 39, 50, 63, 65, 72, **72**, 77, 79, 105, 112, 114, 146, 165; 2010 105; 2012 37, 50, 64, **72**, 115; 2013 37, 50; 2014 37, 50, 64, **72**, 166; 2016 37, 166
DSP (Democratic Socialist Party) 35, 36, 49, 53, 55–6, 60, 61, 69, **70**, 127
Dulles, John Foster 27

East Asia 6, 19, 20, 28, 92–3, 156–9
East China Sea 157–8
Economic Financial Policy Council 145
economic growth 6, 83–95, 100, 141; cultural explanation 2, 86–7, 164; Meiji period 14, 17; Occupation 25–6, 28, 29; political parties and 35, 49, 52, 54–5, 56, 57, 78, 166–7; postwar 35, 38, 46, 52, 55, 56, 57, 83–4; pre-modern 11–12; rates 83, 89, 98, 106, 167; state-led 22–3, 29, 44, 83, 85–6, 94, 106, 164; West's reaction 83, 84, 89–90
economic policy reform 83, 89, 102–6, 146–7, 167
economic relations: East Asia 158–9, 160; EU 156; U.S. 155, 160
economic slowdown 1, 6, 17, 46, 86, 89, 90, 92, 94, 96–109, 149, 165, 167
economy, future issues 166–9
education 4, 25, 46, 76, 77, 93, 118, 143; civil society 123, 124, 126, 129; pre-modern 10, 11, 14
electioneering 51, 54, 63, 68–82
electoral districts 16, 33, 46, 74; *see also* MMDs; SMDs
electoral system 5, 9, 46, 68–74; 1955 system 24, 32–4, 51–2, 68–9, **70**, 73, 136, 137; local government 41–3; Meiji period 15, 16,

17–18; MMD/SNTV system 33, 34, 35, 36, 41, 55, 69, 70, **70**, 72, 73, 79, 80; *see also* lower house; upper house
electoral system reform 7, 34, 37, 49, 60, 68–73, 74, 78, 79–81, 99, 110, 114, 137, 152, 164, 169
emperor 6, 21, 22, 23–4, 39, 139, 163; Meiji period 13, 14, 15, 16, 17, 19
Energy and Natural Resources Agency 85
energy industry 106, 107, 132, 146, 156, 167–8; *see also* nuclear power
Engels, F. 3
enterprise unions 128–9
Environmental Agency 88, 130, 131
environmental groups 123, 124, 125, 127, 128, 129, 130–1
environmental issues 36, 54, 55, 56, 83, 88, 146, 154, 156, 167; *see also* pollution
Equal Employment Opportunity Law 115, 129–30
EU (European Union) 5, 7, 156
exchange rates 25, 88, 89, 90, 102, 106
Executive Council 111, 112
Export-Import Bank of Japan 85
exports 19, 25, 151, 156, 158, 159, 167; economic growth 84, 85, 87, 88, 89, 90, 94, 98, 102; slowdown 98, 102
expulsion tax 142
extraterritoriality 13, 15

factions 35, 36, 51, 52, 53, 164; DPJ 64; LDP 59, 69, 72, 73, 137, 142
farmers 25, 28, 35, 36, 50, 53, 86, 104, 126, 127, 132
Federation of Independent Labor Unions 126
fertility, low 1, 6, 7, 42, 115, 117, 120, 167, 168–9
feudalism 2, 3, 9, 11, 14, 163
FILP (Fiscal Investment and Loan Program) 52, 85, 103, 104, 144
fiscal policy 52, 58, 93, 99, 101, 102–3, 105, 106, 107, 144, 146, 168
fishing industry 83, 88, 104, 132, 157
foreign policy 7, 20, 28, 37, 61, 65, 142, 149–62
France **1**, 111, 156
franchise 15, 16, 17–18, 23, 119
Freedom and People's Rights movement 15–16
free trade 13, 17, 19, 84, 147, 155, 156, 160
friitaa/freeter 100, 128; *see also* irregular workers
FSA (Financial Services Agency) 38, 99, 103
Fukuda Takco **140**, 141
Fukuda Yasuo 104, 114, **140**
Fukushima nuclear disaster (triple disaster) 37, 39, 50, 64, 65, 102, 105, 107, 115, 128, 132, 165, 167, 168
funding: civil society organizations 124, 125, 126; local 41, 42, 43; Meiji period 14, 15; postwar 26, 34, 35, 37, 51, 52, 55, 57, 68,

73, 74–5, 111; pre-modern 12; reform 49, 71, 72, 74–5; scandals 64, 71, 99
Futenma base 154, 155

G20/G8 156
GATT (General Agreement on Trade and Tariffs) 89
GDP (gross domestic product) 1, **1**, 84, 102, 105, 106, 107, 116, 151, 167, 168
gender equality 23, 46, 106, 115–17, 129
George Mulgan, A. 114
Germany **1**, 2, 5, 39–40, 58, 71, 153, 156; democracy 43, 44–5, 46; postwar settlement 21, 22, 27; World War I 19; World War II 21, 150
Great Britain 3, 4, 18, 19, 20, 142, 153, 156; democracy in 31, 43–4, 46, 52, 114; *see also* United Kingdom
Greenpeace 124
GRU (Government Revitalization Unit) 64, 114
Guidelines for Defense Cooperation 153
Gulf War 40, 54, 151, 154

Harbinger Party (Sakigake) 60, 61, 62
Harris, Townsend 12–13
Hashimoto Ryūtarō 98, 103, 107, 113, 137, **140**, 152, 154
Hata Tsutomu 60, 61, **140**
Hatoyama Ichirō 22, 23, 28, **140**, 154
Hatoyama Yukio 64, 105, **140**
health care 89, 103, 104, 106, 107, 118, 124, 126, 141, 144, 146, 167
Heisei period 14
Hideyoshi Toyotomi 10
Higashikuni Naruhiko **140**
Hirohito, Emperor 21
Hiroshima 20, 21, 150
Hitachi 84
Hokkaido Takushoku Bank 98
Honda 84
Hosokawa Morihiro 42, 61, 71, 127, **140**, 150
House of Councilors *see* upper house
House of Representatives *see* lower house
housewives 54, 100, 129, 131
Hyde, S. 151

Ikeda Hayato 84, **140**
immigration 7, 56, 118–19, 120; and labor market 97, 117, 118, 119, 168
imperialism (colonization) 9, 17, 18–19, 26, 92, 149, 157, 158, 159, 160, 163
imports 13, 85, 89, 90, 107, 155, 156, 158, 167–8
India **1**, 94
industrialization 4, 6–7, 30, 84, 128, 130, 141
industrial policy 38, 44, 85, 86, 87, 89, 164

Industrial Training and Technical Internship
  Programs 119
inflation 14, 21, 25, 29, 88–9, 105,
  106, 141
informal power of prime ministers 32, 135,
  136, 138–9, 142, 143, 145, 147
Information Disclosure Act 120
institutions 2, 3, 4, 5, 6, 86, 90, 91, 93, 100,
  122, 164; civil society and 123–4, 125, 127,
  128, 132; democracy and 3, 4, 5, 22, 23,
  31–47; Occupation 22, 23, 25, 37, 46,
  163–4; Meiji period 14, 16; *see also
  individual institutions*
interest groups 2, 3, 5, 6, 7, 33, 34, 46, 50–1,
  52, 58, 76, 110, 111, 123, 138
interest rates 97–8, 99, 104, 106
Internet 75, 101, 125, 145
Iraq 90, 152, 154
irregular workers 100, 102, 105, 107, 128, 130
Ishibashi Tanzan **140**
Ishihara Shintarō 158
Israel 58, 169
Itagaki Taisuke 15
Itai Itai disease 87–8, 130
Italy **1**, 21, 58, 68, 79–80, 139, 141, 156, 169

Japan Development Bank 85
Japan Exchange and Teaching Program 160
Japan Foundation 160
Japan, Inc. 86, 110, 138
Japan Innovation Party (Ishin no Tō) 64–5,
  166
Japan National Railways (JNR) 113, 143–4
Japan New Party 60, 61, **140**
Japan Overseas Cooperation Volunteer
  Program 160
Japan Tobacco (JT) 113
JCP (Japanese Communist Party) 35, 36–7,
  54–5, **65**, **70**, 72, **72**, **116**, 127
Johnson, Stephen 54
JSP (Japan Socialist Party) 33, 34, 35–6, 49,
  53–4, 56–7, 69, **70**, 72, 92; 1989 elections
  32, 54, 137; 1990 elections 54, **70**; 1993
  elections 54, 61, **70**, 151; 1996 elections 62;
  coalitions 49, 53, 54, 60, 61–2, 99, 127, 151;
  formation 28, 34, 49, 53; pacifism 53, 54,
  61, 151, 152, 154; splits 35, 36, 55–6, 63;
  unions and 36, 53–4, 92, 126–7, 143–4;
  U.S.–Japan Security Treaty 29, 35, 53, 56, 61
Jusen scandal 98

Kaifu Toshiki 54, 59, **140**
Kanemaru Shin 59–60, 99
Kan Naoto 64, 105, 132, **140**
Katayama Tetsu 24, **140**
Katsura, General 16
Kawasaki 84

Keidanren (Federation of Economic
  Organizations) 127, 141
keiretsu (conglomerates) 25–6, 91, 93, 155
Kiko network 131
kisha kurabu (reporters' club system) 76, 125
Kishi Nobusuke 28–9, 53, 84, **140**
Kobe earthquake 99
kōenkai (personal support groups) 33–4, 35,
  51, 53, 59, 60, 72, 73
Koga Tatsuhiro 158
Koizumi Junichirō 32, 42, 43, 52, 54, 62, 63,
  99, 100, 103, 104, 107, 114, 137, 139, **140**,
  144–6, 147, 150
Kōmeitō (CGP (Clean Government Party))
  35, 36, 49, 55, 56, 60, 61, 62, **65**, 69, **70**, 72,
  72, **116**; coalitions with LDP 36, 56, 62, 65,
  106, 147, 166
Kōno Yōhei 56–7, 59
Korea 18; *see also* North Korea; South Korea
Korean War 25, 26, 27, 29, 30, 83
Krauss, E.S. 52, 78
Kumamoto 88, 130
Kyoto 10, 12

labor market 92, 99, 102, 106; irregular workers 100, 102, 105, 107, 130; women 92, 100,
  107, 113, 117
labor unions 25, 28, 35, 36, 37, 53–4, 55, 92,
  113, 119, 126–7, 128–9; private sector
  (Dōmei) 36, 53, 56, 126, 127
Labour Dispatch Law 100
land prices 96, 97, 99, 142
Large Retail Store Law 155
law: bureaucracy and 110, 111, 112, 113, 118,
  125; civil society and 122, 124, 126, 129,
  130; electoral system 31, 32, 62, 68, 73, 74,
  75, 80, 112; Meiji period 13, 15, 16, 17–18,
  39; military matters 152, 154, 158; policymaking and 113, 115, 137; pollution and
  88, 130; postwar settlement 24, 25, 28, 31,
  39–40, 42; prime ministers and 32, 43, 112,
  136, 137, 166
LDP (Liberal Democratic Party) 29, 50–3,
  56–62, **70**, **72**, 73, 74–5, 77, 106, 113, **140**,
  143, 154; bureaucracy and 38, 52, 53, 110,
  111, 143; catch-all nature 50, 51, 52, 58, 63;
  civil society 125, 126, 127, 128; corruption
  46, 49, 51, 54, 56–7, 58, 59–60, 99, 135,
  142; daycare 117–18, 120; economy and 35,
  50, 52, 57; electoral reform and 34, 37, 49,
  52, 72, 73; electoral system and 46, 69, **70**,
  72, **72**, 73; factions 35, 51, 53, 59, 69, 72,
  73, 137, 142; fiscal stimuli 99, 101, 102–3;
  formation 24, 34, 49; immigration and 118,
  119; local politicians and 41, 43, 119; and
  New Liberal Club (NLC) 55, 56–7, 59;
  PARC and 51–2, 73, 111, 114; PKO Bill

154, 157; policymaking and 51–2, 110, 112, 113, 114, 115, 120; as political machine 35, 50, 58, 86, 99, 103, 104, 141; pollution and 52, 83, 88, 130; pork barrel politics 35, 51, 69, 99, 103, 110, 144; prime ministers and 32, 63, 104, 137, **140**; privatization 143–5; realignment 34, 37, 49, 60–1, 127; women and 51, 53, 77, 116, **116**, 117–18; zoku politicians 33, 69, 143, 145; *see also individual prime ministers*

LDP (Liberal Democratic Party), coalitions 49, 61–2, 114, 165; anti-LDP 42, 49, 60, 61, 62, 71, 99, 153; with JSP 54, 60, 61–2, 99, 127; with Kōmeitō 36, 56, 62, 65, 106, 147, 166

LDP (Liberal Democratic Party), dominance of 6, 46, 49, 57–8; 1955–1993 24, 32, 38, 49, 50, 51–2, 69, 93; 2012 onwards 165, 166–7, 169; policymaking and 110, 111, 112, 113, 118, 120; prime ministers and 135, 136, 137

LDP (Liberal Democratic Party), elections: 1974 142; 1976 55, 57, **70**; 1989 54, 59, 72, 112; 1990 59, **70**; 1993 55, 60–1, **70**; 2007 63; 2009 63, 65, **72**; 2010 105; 2012 **72**, 105, 146, 164, 165; 2014 53, **72**, 147, 165, 166; 2016 **65**, 147, 166

LDP (Liberal Democratic Party), splits 34, 37, 49, 54, 55, 56–7, 58–61, 73, 99, 112, 120, 127, 165

liberalization 89, 92, 98, 143, 146, 147, 168

Liberal Party (Jiyūtō) 15, 22, 23, 49, 61, 62, **140**; Ozawa's 61, 62,

local government 41–3, 46, 54, 88, 104, 118, 119; and civil society 124, 126, 132; and national government 41, 76, 88, 119, 120, 136

Lockheed scandal 57

lower house (House of Representatives): dissolution 31, 136, 146; DPJ 7, 37, 50, 63, 64–5, 77; electoral system and 5, 15, 16, 23, 31, 32–3, 34, 41, 43, 68–73, 75; JSP 54; LDP 53, 59, 60–1, 63, 136, 165, 166; prime ministers and 23, 31, 32, 136, 146; U.S.–Japan Security Treaty 29; women in 116, **116**

lower house (House of Representatives), elections: 1976 57, **70**; 1990 54, 59, **70**; 1993 60–1, **70**, 151; 1996 62; 2005 165; 2009 7, 37, 50, 63, 65, 77, 160, 165; 2012 37, 62, 64, 80, 105, 165; 2014 53, 64, **65**, 147, 166; 2016 65, **65**, 166

MacArthur, Douglas 21, 27, 28, 139
machine politics 35, 50, 58, 86, 99, 103, 104, 141
Maclachlan, P. 127
Maibaracho 119
Malaysia 155, 159

Manchuria 18, 19
Market Oriented Sector-Specific (MOSS) talks 155
Marxism 3, 36, 53, 54
Matsukata Masayoshi 14
MCA (Management and Coordination Agency) 113
McLaren, S. 77
media 28, 90, 168; and civil society 68, 123, 125, 130, 132; and the electoral system 75, 76–8; and political leadership 59, 112, 135, 138, 145, 146
Meiji Constitution 9, 14–15, 16, 17, 21, 23, 29, 46, 139
Meiji Restoration 3, 12–14, 37, 39, 46
METI *see* MITI
Mexico 155, 159
Miki Takeo **140**
militarism 15, 16, 17, 18–20, 23, 139, 149, 163
military: Meiji period 15, 16, 17, 18, 20; pre-modern 9, 13, 14; *see also* self defense
Minamata disease 88, 130
Ministry of Education, Culture, Sports, Science, and Technology (MEXT) 118, 119, 143
Ministry of Health, Labor, and Welfare (MHLW) 100, 118, 119
Ministry of Home Affairs 41
Ministry of Labor (MOL) 118, 129
Ministry of Land, Infrastructure, and Transportation 119
Ministry of the Environment 52, 131
Minshintō (Democratic Party) 64–5, **65**, 166, 169
MITI (Ministry of International Trade and Industry) (later METI) 38, 85, 86, 87, 93, 118, 130, 131, 132, 168
Mitsubishi 24, 25
Mitsui 24, 88, 91
Miyazawa Kiichi **140**
MMDs (multiple-member districts) 69, **70**, 73, 163, 164
MMD/SNTV electoral system 33, 34, 35, 36, 41, 55, 69, 70, **70**, 72, 73, 79, 80
modernization 2–3, 4, 9–20, 163
MOF (Ministry of Finance) 38, 39, 85, 97, 98
MOJ (Ministry of Justice) 118, 119
monetary policy 97–8, 105–6, 146
money politics 33, 34, 36, 56, 57, 60, 61, 69, 75, 135, 142
Mori Yoshirō 103, **140**
Murayama Tomiichi 54, 61, **140**, 150

Nagasaki 20, 21, 150

Nakasone Yasuhiro 111, 113, **140**, 142–4, 147, 153
National Council of Educational Reform 143
National Housewives' Association 129
nationalism 6, 13, 19, 27, 142, 157
national security 7, 56, 149–62
National Security Forces 27
National Self-Defense Act 27
National Strategy Bureau (NSB) 114
National Women's Shelter Network 130
NATO 27
natural resources 24, 89, 92, 107, 167
neighborhood associations 122, 123, 124, 126, 132
Netherlands 10, 20
New Japan, Inc. 86, 110, 138
New Zealand 52, 155, 159
NGOs (nongovernmental organizations) 120, 122, 131, 132
Nigata Minamata disease 88, 130
Nikon 84
Nippon Telephone and Telegraph (NTT) 113, 143
Nishio Suehiro 25
Nixon, Richard 88
NLC (New Liberal Club) 49, 55, 56–7, 59, 60
Noda Yoshihiko 64, 105, **140**
Nōkyō 98, 127
North Korea 146, 152, 154
NPO Law 124
NPOs (nonprofit organizations) 120, 122, 123, 126, 130, 132
NPR (National Police Reserve) 27, 139
NSO (National Strategy Office) 64
nuclear power 62, 63, 107, 128, 166, 167, 168; anti-nuclear movement 128, 131–2, 133; *see also* Fukushima
Nuclear Regulation Authority 107, 168
nuclear weapons 151, 152, 153, 154
Nyblade, B. 78

Obama, Barack 154–5
Obuchi Keizō 103, **140**, 150
Occupation 3, 5, 21, 22–7, 28, 37, 46, 149–50, 155, 163
Oda Nobunaga 10
OECD (Organization for Economic Cooperation and Development) 84, 106, 156, 167, 168, 169
Official Development Assistance 160
Ōhira Masayoshi **140**
oil 20, 84, 104, 144, 158, 168; crises 88–9, 94, 113, 141
Okinawa 26, 28, 73, 154, 155, 158
Ōkuma Shigenobu 16
oligarchs 13, 14, 15, 16, 17, 18, 163
Omnibus Decentralization Act (1999) 42

one and a half party system 33, 34, 49, 69
one party predominant system 33, 34, 57–8, 60, 78, 169
OPEC (Organization of Petroleum Exporting Countries) 88
Osaka 12, 141
Ozawa Ichirō 60, 62, 64, 77, 151

PARC (Policy Affairs Research Council) 51–2, 73, 111, 112, 114
Parent-Teacher Associations 124
parliamentary systems 9, 15, 17, 23, 31–2, 33, 39, 43–7, 52, 57–8, 112, 135–6
patronage 33, 35, 51, 110
Peace Preservation Law 17–18
Pearl Harbor 20
peasants 9, 10, 11, 12, 16
Pekkanen, R. 52
pensions 58, 103, 104, 105, 106, 107, 141, 146, 167
People's New Party (PNP) 146
Perry, Matthew 12, 13, 18
personal ties 9, 11, 36, 53, 112, 135, 138, 147
PKO (Peace Keeping Operations Bill) 54, 61, 151, 154
Plaza Accord 90, 97–8
Policy Advisory Council (Seisaku Shingikai) 112
policymaking process 2, 5, 7, 32, 37, 38, 64, 110–21; civil society and 122, 123, 124, 127, 129–30, 131; prime ministers and 110, 111, 112, 113, 114, 137, 138
Political Funds Control Law (PFCL) 64, 74
pollution 29, 42, 52, 83, 87–8, 107, 113, 130, 133, 141
population **1**, 12, 84, 107, 117
pork barrel politics 33, 35, 41, 51, 69, 74, 99, 103, 110, 141, 143–4
postal system 32, 43, 50, 52, 63, 77, 85, 103, 104, 114, 144–6, 147
postwar political system 31–47, 139
postwar settlement 21–30, 149, 150, 154
prime ministers 5, 7, 23, 31, 32, 43, 68, 78, 112, 113, **140**, 145; formal power 136–9; informal power 32, 114, 135, 136, 138–9, 142, 143, 145, 147; leadership 135–48
The Prince 138–9
private sector unions (Dōmei) 36, 53, 56, 126, 127
privatization 14, 54, 103, 104, 113, 143–4, 145
Progressive Party 22, **140**
PR (proportional representation) system 34, 44, 45, 55, 62, 65, 71, 73, 78, 165; SMD/PR system 69–71, 79–80, 138, 169
Public Office Election Law 34, 40, 113

Reagan, Ronald 142, 153
realignment 34, 36, 37, 49, 50, 62, 65, 79, 99, 127, 145, 152, 164, 169
rearmament 21, 27–8
recession *see* economic slowdown
Recruit stocks-for-favors scandal 54, 59
Reed, S. R. 87
reform: administrative 7, 38–9, 52, 61, 110, 113–15, 120, 137, 143; economic 83, 89, 102–6, 146–7, 167; electoral system 7, 34, 37, 49, 60, 68–73, 74, 78, 79–81, 110, 114, 137, 152, 164, 169; regulatory 102, 103, 104, 155; structural 103, 106, 110, 113, 114, 116, 117, 124, 144, 145, 146–7, 167, 168
Rengō 36, 54, 61, 63, 126, 129
Resona banking group 103
reverse course 24, 25, 155
RFB (Reconstruction Finance Bank) 25, 26
Rincho (Ad Hoc Commission on Administrative Reform) 113
Rising Sun 90
Roosevelt, Theodore 18, 50
"rules of the game" 3, 5, 31, 71, 123–4, 164
Russia (Soviet Union) 4, 18, 21, 25, 26, 27, 84, 153, 159
Ryukyu Islands 10, 27

Sagawa Kyubin scandal 59, 99
Saigo Takamori 15
Sakhalin islands 18
Sakigake (Harbinger Party) 60, 61, 62
Samuels, Richard 23, 41, 139
samurai (military class) 9, 10, 11, 12, 13, 14
San Francisco Peace Treaty 27, 157
Sanwa 26
Satō Eisaku **140**, 141, 153
SCAP (Supreme Commander of the Allied Powers) 21, 22, 23, 24
Schreurs, M. A. 131
Schwarz, Frank 122
SDF (Self-Defense Forces) 27, 28, 37, 40, 54, 61, 151, 152, 153, 154
SDP (Social Democratic Party) 35, **65**, 72, **72**, **116**
security policy, postwar 26–7, 30
Seikatsu (New Life) Club 129, 131
Seiko 84
seiyūkai 16–17
Sekigahara, battle of 10
self defense 27, 150, 154, 160; collective 151, 152–3, 154, 166; *see also* SDF (Self-Defense Forces)
Senkaku Islands 154–5
Shelter Movement 130
Shidehara Kijūrō **140**
Shimonoseki, Treaty of 18
Shinseitō (New Renewal Party) 60, 61, **140**

Shinshintō (New Frontier Party) 61
Shintō religion 26–7
shogun 10, 11–12, 13; shadow shogun 59, 60, 64, 135, 141
Shōwa Denko scandal 25, 88
Shōwa period 14
SII (Structural Impediments Initiative) 155
Singapore 155, 159
Sino–Japanese war 18, 158
SMDs (single-member districts) system 34, 36, 37, 44, 45, 50, 55, 63, 65, 71, 72, 127, 164, 165; SMD/PR system 69–71, 79–80, 138, 169
Smith, Adam 87
SNTV (single-nontransferable vote) system 78; *see also* MMD/SNTV electoral system
Social Democratic Party 72, **72**
Socialist parties 22, 24, 28, 34, 49, 53, 62, 113, **140**
social movements 7, 46, 76, 88, 93, 111, 113, 122, 123, 125, 127–32
soft power 159–60
Sōhyō (General Council of Trade Unions) 126–7, 129
Sōka Gakkai 35, 36, 56
Sony 84
South Korea 7, 78, 123, 149, 150, 156, 157, 158, 159, 160
sovereignty: Meiji period 15, 16, 17; postwar 23, 31, 46; territorial disputes 154, 156, 157–8
Spring Struggle (shuntō) 128–9
state-society relations 122–34
stock prices 96, 97, 99, 102, 104, 106
structural problems 97, 98, 100–1, 106, 107
structural reform 103, 106, 110, 113, 114, 116, 124, 144, 145, 146–7, 167, 168
Subversive Activity Prevention Law (1952) 28
Sumitomo 24, 25, 91
Sun, J. 159
Supreme Court 39–40, 112–13, 119, 151
Suzuki Zenkō **140**, 142
Sweden 42, 58, 169

Taishō period 3, 7, 14, 15–19, 23, 46, 163–4
Taiwan 18, 27, 68, 78–9, 158
Takenaka Heizō 103
Takeshima islands 157
Takeshita Noboru 54, 59, 99, **140**
Tanaka Kakuei 51, 57, 113, **140**, 141–2, 147
Taniguchi, M. 77
tariffs 13, 15, 85, 88, 89, 94, 155, 156
tax: consumption 54, 59, 62, 63, 64, 98, 103, 105, 106, 167; corporate 106, 146, 167; expulsion 142; local 41, 42, 43, 104; Meiji period 14, 17–18; pre-modern 12
territorial disputes 154, 156, 157–8, 160
terrorism 32, 152, 154

Thatcher, Margaret 142, 144
Tōhoku Earthquake 128
Tōjō Hideki 22, 26, 28
Tokugawa period 7, 10–12, 14
Tokyo 12, 38, 42, 141, 142
Toyama 87, 130
Toyota 84
TPP (Trans-Pacific Partnership) 106, 146–7, 155, 160, 166
trade: feudal 10, 12; free 13, 17, 19, 84, 147, 155, 156, 160; tensions 89–90, 94, 97, 155; world 84, 87, 89
traditional societies 2, 3, 9, 10, 11, 12, 13, 14
triad reforms 42
"Trinity Reform" 104
triple disaster (earthquake, tsunami and Fukushima) 37, 39, 50, 64, 65, 102, 105, 115, 132, 165, 167, 168
twisted Diet 31–2, 43, 62, 136, 137
two-party system 44, 50, 60, 65, 79, 80, 169

unions, labor 25, 28, 35, 36, 37, 53–4, 55, 92, 113, 119, 127, 128–9; private sector (Dōmei) 36, 53, 56, 126, 127
unitary system 41, 44, 136
United Kingdom (UK) **1**, 144; *see also* Great Britain
United States (U.S.): bilateral relations 7, 21, 27, 90, 150, 152, 153–5, 160; checkbook diplomacy 54, 151, 154; East China Sea 158; economic relations 90, 155, 159, 160; environment 131; GDP **1**, 84; investment in 105; Japanese immigration 19; media coverage of Japan 1; military bases 29, 40, 53, 139, 150, 154; on MITI 38; NPOs 123; recession 90, 98, 102; Tammany Hall 50; TPP 106, 146–7; trade tensions 89–90, 97; World War II 20, 150; *see also* Occupation; U.S.–Japan Security Treaty
Uno Sōsuke 54, 59, **140**
UN (United Nations) 37, 54, 116, 119, 129, 149, 151, 156
upper house (House of Councilors): Democratic Party 65; DPJ 37, 50, 63, 64, 105, 137, 146; electoral system and 23, 31–3, 34, 43, 62, 71, 73–4, 136, 137, 166; JSP 137; LDP 54, 59, 63, 105, 112, 146, 147; prime ministers and 137; women in 54, 77

upper house (House of Councilors), elections: 1974 142; 1989 54, 59, 77, 112, 137; 1992 61; 2007 50, 63; 2009 50, 63, 146; 2010 105; 2013 37, 50, 80; 2016 37, 65, 147, 166
urbanization 35, 83, 141
U.S.–Japan Defense Guidelines 154
U.S.–Japan Security Treaty 27, 28–9, 30, 40, 56, 61, 84, 143, 150, 153, 160; opposition to 29, 35, 53, 128

Weber, Max 4, 139
welfare 25, 36, 37, 41, 42, 55, 56, 92, 100, 103, 104, 118, 124, 125, 126, 132, 141
West, Japan opens to 3, 9, 10, 11, 12–13, 18, 163
Western colonization 12, 18; avoided 2, 3, 9, 163
Westminster system 43–4, 52, 114; *see also* Great Britain
women: and civil society 123, 124, 125, 126, 128, 129–30; comfort women 149; Constitution 23, 46; housewives 54, 100, 129, 131; in labor market 92, 100, 106, 107, 113, 115–17, 129, 168; life expectancy 107; in the media 77; and policy 115–17; political parties, support for 36, 37, 55, 75; in politics 51, 53, 54, 77, 115, 116, **116**
Womenomics (umano-mikusu) 115–16, 117
World Economic Forum 116
world trade 84, 87, 89
World War I 19
World War II 19–20, 21, 126, 139; legacies of 149–50, 156, 160
WTO (World Trade Organization) 155, 156

yakuza 99
Yamagata, Aritomo 16
Yamaha 84
Yamaichi Securities 98
Yasuda 24
Yokkaichi asthma 88, 130
Yokohama 42
Yoshida Doctrine 150, 153
Yoshida Shigeru 23, 24, 27, 139–41, **140**, 147, 150

zaibatsu (conglomerates) 14, 24, 25, 26, 91, 93
zoku politicians 33, 52, 69, 74, 76, 111, 114, 115, 143, 145